Video, an Art, a History

1965–2010

Video, an Art, a History 1965–2010: A Selection from the Centre Pompidou and Singapore Art Museum Collections

Published in conjunction with the exhibition at the Singapore Art Museum
10 June to 18 September 2011

The exhibition is part of the **Credit Suisse: Innovation In Art Series**

With support from

Please direct all enquiries to the Publisher:
Singapore Art Museum
71 Bras Basah Road
Singapore 189555
www.singaporeartmuseum.sg

Designed and produced by
Editions Didier Millet
121 Telok Ayer Street #03-01
Singapore 068590
www.edmbooks.com

Managing Editor
Francis Dorai

Editors
Ibrahim Tahir
James Lui
Lindsay Davis

Designer
Annie Teo

Production Manager
Sin Kam Cheong

Colour separation by SC Graphic, Singapore
Printed in Singapore by KHL Printing, Singapore

ISBN: 978-981-08-8493-2

COVER IMAGE: Jun Nguyen-Hatsushiba, *Memorial Project Nha Trang, Vietnam: Towards the Complex – For the Courageous, the Curious and the Cowards*, 2001. © Jun Nguyen-Hatsushiba. Coll. Centre Pompidou. Courtesy of Mizuma Art Gallery, Tokyo, Lehmann Maupin Gallery, New York.

This work is also in the Singapore Art Museum collection.

Video, an Art, a History

1965–2010

A Selection from the Centre Pompidou and Singapore Art Museum Collections

CENTRE NATIONAL D'ART ET DE CULTURE GEORGES POMPIDOU

President
Alain Seban

Managing Director
Agnès Saal

Director, Musée national d'art moderne-Centre de création industrielle
Alfred Pacquement

Chief Administrative Officer, Musée national d'art moderne-Centre de création industrielle
Catherine Perdrial

Delegate, International Relations
Alexandre Colliex

SINGAPORE ART MUSEUM

Chair
Jane Ittogi

Director
Tan Boon Hui

International Relations
Géraldine Hebras

Exhibition

Curator
Christine Van Assche *Chief Curator, New Media Department, Centre Pompidou*

Co-Curator
Patricia Levasseur de la Motte *Assistant Curator, Singapore Art Museum*

Project Management
Sylvie Douala-Bell *Collection and Project Manager, Centre Pompidou*
Liew Wee Wen *Curatorial Projects Manager, Singapore Art Museum*

Technical and Audiovisual Management
Vahid Hamidi *Technical Audiovisual Manager, Centre Pompidou*
Larry Kwa *Senior Exhibition Officer, Singapore Art Museum*

Logistics
Liliana Dragasev *Artworks Registrar, Centre Pompidou*
Astrid Lorenzen *Restorer, Centre Pompidou* in collaboration with Ludovic Heissler

Exhibition Design
Sebastian Zeng *Super Bear*

Catalogue

Concept
Patricia Levasseur de la Motte *Assistant Curator, Singapore Art Museum*

Research and Project Management
Yin Ker

Images, Centre Pompidou Collection
Alain Dubillot *Digital Image Manager, Centre Pompidou*

Artist Biographies, Centre Pompidou Collection
Maria Rachita *Documentalist, Centre Pompidou*

Essays
Toshiya Kuroiwa, Patricia Levasseur de la Motte, Jacqueline Millner, Krisna Murti, Mark Nash, Nguyen Nhu Huy, Adeline Ooi, Steven Pettifor, David Teh, Christine Van Assche, Beverly Yong

Entries
Frédérique Baumgartner, Raymond Bellour, Pascale Cassagnau, Guillaume Gesvret, Diane-Sophie Girin, Erin Gleeson, Caroline Hancock, Gaby Hartel, Yin Ker, Jacinto Lageira, Marianne Lanavère, Patricia Levasseur de la Motte, Sylvie Lin, Marcella Lista, Priscilia Marques, Françoise Parfait, Florence Parot, Yekhan Pinarligil, Mathilde Roman, Lou Svahn, Elodie Vouille, Elvan Zabunyan

Translation
Yin Ker, Simon Pleasance, Miriam Rosen, Yves Tixier & Anna Knight

Acknowledgements

This catalogue was made possible by the efforts of many individuals and institutions.

The **Singapore Art Museum** would like to express its appreciation to a number of artists and other individuals: Sonia Andrade, Aung Ko, Aye Ko, Jean-Paul Battaggia, Edward Beckett, Chris Chong, Davy Chou, Gaëtan Crespel, Daniel Crooks, Juliah Drey, Kenpachi Fujimoto, Diane-Sophie Girin, Erin Gleeson, Jean-Luc Godard, Odile d'Harcourt, Vattey Heang, Ho Tzu Nyen, HONF, Takashi Ito, Isaac Julien, Sonia Khurana, Jompet Kuswidananto, Kyan Nyunt Lynn, Kyi Soe Tun, Kyi Wynn, Jennifer Lam, Ray Langenbach, Dana Langlois, Le brothers, Leang Seckon, Liew Kung Yu, Linda Lee, Liu Wei, Catherine Mancip, Toshio Matsumoto, Lindsay Merrison, Nicolaus Mesterharm, Morihisa Miyamoto, Mohammad Akbar, Hayati Mokhtar, Barbara Moore, Romain de la Motte, Ko Nakajima, Bruce Nauman, Lydia Ngai, Nguyen Minh Phuoc, Nyein Chan Su (NCS), Kamol Paosavasdi, Mike Parr, Lydia Parusol, Phyu Mon, Patricia Piccinini, Po Po, Magalie Poivert, Apinan Poshyananda, Sudsiri Pui-Ock, Reza 'Asung' Afesina, ruangrupa, Hasnul J. Saidon, Michael Shaowanasai, Simon Soon, Sithen Sum, Thant Thaw Kaung, Monika Tichacek, Tran Luong, Trinh T. Minh-Ha, Tromarama, Vuth Lyno, Apichatpong Weerasethakul, Wong Hoy Cheong, Tintin Wulia, Valentine Xenos and Yang Fudong.

The Museum is grateful to the Publications Department of the Centre Pompidou: Francesca Baldi, Matthias Battestini, Claudine Guillon, Françoise Marquet and Nicolas Roche; to the New Media Department of the Centre Pompidou: Etienne Sandrin; to the Production Department of the Centre Pompidou: Annie Boucher.

Many of the images reproduced in the catalogue come from the Centre Pompidou, while others have been handled by various galleries, museums, festivals and photographic libraries. The Singapore Art Museum is grateful to Anna Schwartz Gallery, Artists Rights Society (ARS), Electronic Arts Intermix (EAI), Estate of Samuel Beckett, Film Makers Field, Fukuoka Asian Art Museum, Haunch of Venison Galleries, Karen Woodbury Gallery, Kick the Machine Films, Moongift Films, Mori Art Museum, National Art Gallery of Malaysia, OK. Video Festival, Réunion des Musées Nationaux, Ryllega Gallery, ShanghART Gallery, Studio Square and Yogyakarta International Media Art Festival 2007. The Museum would also like to thank the Alliance Française de Yangon, Asian Art Archive, Bophana Audiovisual Resource Center, Centre Culturel Français du Cambodge, Centre Culturel Français du Myanmar, Java Arts, Kon Khmer Koun Khmer (Khmer Films, Khmer Generations), Meta House, Myanmar Book Center, NNNCL Films and Yangon Film School.

The **Centre Pompidou** would like to express its gratitude to the following persons who have contributed to this project: Bruno Budniewski, Franck Buisson, Louise Coquet, Rafaele Docimo, Catherine Duruel, Danielle Feugnet, Bruno Gonthier, Véronique Landy, Florence Macagno, Valérie Millot, Séverine Monnier, Alain Peron and Jean-Pierre Six.

Lastly, the Singapore Art Museum and the Centre Pompidou thank the Embassy of France to Singapore for its kind support and Jean-François Danis, Cultural and Audiovisual Attaché.

Contents

Foreword

Jane Ittogi
Chair, Singapore Art Museum

This exhibition and accompanying catalogue bring together a comprehensive selection of artworks that chart the history of video as an art form in both the East and the West.

Video art has matured significantly in its aesthetic, conceptual, and technical depth, since the first explorations of the form in the 1960s by Korean-born artist Nam June Paik. With the video camera becoming ubiquitous today, there are more artists exploiting the medium than ever before.

Video art addresses a large public accustomed to television, cinema, the Internet and other tools of mass communication. As a popular medium, video reduces the 'intellectual' distance between the spectator and the artwork, speaking especially to the young who are quick to embrace new technologies. Interactive installations featured in the exhibition further immerse and implicate the spectator in the artwork resulting in a whole new logic of creation.

To promote a better understanding of the history of this young art medium, scholars and other professionals in the field of art have responded enthusiastically to contribute to this major publication, one of the first to give an overview of almost 50 years of video art in Europe, America and Asia. It also breaks new ground, given the emphasis on Southeast Asia through the selection of works from the Singapore Art Museum collection. This publication aims to present a multifaceted understanding of video art through surveys and critical essays, as well as detailed presentations on the works of key artists who have helped bring video art into mainstream art history.

The exhibition catalogue of *Video, an Art, a History 1965–2010: A Selection from the Centre Pompidou and Singapore Art Museum Collections* furthers the mission of the Singapore Art Museum to offer contemporary art and to acquaint the public with new forms of artistic expression. This publication marks one of the first steps in developing scholarship on video art. It is also hoped that it will inform, engage and inspire readers from all walks of life to see video art from fresh perspectives.

Foreword

Alain Seban
President, Centre Georges Pompidou, France

Alfred Pacquement
Director, Musée national d'art moderne-Centre de création industrielle, Centre Georges Pompidou, France

The Musée national d'art moderne has always sought to diversify its approaches to artistic creation by doing its best to stay in tune with artists. Propelled by its relocation to the Centre Pompidou in the late 1970s, the Museum has been steadfast in establishing itself in the contemporary scene, even if it meant adjusting its approach to artworks. Contemporaneous generations of artists during the Centre's early years saw a redefinition of the frontiers of contemporary art – the dematerialisation of the work of art and its distancing from museum space. Against this context, there emerged works involving audiovisual techniques and which were presented in museums rather than in dark projection rooms.

Very soon, the Musée national d'art moderne wanted to integrate these artistic practices into its collections policy, thus placing itself at the forefront of its field. These 'video' works, as they were referred to at first, were initially the result of peripheral experimentations primarily intended to document ephemeral performances. However, the televisual object, image manipulations through the cathode ray tube, the idea of the projection of the moving image and the self-perpetuating capacities of its mise en scène developed in time to become one of the most forceful artistic forms over the last decade. No contemporary art biennale, no art fair, no exhibition in a museum would be without projections, television sets, flat screens and computers, or installations in which the image takes on monumental dimensions.

With more than 1,600 videotapes and 120 multimedia installations, the Centre Pompidou's collection is rare in both its size and scope. This range is what makes this exhibition possible today at the Singapore Art Museum. For the first time, our collection – represented by a large selection of 41 videotapes and installations – partners a selection from the Singapore Art Museum collection that is more specifically orientated to the Southeast Asian region. The exhibition, proposed by Christine Van Assche, Chief Curator of New Media at the Musée national d'art moderne and responsible for this collection since its inception, assisted by Sylvie Douala-Bell, is thus truly remarkable. Through six thematic sections, she recounts this trajectory through a large selection of works from the mid-1960s to the present day. With the recent technological revolution upon the arrival of digital images, this project has the double merit of tracing a history that is truly topical and of presenting both renowned and new unseen works to the public.

We take the opportunity to extend our warm gratitude to Mr Tan Boon Hui, Director of the Singapore Art Museum, as well as Patricia Levasseur de la Motte, co-curator of the exhibition, assisted by Yin Ker, and the entire team from the Museum who have made this project possible.

Foreword

Tan Boon Hui
Director, Singapore Art Museum

The history of contemporary art as written in the West is still predominantly a Euro-American one. Asian artists, where they do appear, such as Nam June Paik or Yayoi Kusama tend to be rare individuals who have spent important periods of their artistic career in Europe or America and hence have been anointed as part of *international* (read: Western) contemporary art history. The rising prominence of China and India in the closing decades of the 20th century has somewhat altered the trajectory of this monolithic goliath. Nevertheless, the vibrant artistic traditions of many regions including Southeast Asia have often been passed over still, or relegated to the antiquities or ethnographical spheres of knowledge. This collaboration between the Singapore Art Museum (SAM) and the Centre Pompidou has enabled SAM to work with our museum partners to insert some of the key videos from Southeast Asia in the SAM collection into the larger narrative of video art development presented in this exhibition. The recasting and disruption of contemporary art history that results from the inclusion of non-Western practices is only beginning, and as Southeast Asian artists continue their push to be seen and heard beyond the region, SAM is well placed to be a focus and crucible for this charge.

We thank our excellent partners from the Centre Pompidou for their professionalism, knowledge and openness to embarking on this journey with us. Most of all, SAM thanks all the artists, especially our Southeast Asian friends, for their trust and partnership, without which this project would not have been possible.

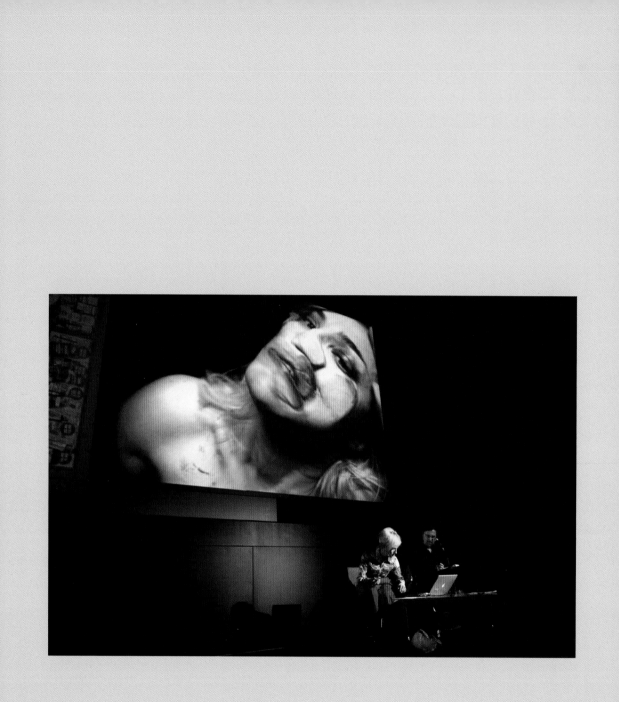

Vidéo et après: Pipilotti Rist, Centre Pompidou, 2006.
© Coll. Centre Pompidou. Photo Bertrand Prévost.

Video, A "Global Groove", An International History

☐ **Christine Van Assche**
Chief Curator, New Media, Centre Pompidou

"Art shows philosophy today how to circulate in the diversity of cultures in order to reinvent itself by breaking with its atavisms."[1]

François Jullien

I. Introduction to the Exhibition

The exhibition *Video, an Art, a History 1965–2010* presents at the Singapore Art Museum a selection from the collection of Centre Pompidou, in resonance with works selected from the Singapore Art Museum collection. A total of 53 works are shown at the museum's two spaces. It is a pilot exhibition bringing together two collections: one that began in France in 1976 with works from 1965 until today, and the other since 2008 in Singapore; one turned towards major international trends, the other steered towards Asian works – more specifically, those from the currently very prolific region of Southeast Asia.

Video, an Art, a History 1965–2010 fans out in the museum's two buildings, linked by distinctive scenography and signposts. Historical works created in the context of television as laboratory, or critical works preface the exhibition. The next section is on identity and examines investigations of the representation of the self and the other, and the documentation of performance. The third section invites us to experiment with the relation between the videotape and installation in space. The fourth section explores landscape as a metaphor, retranscribed in a spatiotemporal installation, while the fifth section surveys geo-political questions, history, memory and archive. With a work by Jean-Luc Godard as a departure point, the last section focuses on the deconstruction of the narrative, as well as the attempts at fiction by certain contemporary artists.

Most international exhibitions, all biennales, almost all museums of contemporary art, the majority of large museum collections, some private collections and even contemporary art fairs exhibit and present video works in diverse forms. On visits to art schools, festivals and discovery exhibitions – whether in France or elsewhere in the world – we cannot help but notice the proliferation of works or attempts at works using digital tools such as video, photo and sound. The only resistance is from the auction houses and certain contemporary museums of 'fine arts'. In the case of the former, it is not difficult to imagine that this art of the day is not 'saleable' at auctions. For the latter, there remains the same old reticence – indeed – against new or relatively new media. It took a century for photography to be recognised as a fully fledged artistic practice. Video has been in existence since 1960, for already half a century.

Nonetheless, during this half-century, video has made considerable progress, not only in pushing against the frontiers of aesthetics but also in the field of technology and economics, as we shall see later in this essay.

II. Definitions and Limits

The term 'video' has evolved so much that it is

important to redefine it today. During the 1960s and 1970s, 'video art' was the term used when television was applied as a medium of art, or in the words of Korean artist Nam June Paik, as a 'metaphor of vision'. While in the 1960s and 1970s, the video recording was a reflection of what the artist saw. In the 1990s, video manipulation transformed the recording into an artefact whose links with the filmed object are increasingly weakened.

With the advances in technology and the infiltration of information technology techniques in video, the term 'new media' became more apt in the 1990s, covering not only video and its offshoots – hybrids of video and sound as artistic practice, as well as of video and the Internet – but also older forms like cinema which have been converted to digital formats for the purposes of both creative work and dissemination. The term 'new media', theorised in 2001 by Lev Manovitch in *The Language of New Media*,[2] has been adopted by a considerable number of museums and collections, as well as other theoreticians since the middle of the 1990s.

In the 2000s however, the term 'video' resurfaced – independently of the word 'art'. Video became an artistic practice in continuity with creations from the 1960s and 1970s, that is to say, not just coming from the artistic context and presented in this environment, but also in connection with a much more discursive framework. Admittedly, there was a shift from the magnetic tape to the digital file, from the analogue signal to the pixel, from analogue devices to laptops. Today, there are artists who disseminate their works without recourse to the world of art and who prefer to create and distribute their works on websites like YouTube, Dailymotion and MySpace. Above all, aesthetic practices are

evolving in the global world in which we live – in which their authors live. We will return to this shortly.

As Jacques Rancière wrote, "A medium is not a 'proper' means or material. It is a surface of conversion: a surface of equivalence between the different arts' ways of making, a conceptual space of articulation between these ways of making and forms of visibility and intelligibility determining the way in which they can be viewed and conceived."[3]

At a time when conceptual definitions are in the process of elaboration, it is logical that the frontiers in themselves are zones of thought and experimentation. Obviously, the frontiers of video with cinema – whether experimental, documentary or fiction – are very porous, as is the case with television, photography, information technology and even sound. In our postmodern era, the questions and issues connected with boundaries are subjected to permanent revision from cultural and subaltern studies, and crossings with sociology, anthropology and geopolitics.

III. Centre Pompidou's New Media Collection

Since 1976, a year before opening its doors to the public, the Centre Pomopidou has been interested in artists of other cultures. Pontus Hulten, the first director of the Musée national d'art moderne, acquired the first tapes of Nam June Paik under the premonitory titles of *Global Groove* and *Guadalcanal Requiem*, as well as the installation *Moon is the Oldest T.V.* (pp. 114, 196 and 108). In 1978, the museum director organised Paik's *TV Garden*, an exhibition of unprecedented impact.

A few years later, festivals organised in Japan – for example the *Rencontres Internationales de Vidéo*

Pipilotti Rist, *A la belle étoile (Under the Sky)*, Centre Pompidou Piazza, 2007.
© Coll. Centre Pompidou. Photo Georges Meguerditchian.

in which Nam June Paik and Bill Viola participated amongst other artists – allowed me to discover the works of pioneers of video in Japan: Shigeko Kubota, Mako Idemitsu, Toshio Matsumoto, Ko Nakajima, Shuntaro Tanikawa and Shuji Terayama. In the exhibitions and international biennales of the 1990s and 2000s, I was able to see and acquire the installations of Asian artists: Jun Nguyen-Hatsushiba, Fiona Tan, Jianwei Wang, Apichatpong Weerasethakul and Peili Zhang.

The Centre Pompidou consequently acquired an exceptional corpus of unique video installations by incontrovertible artists like Nam June Paik, Dan Graham, Bruce Nauman, Martial Raysse, Vito Acconci and Peter Campus. This corpus of installations, together with a collection of video tapes (from M. Abramovic/Ulay, J. Beuys, R. Filliou, T. Matsumoto, N.J. Paik, etc.), make the Centre's new media collection one of the world's most important, alongside New York's MoMA (Museum of Modern Art) and Amsterdam's Stedelijk Museum. Throughout the last three decades, when this type of work had a conceptual importance but no market value (or rather, not the financial value accorded by the market today), the Centre's devotion to these works has been exceptional and continuous.

Complete with a significant ensemble of video and audio tapes, CD-ROMs and websites (numbering 1,800), this corpus of 120 installations presents to the Centre's audience, as well as those beyond the Centre, a fairly complete vision of the Fluxus researches, happenings and filmed actions, minimalism, international conceptual and post-conceptual preoccupations from the second half of the 20th century to the beginning of the 21st century.

The task of global prospecting is similarly carried out in North and South America, North Africa, the Middle East and Australia. Before the exhibitions and biennales, and before the propagation of Internet websites, videos were disseminated through festivals. These festivals were international exhibitions that presented a panorama of works from diverse cultures and functioned as forums for international artists.

Video was first established as an artistic tool in North and South America, Western and Eastern Europe, and Japan during the 1960s, 1970s and 1980s. The language of the medium was able to develop over the course of realisations, critical analyses and exhibitions on these continents. Similar developments in the Middle East, North Africa and Asia only took place later in the 1990s and 2000s, following the transition to the digital platform, to information technology, and to mobile devices that are increasingly made in Asia.

IV. Video, an Instrument of Critique

In the era of computational reproducibility, the establishment of video as an instrument of critique remains very much linked to the evolution of technologies, and this is true of its entire trajectory. Briefly, in the beginning, video artists appropriated television sets (sometimes the television even) and then the monitors to 'exhibit' their work: Nam June Paik, Vito Acconci, Valie Export, Dan Graham, Mako Idemitsu, etc. The arrival of the DVD and the video projector in the 1990s considerably revolutionised the presentation of video in public museums and exhibition spaces in terms of a more effortless integration; an egalitarian coexistence with other fields of practice.

The artists of the 1990s conceived video works projected in dark spaces, isolating them from other plastic works. One or more combined projections allow for 'montages' within the space

Espace Nouveaux Médias, Centre Pompidou.
© Coll. Centre Pompidou. Photo Bertrand Prévost.

and lean towards a certain 'spectacularisation', thus entering into direct competition with cinema projections. Contrary to the cinema spectator who is constrained by a passive receptivity – certainly physically passive – the spectator of the installation is 'psychologically and sociologically' engaged in the spatial montage proposed by the installation artist. There is no lack of examples. Amongst the most eloquent works, we cite those of Eija-Liisa Ahtila, Doug Aitken, Stan Douglas, Gary Hill, Pierre Huyghe, Isaac Julien, Mike Kelley, Dinh Q. Lê, Steve McQueen, etc.

The 2000s appear marked by resistance on the part of artists to dark confines. Henceforth, they seek to integrate their works into museum galleries without isolating them from the context, and pursue materials and configurations that allow smooth integrations. Francis Alys, David Claerbout, Gary Hill, Aernout Mik, Pipilotti Rist and Tony Oursler are a few of the many artists examining the integration of their works into museum spaces.

The 'phenomena' of the 2000s are flat screens and the diffusion of websites. The flat screen has become commonplace, and artists and curators unfortunately confuse it with painting. Self-evidently, the suspension of the flat screen on the museum walls and in the residences of private collectors is the perfect integration of video with collection display: it no longer disrupts!

It is the ideal support at fairs whereby merchants can thus introduce a number of videos amongst the multitude of works to the public. This said, the flat screen integrates so well that it 'irons out' certain parameters of critique and the aforementioned dynamic relationship with the spectator at the same time.

Over the past few years, the spaces of diffusion on the Internet have most certainly become the new spaces appropriated by artists to create and disseminate specific works which are highly critical of the media, or to present existing works which gain a much larger visibility worldwide.

V. A Contemporary Global Art

"Art is politics by means of a distance it keeps from its own functions as well as of a specific time and space it creates and by means of the way in which it distributes the time and populates the space."[4]

Jacques Rancière

Of the proliferation of works from all over the world, a few important conceptual and post-conceptual trends can be spotted today. However, not having the time to be exhaustive, we highlight a few major trends in the works from the 1990s and 2000s in an art history hesitating between the established and accepted modes of representation, and the dissenting, experimental, prospective, pragmatic and speculative modes.

1. Space and time

Video, writes Fredric Jameson, is unique in our times of late capitalism "because it is the only art or medium in which this ultimate seam between space and time is the very locus of the form, and also because its machinery uniquely dominates and depersonalises subject and object alike".[5]

The ontological parameters of video works since its beginnings – and which persist today – are the phenomenological parameters of space and time in relation to the spectator's critical perception. The space of a work is not only that conceived by the artist to link the different elements, but also that conceived by the artist within the work to create this complex relationship with the spectator.

Time – a notion and concept traversing all cultures – is one of video's essential parameters. All the same, it is highly subjective. Here, the spectator plays the role of an active agent, becoming a parameter which is indispensable to the work's existence, thereby attributing its temporality.

In *Hatsu Yume (First Dream)* (1981) which Bill Viola realised in Japan while as artist in residence at Sony, he worked on the subject of the video image to transform it into space-time, according to a very Deleuzian concept. He imperceptibly integrates the viewer into the Japanese landscape, evolving very slowly with the rhythm of nature (p. 170).

As for Thierry Kuntzel, in the installation *Autumn (Mount Analogue)* (2000), a work which is part of *Four Seasons*, he links a dream landscape which calls to mind Asian drawings and paintings with micro-variations of light and colours to Ken Moody's face shown in close-up as well as the eye movements of Moody, a famous model. Time is given rhythm by the movement of the eyes, while space is placed within another space by the extreme presence of Moody's visage (p. 176).

Space seems to have no limits for Pipilotti Rist who uses museum spaces with the greatest liberty, be they outdoors (Centre Pompidou, 2007; Singapore Art Museum, 2011) or indoors (MoMA,

2008), on walls, on the ground (Musée d'art et d'histoire de Genève), on ceilings, etc. From now on, images circulate on the entire horizontal or vertical surface. For Rist – as for others – the screen's verticality has disappeared, and the spectator's rapport with space is without the depth of the field.

Jun Nguyen-Hatsushiba suspends time in a no man's land that is contextualised by geopolitical questions (frontiers, exile and migration) in a specifically created undersea space where the spectator becomes a participating actor, as in the previously mentioned works.

2. Political and poetic

In the post-Marxist era, in countries with emerging cultures where technologies undergo an accelerated development, artists choose reproducible digital media like photography and video as their preferred fields of expression. The new geopolitical map of creation is far from exhaustive but is found in countries and regions with emerging economies such as the Balkans, the Middle East, certain countries of Asia and Southeast Asia, Eastern Europe … Let us be reminded that between the 1960s and 1980s, the productive regions of video works used to be clearly found in Western Europe, North America and certain countries of South America like Argentina and Brazil.

According to Fredric Jameson in his publication titled *Postmodernism, or, The Cultural Logic of Late Capitalism*, late capitalism begot postmodernist cultural forms, which have taken over art as well as occasionally new forms of resistance based on the parameters of micropolitics and latent poetry.[6]

A postcolonialist vision of the world encouraged artists to create an 'ethical and poetic' intermediary space between the spectator and the other, and to take interest – whether closely or remotely – in the questions of history, memory, archives, rites, anthropology and sociology (as can be seen in the works of Nam June Paik, Chris Marker, Johan Grimonprez, Liu Wei, Dinh Q. Lê and Trinh T. Minh-ha).

The last three *Documenta* in Kassel amongst others, as well as the last biennales of Venice and Istanbul, have highlighted such works by selecting a considerable number of artists without excluding any geographical zone. As Okwui Enszwor, director of *Documenta XI*, writes in the catalogue of this exhibition, it is in the postcolonial period that we find the most critical statements and we see the radicalisation of notions of spatialisation and temporality.[7]

3. Attempts at fiction

Certain artists have attempted short fiction (at least once in their artistic career) or a fictional feature-length film, with actors, stage set, scenarios, etc. Their works are the test of cinema's founding parameters – or rather those of fiction films – by bringing on a critical reflexion on the roots and methods of the narrative (the McGuffin, absurdity, the surrealist narrative and so on). Pierre Huyghe's *The Third Memory*, Yang Fudong's *Backyard - Hey! Sun is Rising* or Isaac Julien's *Baltimore* are cogent examples from this category (pp. 238, 242, 246).

Indeed, these creations reflect with nostalgia a bygone modernity, but reinvent with reconstructed data a new real, an amplified real that is deliberately dehumanised and filled with new micro-narratives. "Fiction is not something unreal that we add to items on the register of illusion: it is part of the very fabric of the real,"[8] writes philosopher Elie During.

VI. Conclusion

From the 53 works, the exhibition endeavours to reconstruct a history based on data derived from two continents of two different histories that have effected crossings through the intermediary of artists from the pioneer generation such as Nam June Paik, Chris Marker, Mako Idemitsu, Toshio Matsumoto, Ko Nakajima and Bill Viola.

In the future, crossings will become more numerous and the articulations, though at times less traceable, will be effective in the elaboration of a shared and universal world in terms of aesthetic, philosophical, poetic, ethical and political concepts. Art is capable of proposing these transfers that announce this utopian 'philosophical globalisation'.

Translated by Yin Ker

1. *"L'art montre aujourd'hui à la philosophie comment circuler dans la diversité des cultures pour se réinventer en rompant avec ses atavismes."* Jullien, François, *Nourrir sa vie à l'écart du bonheur* (Paris: Seuil, 2005).

2. Manovitch, Lev, *The Language of New Media* (Boston; London: MIT Press, 2001).

3. Rancière, Jacques, *The Future of the Image* (London, New York: Verso, 2007).

4. Rancière, Jacques, *Aesthetics and its Discontents* (Cambridge: Polity Press, 2009).

5. Jameson, Fredric, *Postmodernism, or, The Cultural Logic of Late Capitalism* (Durham: Duke University Press, 1991).

6. *Ibid.*

7. Enzewor, Okwui, *Documenta 11: Platform 5: Exhibition* (Kassel: Hatje Cantz, 2002).

8. *"La fiction n'est pas quelque chose d'irréel que nous ajouterions aux choses sur le registre de l'illusion ; elle fait partie de l'étoffe même du réel."* During, Elie, "Sur les franges du monde: fictions de Laurent Grasso" in *Laurent Grasso* (Dijon: Les Presses du Réel, 2009).

Ho Tzu Nyen, *Utama – Every Name in History is I*, 2003.
Courtesy of the artist and Fukuoka Asian Art Museum.

Recalibrating Media: Three Theses on Video and Media Art in Southeast Asia

☐ **David Teh**

Recently, a meeting was convened to discuss the institution of Singapore's new national gallery for modern art. The gathered arts and museum professionals debated many things. What should be the museum's historical scope? How should it address Singapore's geographical situation? Should it restrict itself to the *beaux arts* media of the Western tradition? But the delegates seemed unanimous about one thing: that the *art history* of Southeast Asia did not yet exist, or was at any rate too paltry, for the purposes of a regionally focused modern art museum. For anyone who has been frustrated by the patchy nature of art's written archives in the region, this consensus might have passed unremarked. But such a proposition – an art museum without art history – must be hard to conceive for anyone from a place (such as France) known for building art museums well. Even in the field of media art, which for decades suffered a comparable amnesia, historicisation is these days an essential part of what art institutions offer.[1] Comparisons may be odious, but Singapore and its neighbours probably have some catching up to do. And much as we might wish to throw off the curse of belatedness and come up with new ways of making history, the situation throws a spotlight on the core question of what a museum and its collection are for, a question salutary for a nation in such a hurry to build them, but lacking a confident vision as to why.

The present exhibition therefore offers a cautionary exercise, composed as it is of two collections with rather little in common. On even a cursory inventory, differences far outweigh similarities: the Singapore Art Museum's (SAM) collection contains nothing made before 1998, suggesting that media art, and the idea of collecting it, belong to the period after the Asian Financial Crisis (1997–98). The Centre Pompidou's collection, of course, reaches back through four decades to media art's genesis, reflecting the social and economic upheaval of Europe and North America in the late 1960s and early 1970s. SAM's collection is sensibly restricted to Singapore's geographical vicinity, with one stretch to Asia's Western extremity (Iran); whereas the Pompidou collection reaches eastward to India and beyond, from its strong Euro-American axis. Historically, two points of contact are particularly noteworthy: the foundational role played by (Korean-born) Nam June Paik, and the inclusion of Japanese media art from the 1980s. Yet it's clear that this inter-continental collection is not without its gaps, some of which this exhibition will illuminate, but cannot fill. Nevertheless, the juxtaposition suggests some parallels and divergences that may guide the study of video and media art in this region. I will outline three of these, but first we should address some of the difficulties inherent in such a 'regional' framing.[2]

Medium as Figure and Ground

Art history is always, in a sense, meta-history: it only takes shape on the background of some other sort of history, be that economic, political or social.

Hence, behind Raphael we find a Medici pope; behind Courbet, an emergent bourgeoisie; behind modernism, the political and psychic trauma of the world wars; and so on. The formalism championed by Clement Greenberg was perhaps the closest art came to autonomy, to peeling itself off these backdrops and standing on its own feet. But as it internalised and digested its own historicity – as the critic Arthur Danto diagnosed in Pop – the need for backdrops was put beyond doubt: *topos* (in the case of land art); art history itself (in conceptualism); *ethnos* (in the "global" art of the recent biennale boom); or social dynamics (in "relational aesthetics"). Media art was not immune to this imperative, nor too far behind. It too emerged from the experiments of the 1960s, on the critical fringes of the ascendant broadcast and popular cultures – what Guy Debord called the "Society of the Spectacle" – and while it sometimes strove for autonomy, this backdrop of modern media history is crucial to our understanding of media art generally, and of the pivotal medium of video in particular.

But without a satisfactory regional art history, how can we begin to historicise video art in Southeast Asia? A volume like this is perhaps not the place for it, but given that many of my fellow contributors speak from geographical positions, it seems reasonable to ask how and why they might have come to be assembled in one place. What is the appropriate backdrop for Southeast Asian media art? The region itself is hard to define, the difficulty not simply geographical, but political and historical. Starting as a figment of the imperial-military imagination (British, Japanese and American), what we now call Southeast Asia is a creature of World War II and the Cold War. But the area was linked up in all sorts of different configurations before that – its already diverse indigenes played

host to Chinese, Indian and Arab visitors for centuries before the Europeans arrived – and these earlier shapes have left strong cultural imprints and a deep hybridity that make pre-modern Southeast Asia incomparable to pre-modern Europe or Japan. Regional intellectual enquiry inevitably leads beyond the present frame to these other, older ones. Start with the wrong chronology, and your map will be distorted, full of mysterious holes and unexplained correspondences. Start with the wrong geography and you will struggle to make sense of the cultural continuities.

Southeast Asian media art may seem immune to these quandaries, emerging as it has rather recently (mostly since the end of the Cold War), in a period marked by brisk global and intra-regional exchange in both economic and cultural spheres. But a quick, regional survey proves otherwise, revealing how closely media artists are tied in to their local cultural matrices. Few may fairly be called traditionalists, yet fewer still ignore their traditions altogether. In fact, tradition is often the pretext – we might say the *screen* – for the most modern of gestures, as in Arahmaiani's eerie, feminist-informed revision of the *Ramayana*, an Indian epic that is part of the DNA of narrative across the region (p. 216); or Ho Tzu Nyen's theatrical deconstruction of Singapore's foundation myths, treading the uneasy fault line between colonial and oral histories.[3] From these two examples, it's clear that to privilege *beaux arts* forms to the exclusion of, say, performance – or of music, textiles, or even ritual traditions – will be ruinous for art history. Much will therefore hinge on the amplitude of our notion of media itself. It will need to be reflexive and locally inflected, unencumbered by colonial chronologies, Cold War geographies, or Western fine art hierarchies. In places where the written record is slow and incomplete, media artists, who tend to be attuned to their mediums' pre-histories, could moreover be pivotal in the recalibration of the *dispositif* of art history.

At any rate, where the technical and cultural landscapes are so varied, a formal overview of video practices will not be of much use. Regional coherence is more apparent at the level of theory and history, than in the mix of artistic styles. It might be more fruitful then to try to discern the *programme* of video, in the sense of what Vilém Flusser called the "programme of photography": characteristics not just of the video image, but of the socio-technical parameters within which it is made.[4] Who has had access to video, as producers or consumers? How has it been distributed, and how has it interacted with other, older media? What does it make possible, that was not possible with earlier technologies? And if this activity is not much informed by the medium's Euro-American history and aesthetics, what are the local conventions and histories that inform its production and secure its legibility?

Dissemination and Reflexivity

In one of the works in SAM's collection, Araya Rasjdamrearnsook's *Two Planets Series* (2008–09), villagers from the artist's neighbourhood in northern Thailand sit in peaceful rural settings before reproductions of some masterpieces of early modern painting (p. 224). As they try to make sense of the images – and frequently digress – we observe with delight what happens when an oral culture confronts the stuff of a literary art history. How vain seem all our academic readings of Van Gogh and Millet, how removed from the lives of the people and places they depict! In these irreverent encounters, art is temporarily demystified – it becomes a mere thing-in-the-world again, a pretext for idle talk, local gossip and bawdy jokes

– refreshing our sense of what it might *mean*.

I first saw this work in 2008, in a hopelessly jumbled exhibition called *Traces of Siamese Smile* at the then new Bangkok Art and Culture Centre. The following year I saw it again, this time as a single-channel video in a short film festival in Germany. More recently, I saw it installed multi-channel in a cramped room at a museum in Sydney, as part of the biennale there. In each iteration, its presentation – not to mention its context – was drastically different. Media artists and theorists have long grappled with the question of what, in such cases, constitutes the actual work of art. Mounting it on a large flat screen on a gallery wall emphasises the artist's play on notions of the picturesque; showing it in a cinema might draw us closer in to the narratives and personalities of those on screen; while an immersive installation will yield more disjointed narratives, but provides a richer sense of the place in which it was made. But if no one permutation is definitive, what is it that the museum has collected?

Araya's work is not even at the slippery, site-specific end of the spectrum. But this constant shifting of the work's material, social and spatial parameters is a fundamental condition of media and video art. And it is exacerbated by the ease with which moving images now cross between the formats of film and of art, as well as by their deployment in performance, installation or online. This exchange has been the subject of vigorous discussion in the West – prompted as much by contemporary art's constant rediscovery of the cinema as by the explosion of video-making – and has demanded a major rethink of the space-time of the gallery and the museum. If all this gives artists, curators and conservators a few headaches, it also energises the work, allowing it to adapt to the spatial and social

Apichatpong Weerasethakul, *Morakot (Emerald)*, 2007.
Courtesy of Kick the Machine Films.

dynamics of each new exhibition context.[5]

Araya's continuously morphing art work reveals two key tendencies that shape video art globally: reflexivity and dissemination. These forces sometimes pull the medium in opposite directions. They were visible, and visibly opposed, in its experimental heyday, the late 1960s and 1970s. The reflexive instinct was exemplified by the work of, say, Bruce Nauman, Vito Acconci, or Dan Graham. Here, video had to find its place in the artist's toolkit, in the studio and the gallery. The result was a new anthropometry, characterised by Rosalind Krauss as a kind of narcissism, and marked by a keen self-awareness – both on the part of the artist whose actions it captured, and of the machine itself, whose materiality and functionality were often foregrounded.[6] Meanwhile, many artists and activists were more interested in what video could do *outside* the studio, allowing them to engage with theatres of social and politi-

cal struggle, and even plug these into broadcasting infrastructure, in ways that seem to us now – especially in contemporary Singapore with its emaciated public sphere – quite radical.

Along both avenues, video was used to document with a new immediacy, trumping the slower and more expensive *enregistrement* of celluloid film, and short-circuiting the hitherto much slower feedback cycles of art and society respectively. But these two tendencies point towards different historical backdrops: dissemination (often hastily characterised as 'democratic') highlights what is fundamentally modern about the medium – its reproducibility – and thus, its *social* and *economic* valence. Reflexivity, on the other hand, points to a history more specific to art, emphasising video's *aesthetic* valence. Southeast Asian video art is more beholden to the former tendency than the latter; formal reflexivity is not high on the agenda – a generalisation we could not make about the Euro-American video canon. This divergence can be explained with reference to the historical trajectory of video in the region.[7] (Hence also the significance of an artist like Ho Tzu Nyen, whose practice combines the drive to dissemination with a keen awareness of video's specificity, and its pre-histories in film, visual art and theatre.)

One of Western media art's master narratives – from Fluxus, through the activist work of the 1970s, to networked video today – concerns the radical dilation of access to media tools. Video production in Southeast Asia has certainly developed in tension with broadcast media, but the historian looking to tease out a similar story will be disappointed. Here we must take account of the very different economic realities into which it was received, and the timing of its arrival and popularisation. Although some pioneers gained early access to analogue video recorders, the time-lapse between this (before the emergence of a significant middle class) and the mass take-up of DV (after it), was much shorter than in the West. The vectors imagined for the video image have thus had less to do with broadcast media and more to do with PCs, VCDs, mobile phones and the Internet – consumer technologies already widely disseminated when DV arrived. And while we should be wary of essentialising the opposition between "passive" television and "interactive" computer-based media, the terms of engagement have certainly shifted. The DIY ethos that flavours much digital media art does not imply the same revolutionary stand against media hegemony as was found in much of the Western video canon. In Southeast Asia, video art tends to sit alongside popular screen culture more comfortably than early video art did in the West.

The wider ramifications of this accelerated dissemination will have to be elaborated elsewhere.

For now, it provides a suggestive point of departure for three more speculative propositions.

First Thesis: Video is (and is Not) Film

It is a key tenet of Euro-American video art that video is *not film*. This negative definition has encouraged video-makers – especially in the pre-DV and early-DV eras – to do things that filmmakers could not do. This bolstered video's claims to experimentality, underwriting its rejection of narrative and other cinematic conventions. While this formal predisposition can be discerned in Southeast Asian video, it is certainly not dominant. For the historian to project onto the region the same antagonism with film would be a big mistake. If an earlier generation of artists, exposed (like Arahmaiani) to the video art of the 1970s and 1980s, were conscious of it, younger ones trained in the 1990s and since are more relaxed. Apichatpong Weerasethakul and Ho Tzu Nyen, for example, while attentive to the distinctions between film and video, explore the characteristics and the genres of both.

Much of the Centre Pompidou collection is native to the video medium; much of SAM's collection is not, especially if we disqualify video installations. We would not describe Lee Wen's performance videos as 'video art', yet this does not mean they are any less worthy of collection (p. 204). They remain important records of an artist's engagement with the electronic moving image within the parameters of, and challenging the parameters of, his practice – even if they are not especially reflexive about the medium of video. Moreover, they tie Lee Wen's work into another genealogy, that of performance art and *its* encounters with the moving image. This suggests one way that media theory might be recalibrated for this part of the world: through a focus on *remediation* – rather than medium specificity

– a more coherent geography of video may come into view. For example, in the Malay world (which includes Singapore), we might survey its constant re-channelling of performance traditions such as the puppet theatre (*wayang*), a heritage common across mainland and insular Southeast Asia. This in turn suggests a second line of enquiry.

Second Thesis: Video as an Oral Medium

In Marshall McLuhan's vision of the global village, electronic media such as video promised to return us to a more organic ("tribal") mode of social connection. Whether this has materialised in Western media culture is a matter for debate, revived now by the "social web", and the proliferation of portable media devices. In Southeast Asia, though, we can see that the oral capacities of video are more pronounced, and do more to shape its use, since the advance of an older literacy (associated with modern print media) has been less comprehensive. In most of the region, notwithstanding the modernisation and rationalisation of communications during and since the Cold War, oral transmission is still preponderant in everyday life. Important dialogues occur face-to-face; friendships are maintained over the phone, rather than by e-mail; memories are embedded in narratives that are less likely to take objective form. Hence, the persistence in media art of certain narrative modes, another of the obvious distinctions between the two collections assembled here.

Rather than historicise video as a tool, we will be better off examining it as a *social process* – a process of mediumship – that is, not merely a channel but a *channelling* that may be corporeal, social and spiritual.[8] Video's prodigious amplitude as a medium rests upon its capacity for plugging into, and remediating, older, oral forms: the performance traditions mentioned above, the folk art of story-telling, and local spiritual traditions. While none of these channels emerged from the 20th century unscathed, they still draw from wells of cultural meaning (and artistic ingenuity) that are either pre-national and indigenous, or multi-ethnic and cross-cultural, or both.[9] While film studies struggles in the straitjacket of "national cinema", the study of video will lead more readily to this pre-history, displacing the national framings that have militated against regional correspondence for decades.

Third Thesis: The Long Shadow of Authoritarianism

Even within the national logic, though, there may be some regional coherence. Whereas video emerged in the West in dialogue with upheavals in bourgeois civil society (such as the anti-war and civil rights movements), its emergence in Southeast Asia has been in dialogue – though not always as directly – with authoritarianism. This is perhaps the only structural condition shared throughout the region, from the "soft" authoritarianism of Singapore or Malaysia, through the strongman cronyism of the Philippines under Marcos, or Indonesia under Suharto, to the openly repressive military regime of Myanmar or the post-socialist bureaucracies of Vietnam and Laos. The Cold War saw media power jealously guarded by government and the military, forces inimical, of course, to creativity, and which continue to shape the programme of video to this day. The broad legacy of this centralisation has been that history, insofar as it took the form of moving images, has conformed more to the official than to the popular imagination. (In some places it would be more accurate to say that the popular itself has been largely an official production.) This has tended to streamline ethnic diversity and political differences, and in many cases efface them altogether. In much of Southeast Asia, however, the situation has now thawed considerably. Media power has been decentralised – in some cases rapidly – with the arrival of corporate players, and competition from new supra-national channels such as cable, satellite and now the web. This has coincided with the mass dissemination of DV, with some exciting results. Citizen journalism has taken root online, challenging the official picture even where there is no free press.[10]

For artists, however, the state's stranglehold has long cheapened the moving image's epistemological value; and where this grip has been relaxed, they now seem disinclined to try to restore it. Few artists use video to compete with, or correct,

the official record. Instead of objectivity, they pursue a new *immediacy*, characterised by improvisation, play, found and "mixed" realities. Most video artists, even politically engaged ones, avoid didactic aesthetics, in favour of either observation, or narrative forms derived from popular and folk traditions – compare, for example, Arahmaiani's work to Martha Rosler's *Semiotics of the Kitchen* (1975).[11] Such comparisons are unlikely to furnish us with the tools necessary for a regional media analytic. But they underscore that what a moving image *says*, and its purchase on the real, are contingent not just on technical conditions but also on social and political ones. For a Southeast Asian media art history, cultural specificity will be at least as important as medium specificity.

---

1. Introducing one of the more ambitious attempts to date to bring media art into the art historical mainstream, Oliver Grau laments how much of the field remains uncharted. Grau, Oliver (ed.), *MediaArtHistories* (Cambridge; MA; London: MIT Press, 2007). It is notable, though, that amidst the "many-voiced chorus" he assembles for the purpose, only two (out of 21) voices are singing non-Euro-American tunes. Southeast Asian media art is doubly marginal, then, peripheral with respect to a media art history that is itself peripheral.

2. It is worth noting that many Southeast Asian artists feel no particular need for this regional framing. They have good reason to be skeptical, given that geography's origins. But for art historians, critics and curators, "Southeast Asia" provides a suggestive horizon for describing, criticising and collecting art from these countries whose historical experiences, and cultural inheritance, so richly overlap.

3. Arahmaiani, *I Don't Want to be a Part of Your Legend* (2004) (p. 216); and Ho Tzu Nyen, *Utama – Every Name in History is I* (2003).

4. Flusser, Vilém, *Towards a Philosophy of Photography* (London: Reaktion Books, 2000).

5. Of course, video-makers may stipulate requirements for exhibition, but in Southeast Asia, where institutions have been slow to collect even the most outstanding video work, we can imagine few artists being very prescriptive.

6. Krauss, Rosalind, "Video: The Aesthetics of Narcissism", *October*, Spring 1976.

7. This holds *a fortiori* for *new* media art. As Southeast Asian artists have been further from the bleeding edge of technical innovation, in their experiments they tend to start, like the rest of us, as consumers rather than developers of new media. Pioneering video artist, Krisna Murti, confirms this from an Indonesian standpoint in his recent volume, *Essays on Video Art and New Media: Indonesia and Beyond* (Yogyakarta: IVAA, 2009), p. 37.

8. See Morris, Rosalind C., *In the Place of Origins: Modernity and its Mediums in Northern Thailand* (Durham; London: Duke University Press, 2000).

9. That is, they combine knowledge from afar with knowledge of the distant past, the two essential components of artisanal storytelling that Walter Benjamin saw united in the mediaeval journeyman. Benjamin, Walter, 'The Storyteller: Observations on the Works of Nikolai Leskov'. In *Illuminations*, trans. Zohn, Harry (London: Fontana, 1992).

10. For examples from two very different national contexts, compare the escapades of Singapore's Martyn See with the clandestine video journalism of the Democratic Voice of Burma: http://singaporerebel.blogspot.com and http://burmavjmovie.com.

11. Araya's videos are exceptional here – both *Two Planets* and her well-known series featuring corpses (c.1997–2006) are composed along deliberately pedagogical lines. Yet in both, authority is subverted through oral play: in the former, masterpieces are submerged in village banter; in the latter, the artist's poetic and philosophical lectures fall on deaf ears.

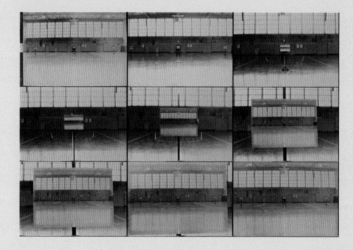

Takashi Ito, *SPACY*, 1981. © Takashi Ito.

Japanese Experimental Film: Fukuoka

☐ Toshiya Kuroiwa

Introduction: Experimental Film and Video in Fukuoka

First of all, I would like to speak about experimental films. Experimental films have different goals from popular film media such as television or movies on DVDs or online streaming. Their objectives have nothing to do with commercialism and consumerism; they try to be more expressive and visionary, exploring new ideas and techniques. This can appear as something absurd, but gives us a chance to expand the possibilities of art.

Cinema was born in the late 19th century, a chaotic time when many new technologies and social circumstances were introduced to the world. You could say that cinema itself was an experimental product. Business has always been an important aspect of moviemaking, but to make significant enough progress for the images to be shown to the public, there were difficult trials and errors. In those days, the audience had no fixed ideas on how movies ought to be, and every projection booth seemed like a laboratory providing endless surprises and excitements. Experimental film is not a different or separate entity, but a part of film history.

The essential concepts of experimental moviemaking appeared during the 1920s and lasted until the 1930s. In art, cubism, structuralism, dadaism, surrealism, futurism, expressionism and other avant-garde movements led to the destruction of the common code and context of art preceeding them. They destroyed and reconstructed the rules of traditional arts. Therefore, it is not difficult to understand those artists' interest in the new attractive media. Salvador Dali, Marcel Duchamp and Hans Richter, for example, made several impressive films. Their work was extremely abstract and hardly contained any narrative or element of entertainment. Nevertheless, their stance and action were already an artistic statement and taught us the essentials of a film. This is because it has consequences upon the origin of film: the holding of time. Movements and colours were expressed through time, something that could not be achieved through canvases or sculptures. Their works were very different from our general perception of films.

In Japan, many experimental film and video artists surfaced in the 1960s. Toshio Masumoto, Takahiko Imura (Taka Imura), Nobuhiro Kawanaka, Shuji Terayama and Katsuhiro Yamaguchi are a few of them.

Toshio Matsumoto's avant-garde films remain influential on the Japanese art scene. His early works *Nishijin* (1961) and *Ishi no uta* (1963) contain characteristic experimental film methods, such as daring cutting and framing, structuring, close-up shooting, double-imaging and reshooting of still photos. You can see how it was inspired by European and American experimental films. Through many discussions and criticism, it formed a unique Japanese style.

From the 1960s until the 1970s, reviews like *Eizou no hakken* (*The Discovery of Film*) (1963) and

Hyougen no sekai (*The World of Expression*) (1967) had an intense impact on students and movie-makers of that time. Their unrestrained language and way of thinking demonstrated resistance against the old theories and provided a new refreshing sensation.

Something else characteristic of filmmakers from that period is that not only did they present films, but also video art and other forms of art now referred to as media art. The filmmakers were less interested in arriving at a perfect movie than in discovering more ways of expression through new media. Most of them focused on controlling the frame (space) and time in a technical way, often by designing their own screens and projectors. The complicated and extreme ideas of the experiments were always in reaction to the commercial movies; they were strong antitheses to them. The works always left the audience with the same question: what is film?

The way experimental film developed in the United States and Europe differs from the way it did in Japan. Artists from the United States and Europe place emphasis on the individual while those in Japan place emphasis on the collective. This might explain the different styles. In the United States and Europe, people try to return to the origin, simplifying the technologies and methods of these days. In comparison, Japanese artists tend to reconstruct existing images and impact contemporary perception by reintroducing them. This Japanese aspect is later used in the sampling of electronic music in the 1980s, as well as in their constructive expression. These characteristic features of Japanese experimental film can be seen in the film scenes of Fukuoka from the 1970s and 1980s. The following chapters will examine the conditions that set Fukuoka apart.

Experimental Films of Kyushu Institute of Design: the Accomplishments of Toshio Matsumoto

The Kyushu Institute of Design (KID) merged with Kyushu University in 2003 and is now called Kyushu University, Faculty of Design, Graduate School of Design. It is located in the south of Fukuoka and is one of the smallest national universities in Japan. The idea of their interdisciplinary education is the humanisation of engineering and the assimilation of fine art and science.

The year 1980 marked a major turning point for the University when filmmaker Toshio Matsumoto was installed as professor. Matsumoto's theoretical perspectives and avant-garde expressions were cutting edge at that time. He helped many students become distinguished filmmakers; for example Takashi Ito, Shinsuke Ina, Akihiko Morishita, Takashi Inagaki, Masaru Ohashi and Yasuo Torikai.

The structuralism of Takashi Ito's work *SPACY* (1981) shot on 16mm is representive of the works produced at the Kyushu Institute of Design. Takashi took about 700 still shots, developed them by himself, and then shot a film frame by frame to create this work. The movie begins with a vacant gymnastic hall with photos of the hall placed on easels at regular intervals in a circle. The camera proceeds to approach each photo (with minimal noises of an analogue synthesiser) until the photo fills the screen, before jumping to a new perspective of the hall and then moving on to the next photo on the easels. The continuing frames and changing spaces which are created through the combination and to-and-fro of several photos create many different perspectives. The use of different speeds, playbacks, reverse playbacks and colour filters generates a wide range of variations as well. Most audiences experience being propelled into the screen and into the gymnastic hall. The relation between watching and being watched becomes shuffled and the audience experiences a whole new sensation, as with the painting, Velasquez's painting *Las Meninas*.

The pictures of *SPACY* were taken according to a calculated framing, and then shot again in a row, frame by frame, to complete the movie. The length of the frames and shots, as well as their variations, were planned mathematically. This is called a "structural film": the artist did not merely rely on his instinct but also used programmes based on theories to control space and time. This can also be seen in the works of other students.

While a professor at the Kyushu Institute of Design, Toshio Matsumoto discovered unique film techniques and inspired students and other creators with theoretical approach to film. He also provided the opportunity to experience the excitement of films and the exhilaration upon a film's completion. This allowed one student with a big dream to become a true artist: *SPACY* won international acclaim and is now in the collection of the Centre Pompidou in Paris. Toshio Matsumoto established the golden age of experimental film in Fukuoka within a short term of only five years until his retirement in 1985.

Film Makers Field: Experimental Film for the individual

The Film Makers Field, also known as FMF, is an organisation dedicated to the screening of independent films. It was founded in 1977 by Yoshihiko Noto, Ryoichi Morita and Yoshio Fukuma. They used to have 10 members, including current leader Yasuko Miyata, and was active in holding screenings in the name of "FMF cinematheque". The organisation was broken up in 1980 due to financial troubles but was reopened in

Kyushu Institute of Design.
Courtesy of Morihisa Miyamoto.

1982 by the same three persons who first founded it. Since then, they have been part of Fukuoka's film-screening history of over 25 years. Unfortunately, Yoshio Fukuma passed away in 2007; Yasuko Miyata and some volunteers now manage FMF. To date, FMF has held 114 screenings.

Their most famous festival is called *Personal Focus*; a festival of 8mm film movies of only three minutes or 50-feet film length. Any creator can participate as long as they fulfil these requirements. People come from Fukuoka, Tokyo, Osaka, Kyoto, and even all the way from Hokkaido and Okinawa to join this festival. Sometimes the number of participants went beyond a hundred, including students of the the Kyushu Institute of Design and famous filmmakers. *Personal Focus* has been held annually since 1978, but is recently a non-scheduled festival.

The FMF succeeded in opening the door to the world of independent films, and in continuing their activities in spite of multiple adversities.

Personal Focus 2007 by Film Makers Field.
Courtesy of Film Makers Field.

The effort they have been making to maintain their grassroots activities under despite extremely difficult financial circumstances throughout the 30 years is almost indescribable. Thanks to the sympathetic personalities of Fukuma and Miyata, many young creators gathered at the FMF to exchange valuable experiences on history and work, and to encourage the development of the FMF. The FMF was an excellent platform for Fukuma and Miyata – filmmakers themselves – to create a strong connection with Fukuoka's artists, museums and organisations.

Another factor that had a huge influence on experimental film in Fukuoka were the film-screenings at the Fukuoka American Center. The Fukuoka American Center is a part of the American Consulate Fukuoka (Public Affairs Section). It was founded in 1948 and its beautiful traditional American-style building has always been admired by the Fukuoka citizens. From 1973, the Fukuoka American Center started a series of lectures, inviting famous artists and critics. They discussed

various themes (politics, economy, diplomacy, environment, fine art and culture) from both the American and Japanese persepctives. The following Japanese and American artists and authors were amongst the many who were invited: art critic Yoshiaki Tono (Homei Tono) in 1973 and 1974, architect Michael Ross in 1973, author Peter Neel in 1973, movie critic Donald Richie in 1973 and 1974, musician Toshi Ichiyanagi in 1973, experimental film critic Henry Keizer III in 1975, dancer Stacia Thoroughbred in 1975, film anthropologist Sol Worth in 1977, art critic Yusuke Nakahara in 1977, sculptor Donald Judd in 1978, video artist Bill Viola in 1978 and 1990, art historian and photographer Dawn L. Cohen in 1979, architect Akira Isozaki in 1979, filmmaker Takahiko Imura in 1980, movie producer Joan Micklin Silver in 1982, filmmaker George Landau in 1984, video artist Shinsuke Ina in 1989, environmental artist Christo in 1991, and leader of Art organisation Carl E. Loeffler in 1989.

America started producing a lot of experimental films in the 1940s. The American Center has its own film archives within the library, with several experimental films including *Meshes of the Afternoon* (1943) by Maya Deren, *Dog Star Man* (1961–1964) by Stan Brakhage, *Eaux d'Artifice* and *Scorpio Rising* (1953 and 1963) by Kenneth Anger, *Chelsea Girls* (1966) by Andy Warhol, *The Flicker* (1966) by Tony Conrad, *T·O·U·C·H·I·N·G* (1968) by Paul Sharits, *Arabesque* (1975) by John Whitney, *Wavelength* (1967) by Michael Snow and *Reminiscences of a Journey to Lithuania* (1971–72) by Jonas Mekas.

These are the fruits of labour of the director and staff who worked as producers. For example, Akira Ogata and Mari Kaigo are people we should not forget. The American Center is part of the American government agency and changes its director every few years. The unwavering commitment to art and experimental films for nearly 20 years is also due to the efforts of the Japanese staff.

The many lectures and experimental films introduced by the Fukuoka American Center created a valuable opportunity for artists living in a local area like Fukuoka. They also influenced students and creators. Shinsuke Ina speaks of this period and its importance in his book *Media art no sekai jikken eizo 1960–2007* (*The World of Media Art: Experimental Films 1960–2007*). Unfortunately the elegant building was torn down in 1993 due to land redevelopment. The Center is now managed at its new premises.

Fukuoka American Center.
© Kenpachi Fujimoto.

Fukuoka's Experimental Film and its Region and People

We have explored the development of Fukuoka's experimental films from the late 1970s to the 1980s. We looked at how educational, civil and public institutions such as the Kyushu Institute of Design, the Film Makers Field and the Fukuoka American Center made the most of their individual potential while respecting the others and functioned in harmony.

The Kyushu Institute of Design – with Toshio Matsumoto as its core – introduced the world to a completely new sense of experimental film, manoeuvering structural time and space. The Film Makers Field opened up many young artists to experimental films, continuing their activities despite many adversities. They also complemented Fukuoka's rising modern art scene and stimulated artists of both fields. The Fukuoka American Center introduced many experimental films produced by the counter-culture of America. Their influences are still noticeable among Japanese experimental filmmakers.

When the medium of movies changed from film to video (electronic devices), both the advantages and disadvantages became clear and stimulated each other positively. While high expectations were made of new media, traditional film technology became a success and finetuned its expression.

In these circumstances, independent creators worked hard in competing against one another. Fukuoka's size and character as a provincial city has much to do with this. Located in the north part of Kyushu, Fukuoka has always been a site for cultural exchanges for the mainland, a place where various cultures meet. It has a nomadic side that makes it open to new and foreign things. The young creators and students form a tight community network based on the hunger for information and the stimulation that provincial cities create. Experimental film in Fukuoka was born when the three elements of location, technology and talent came together. The fact that Fukuoka became a global place in such a short time is a miracle after all.

Nguyen Minh Phuoc, *Red Etude*, 2009. Courtesy of the artist.

Video Art in Vietnam: A Brief Report

☐ **Nguyen Nhu Huy**

Video Art Before 2008

One of the most uneasy things for me when I look at the condition of video art in Vietnam is that there was virtually no practice of it in the history of approximately 30 years of Vietnamese contemporary art. It was only recently, or to be more exact, two or three years ago that I first observed the real emergence of video artworks and short documentaries by local Vietnamese artists in some international exhibitions.

It is necessary to clarify that in discussing local Vietnamese contemporary artists, I am primarily commenting on those who were born, brought up and received most of their education in Vietnam. This classification is just a strategy to highlight the key difficulties faced by Vietnamese artists when they practise contemporary art in general and video art in particular; I believe that those with dual citizenship are not confronted with as many challenges because they have more options.

To see the reasons for the poor development of video art in Vietnam, it is necessary to take a brief look at the social context in which Vietnamese contemporary art exists and the struggles to keep it viable.

From both the theoretical and practical perspectives, Vietnamese contemporary art has had a relatively short history beginning with its indistinctive establishment in the last decade of the 20th century, which parallels the opening-up policies of the Vietnamese government. This is a rather fledgling history when compared with those of neighbouring nations, such as Indonesia, whose contemporary practices date back to the 1970s and 1980s.

Looking further, I would say that the history of both Vietnamese art and its contemporary counterpart is a history of importation. It was not until the early 20th century that the word *nghệ thuật* meaning "fine art" or *beaux arts* first appeared in Vietnamese vocabulary. It was only until the French establishment of the Ecole supérieure des beaux-arts de l'Indochine (Indochina College of Fine Arts) in the 1920s that the concepts of painter, artist, art and artwork made their first appearance in newspapers and social life. Similarly, in the early 1990s when Vietnam was progressively opening up to the global market, foreign artists started to visit Vietnam as tourists or, in many cases, as guests on cultural exchanges with local institutions like the Hanoi University of Fine Arts. Inspired by these new contacts, young Vietnamese artists came to be increasingly exposed to a much wider spectrum of art which was totally different from what they were taught in the art universities, especially from the formal perspective.

In any process of importation, it is worthwhile to observe the adaptation from two angles, as both the imported subject and its new destination of reception have to change to fit each other. If we treated new art forms – namely performance, installation and video art – as the imported subjects to the Vietnamese art context in the 1990s, when teachers at the art universities were still lecturing the same curricula as in the 1930s, we would see the problems of this importing process because the necessary theoretical and practical platforms for these new things were simply inadequate, if not totally absent. This led to a situation whereby, despite the eagerness to receive new art forms, Vietnamese artists remained incapable of articulating their own discourse and continued to struggle with mere superficial imitation.

The next question would be why performance and installation, although facing the same difficulties, have made a much easier quantitative and qualitative development amongst young Vietnamese artists as compared to video art. The only feasible answer is that performance and installation are not technology-dependent. In other words, they are not under the umbrella of what is referred to as "the age of mechanical reproduction" and "the digital age". Therefore, they were adopted more easily and quickly than video art.

From the economic perspective, it could be rather simple to gather materials for a performance or an installation artwork (which might be just some ready-made items or the artist's own body), whereas, if an artist wanted to make a video – even the simplest one, he would need at least a personal camera, a computer, a projector and a sound system, which were too expensive for most artists then.

In fact, video art did germinate in Vietnam in 1998 and between 2002 and 2004. There were several workshops on video art such as the one between Vietnamese and Swiss artists in 2002 at the Hanoi Centre of Contemporary Art or *The Fairy Tales' Soup Project*. Led by artist Tran Luong in 2003 and sponsored by the British Council on the occasion of the 30-year friendship between the two nations and the 10th anniversary of the British Council in Vietnam. Each artist participating in the latter project made a video based on their own interpretation of a fairy tale. Those videos – around 10 altogether – were all presented in local public areas for a large audience. However, after this attempt, almost all Vietnamese artists stopped doing artworks using moving images.

Another important reason why very few young Vietnamese artists chose video art and moving images as their key practice was because the government strictly controlled all activities related to moving images. According to Tran Luong, *The Fairy Tales' Soup Project* would not have been possible without the strong 'umbrella' of the British Council and the Embassy of United Kingdom.

In his famous 1936 essay "The Work of Art in the Age of Mechanical Reproduction" Walter Benjamin stated that the "mechanical reproduction of art changes the reaction of the masses toward art" and "with regard to the screen the critical and the receptive attitudes of the public coincide". For me, this is the key reason for Vietnamese official institutions' enforcement of strict censorship policies on video art and independent documentaries: the authorities are aware that moving images' descriptive and critical capacity over social reality could strongly stimulate the masses' critical capacity. Obviously, this external factor did prevent Vietnamese artists from incorporating moving images into their practice because it was very difficult for them to gather art materials and to exhibit their artworks here.

The absence of Vietnamese video art in both the local and global art scene is also the result of the scarcity of foreign curators or experts on Vietnamese contemporary video art, in comparison with Indonesia, Malaysia, not to mention China,

Nguyen Nhu Huy, *Emotion*, 2010. Courtesy of the artist.

Le brothers, *The Bridge*, 2009. Courtesy of the artist.

Tran Luong, *Flowing*, 1998. Courtesy of the artist.

Video exhibition of artist Nguyen Duc Loi at Ryllega Gallery in Hanoi.
Courtesy of Ryllega Gallery.

or even Thailand. The above analyses have shown that weak theoretical and practical platforms, strict censorship, as well as technological and economic difficulties in Vietnam before 2005 made it almost impossible for Vietnamese artists to make and exhibit video artworks publicly in Vietnam. Logically, when the opportunity was closed in Vietnam, the artists became dependent on exhibitions outside of the country, which basically means that they were dependent on the opinions and analyses of foreign curators.

Here, we should also highlight the fact that Vietnamese artists could barely compete with so-called "Vietnamese" artists who received their full education overseas and practised abroad. This gap can be seen in all aspects: the quality of their artworks, especially the technical aspects, their public relations skills, their (in)ability to verbally present themselves and to use English to establish new professional relations, etc. Consequently, it was very rare for a Vietnamese artist to take the initiative to submit his or her video to foreign curators because they anticipated their own failure. This is one more reason why Vietnamese artists hesitated to choose video art as their voice at international forums.

Changes Between 2008 and 2010

However, things have changed at a much faster pace recently.

Truong Thien, a young lecturer at the Hue University of Fine Arts told me in an interview in September 2010 that he was going to the United States to visit the Indiana University to study its method of teaching video art. According to Do Ky Huy, a colleague of Truong Thien, the reason why his university chose to open a new faculty of video art is that it relates to both photographic and digital art which can help students learn more than one medium at a time.

In October 2009, DOCLAB, an independent art centre at the Hanoi Goethe Institute, debuted its rich programme with short training courses, workshops, film presentations, studios and a video library. The idea came from Trinh Thi, a young filmmaker and video artist whose foremost aim was to create more opportunities and provide better training for Vietnamese artists so as to inspire them to be more confident in the use of moving images.

Since August 2009, a group of independent artists in Ho Chi Minh City under the name Passionate About Film have been holding weekly screenings of video artworks and international art movies for a large audience. In May 2010, Yxine, a group of cinema lovers organised an online festival of short films and documentaries which attracted a large number of young filmmakers in Vietnam. This group has also been presenting films online on a regular basis of three times a week.

Some artists have started to focus on moving images professionally, gradually forming a group of independent artists working on documentaries and video art in Vietnam, such as Nguyen Minh Phuoc, Nguyen Trinh Thi, Le Quy Anh Hao, Nguyen Duc Tu, Hoang Duong Cam, Nguyen Nhu Huy and Le brothers Thanh-Hai.

This significant change is not due to any modifications in the authority's censorship policy. Some believe that it is even stricter than it was in the 1990s. The difference actually lies in the fact that there are more social "oases" beyond the hands of the controller: for instance, the Internet and social networks which somehow make it much easier to popularise the art form of moving images with the Vietnamese audience, thus creating a much wider audience than ever before.

The second reason is the evolution of the artist's awareness itself. Over time, they have developed a more mature perception; they no longer reckon video art and other contemporary art forms as tools to pursue formalist newness, or to gain entry into international exhibitions, as affirmed by the twin brothers Thanh-Hai, "I don't care what video art is. I just know that I have been painting and doing performance for over 20 years but no one has cried when they see my artwork. But just now, when I presented one of my video artworks, some people couldn't hold their tears. This makes me understand the power of moving images. We want to use this medium to tell our stories. We aren't pursuing fame or anything, but just want to share our stories with people around us."

Yes, from this genuine need to tell personal stories – and first and foremost for those around us, I firmly believe in a brighter future for moving image as an art form in Vietnam.

Aye Ko, *IT Boat*, 2007. Courtesy of the artist.

Emergence and Emergency: Video Art in Cambodia and Myanmar

☐ Patricia Levasseur de la Motte

It is only recently that the Mekong region has drawn the attention of the international art scene. One international event that comes to mind is the Asia Pacific Triennial of Contemporary Art at the Queensland Art Gallery, Brisbane, which first featured in 2009 a stage for the region that included Cambodia, Laos, Myanmar[1], Vietnam and Thailand.

Contemporary art practice got underway in Cambodia and Myanmar later than in the other countries in Southeast Asia. Both countries went through turbulent periods which were not conducive to artist development. In Cambodia, contemporary art carries the burden of the glorious past of ancient Angkor and the turmoil of the Khmer Rouge, during which time most of the artists either left Cambodia or were killed. Consequently, the concept of 'art for art's sake'[2] has been slow to take root in Cambodia, a country with an economy that is now heavily dependent on tourism[3]. Nevertheless, over the last few years, the contemporary art scene in Cambodia has been growing slowly but confidently.

Similarly, Myanmar suffers from repression, isolation and economic problems that have all made the country distanced from developments in the international art scene. The art community endures the lack of state support, severe control and censorship and lack of teaching of contemporary art practices in the local art academies, whether in Mandalay or Yangon. Yet, the country has an emerging generation of artists, flourishing art spaces, fresh artistic innovations and has been increasingly participating in international events. Yangon now appears as a dynamic city for contemporary art development. However, the restrictive issuance of travel visas remains a hindrance for artists.

For people in Cambodia and Myanmar, television sets remain rare and expensive. In Myanmar for example, while 66.4%[4] of the population watch television (mainly the national channel Myanmar Radio and Television), only 38.5% actually own television sets. In parallel with Vietnam[5], video art emerged in Cambodia and Myanmar just a few years ago. The pioneers in video art in these countries are actually multi–disciplinary artists who also work with painting, photography, installation and performance. Whereas Cambodian video works often deal with the catharsis of the war or the country's long culture, in Myanmar the themes explored in the videos are often related to Buddhism, the main religion in the country. And unlike Cambodia, Myanmar cannot count on tourism to help with the development of the art scene.

This essay aims to provide a survey of the video art scene in Cambodia and Myanmar, two countries facing similar issues and challenges. The purpose is to understand the reasons for the late and tremulous emergence of video art in that area, relative to other countries in Southeast Asia. To accomplish this survey, we need to extend the field of study to video-related domains like performance, documentation, cinema and mixed-media installations.

Twin Diamonds, Cambodia, 2009. © Davy Chou and Kon Khmer Koun Khmer.

I. Challenges
Video Art Teaching

While students may attend courses on video techniques at the Department of Media and Communication (DMC) established in 2001 under the Royal University of Phnom Penh, it is primarily an academic institution for journalists and communications practitioners. Phare Ponleu Selpak Art School[6] in Battambang is a visual art school for performing arts as well as video and graphic arts; the animation studio develops animated movies. Artist Srey Bandol is one of the co-founders.

Apart from universities and schools, other institutions provide training and workshops in video like the Bophana[7] Audiovisual Resource Center (Phnom Penh), the French Cultural Center (Phnom Penh), Meta House[8] (Phnom Penh), the Yangon Film School[9] (Yangon) and the Alliance Française (Yangon). Courses and workshops also welcome overseas artists and filmmakers. Video is acomplex medium that combines conceptualisation, creation, writing and technical mastery. According to

Nicolaus Mesterharm[10], director of Meta House: "To learn the media takes time. We live in a society of consumerism, we want everything right now. It is the same for the artists, but they must learn to be patient. There are a lot of technical skills to acquire and digest. This takes time."

In 1999, the Population Services International Myanmar (PSI) was created by Grace Swe Zin Htaik[11], a former famous actress in Myanmar and founder of the Motion Picture Association in 1988. As a producer of television programmes and documentaries, PSI also provides workshops and training in video production. Artists from different backgrounds have participated in them. PSI also collaborates with neighbouring countries, such as Thailand.

Resources and Documentation

Libraries and resource centres on contemporary art are lacking in both countries. To remedy this situation, the Bophana Audiovisual Resource Center in Phnom Penh was created to preserve and archive Cambodian memory through films, photographs and videos. But artists still lament the lack of art publications and information. Burmese video artist Wah Nu[12] says, "We want to read and learn about cutting-edge art events. But we can't find any contemporary art books, magazines and newspapers in bookstores except those with titles like *How to Create a Painting*". In Myanmar in particular, access to information and publications about contemporary art is severely limited, or even nonexistent especially when the Internet, the main source of information for a number of artists, is frequently shut down. Artists struggle to build small libraries that they share with others in the community. Artists who are fortunate enough to travel overseas often see contemporary art publications as precious things and bring home as many as they can.

Exhibition Spaces and Art Communities

The first exhibition space to show contemporary art in Cambodia was the Reyum Institute of Arts and Culture[13]. The French Cultural Center in Phnom Penh, Reyum, Java Arts[14], and Meta House have organised exhibitions[15] of contemporary artists both local and international. Other art communities like Cambodia Living Arts[16] (CLA) also aims to support the revival of Cambodian traditional art forms and to inspire contemporary artistic expression. CLA commissions artists to create new works that dovetail traditional and contemporary styles, bringing new life to ancient forms. In 2005 artist Sopheap Pich founded the Cambodian Contemporary Art Association with fellow artist Linda Saphan. Saklapel, the Cambodian Gallery of Cambodian Art[17], seeks to exhibit and encourage contemporary artistic expression in Cambodia and beyond. It also seeks to create a sense of community amongst visual artists. In 2005 Saklapel launched the Visual Art Open (VAO), an annual event which features work by Cambodian contemporary artists.

In Myanmar, alternative spaces providing support to the local community working with contemporary art expressions have been opening recently. Among them are New Zero Art Space[18] and Lokanat Art Gallery in Yangon. Located in a residential building, Axis Alternative Space hosted in January 2008 an exhibition entitled *Another Seven Artists* curated by NNNCL (Wah Nu and Tun Win Aung). Among the contemporary works on display were Wah Nu's *Cloud and the Sea*, an installation that included a small video component and Wai Mar Nyunt's video work *Untitled (Shwedagon by Night)*.

Support

In Cambodia and Myanmar, painting is still dominant. Video as an art medium is still not enjoying support in terms of buyers and collectors. While recent technological advances allow artists to use simple cameras or even phones to record images, edit and publish them via the Internet, video remains a relatively expensive medium.

With little state support, young local artists and art spaces receive some backing from the older generation (for example from Po Po or Kyi Wynn), a few foundations and art organisations[19]. Moreover video art is hardly understood by the officials and censorship is also one of the artists' main concerns, along with exposure.

II. Diversity of Inspirations
Cinema

Cinema in Cambodia began in the 1950s at the time of the country's independence after 90 years

Wah Nu, *Universe is Just a Fathom*, 2008. Courtesy of the artist.

as a French protectorate[20]. Many Cambodian films were screened in theatres throughout the country in the 1960s and early 1970s, a period now regarded as the golden age with more than 400 films produced. The films were popular and had themes of love, Khmer legends and folktales. Davy Chou, a Cambodian filmmaker who studied abroad and the grandson of famous filmmaker Van Chann (active in the 1960s) recalls the golden age of Cambodian cinema in his film *Twin Diamonds*[21].

In Myanmar, films with socio-political themes became popular in the 1930s. In the era that followed the 1988 pro-democracy uprising, the film industry has been increasingly controlled by the government. Over the years, the movie industry has also shifted to producing low-budget films to be distributed cheaply as video tapes and VCDs. These serve as substitutes for the lack of television and cable broadcasting in Myanmar. Most of the movies produced nowadays are comedies. Coming from a long tradition family of filmmakers[22], Wah Nu[23] is one of the leading video artists in Myanmar. She studied music at the University of Culture in Yangon and for her, music is an important supporting media for video and film. Her parents' involvement in filmmaking and production has given Wah Nu intimate insights into the film industry. Recalling this, Wah Nu said, "When I started to do my video work, at that time, I never saw video

art before … That kind of art is very new for our country till that time. But I know about this technique because I grew up in a film industry family. I know where I can find the materials such as cameras. This is a good reason why I can present my idea in this new media."[24] *Kekeke! Kebalaba!*, the video installation done with her partner Tun Win Aung, illustrates the link between her family background in filmmaking and her practice of video art (p. 250).

Performances

Performance art started in Cambodia and Myanmar in the late 1990s with pioneer artists like Aung Myint and Po Po. Performances were hardly recorded, and when they were, it was mainly with photographs. Recently artists are starting to think of video as a way to record their performances and even to integrate video in a full installation. In June 2010, in cooperation with the French Cultural Center in Phnom Penh, Meas Sokhorn realised a personal project using garbage disposal as a metaphor for apathy. The project entitled *Trash-fix* included a performance with a bicycle trash removal service, a video and an installation of the collected trash.

Music

Some artists of the younger generation in Cambodia are inspired by famous songs from the 1960s. Leang Seckon[25] for example sings traditional songs in his work to express all his "feelings about life"[26]. In his video *The Heavy Skirt* (2010) that is part of a larger installation, Seckon revisits his painful life when his mother was pregnant during the bombing campaigns of the Vietnam War. In the video, as his mother speaks of the war, we see images of flowers and the karaoke-style singing performance of the artist himself. Seckon says, "My work is showing my

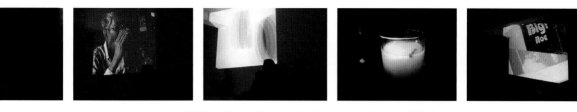

Off, Flash Memory & Light at Studio Square in Yangon, 2007. Courtesy of Studio Square.

feeling that all of us suffer and have pain. Women are our life source. We all come from the skirt." At the end of the 1980s Seckon found his musical inspiration watching a group perform in the province. It is poignant that music was used by the Khmer Rouge army during their marches to mask the sound of the gunshots. Seckon does videos karaoke-style, and talks about love stories and folktales, and also draws inspiration from the dancing and singing in Indian movies.

Documentary Video and Art

The boundary between documentary video and video art is sometimes blurred. In Svay Sareth's[27] recent exhibition *Tuesday*[28], the centrepiece was a 200-kilogram boat constructed in 2009 while the artist was studying at the Ecole des beaux-arts de Caen in France. Unsure if his boat would sink or float, Svay Sareth put the boat on a cart that he had also built and pushed it 27 kilometres for 11 consecutive hours through rural and urban Normandy in France, until he reached the sea. A video that documents his trek, *Adieu/ Goodbye*, accompanied the exhibition[29].

In Khvay Samnang's video projection *Reminder* (2008) a seemingly endless number of students appear in front of the viewer in a slideshow format. Dressed identically in school uniforms, the students wear hand-written nametags, and pose against a blue backdrop. *Reminder* occurred to the artist when he was employed to photograph 800 students for their high school graduation. While posing, students expressed shyness typical of self-con-

scious youth, but at the same time the setting was reminiscent of a culturally specific response. Their resistance to being portrayed as prisoners was a palpable reference (generations later) to the iconic black-and-white mug shots taken at a former high school turned prison during the Khmer Rouge where 14,000 people were numbered, photographed, and then murdered. The video stands between reality and fiction.

Culture and Religion

In both Cambodia and Myanmar, while Buddhism is the main religion, other local beliefs and religious practices are observed. This diversity is reflected in some video works like *Negligence Leads to Loss; Attention Preserves* by Cambodian artist Than Sok (p. 226). Nyein Chan Su's[30] video *Near Mandalay* (2009) is a short documentary video on the *nat* (spirit) festival, showing crowds at temples praying and paying respect to the *nat*[31]. Nyein Chan Su[32] used an unobtrusive hand-held camera to shoot his video documentation of both the festival and the conditions within which it takes place. The myth of the old Buddhist kingdom encounters modernity in a twofold sense: *Near Mandalay* reveals the mechanisms of commercialising faith and religion while framing an ancient ritual with contemporary video art[33].

In Wai Mar Nyunt's *Untitled (Shwedagon by Night)*, a single-channel video records the circumambulation of worshippers at the Shwedagon Pagoda in Yangon. The artist recalls, "all the worshippers who are moving around have their own stories, worries and wish for peace in mind"[34]. Here the artist takes an outsider's eye, and video is used as a social documentary.

In *Universe is Just a Fathom* (2008), realised with her partner artist Tun Win Aung, Wah Nu[35] reflects on Buddhist ontology while inspired by invasive medical technologies, creating a compelling journey that escapes its simple visual aesthetic. The work was developed when Tun Win Aung's father had to undergo an endoscopy and is inspired by an excerpt from Buddhist scriptures. The Buddha once replied to a recluse seeking the end of the universe that within the fathoms of the body all could be found: within the body lies the world itself, its beginning, its end and the ways around it. Accompanied by hydro-music by Kyaw Ko Ko (made by the sounds of water in its different states of matter), the work presents images of the universe both within and without[36].

Experimental Video Art

The younger generation of upcoming international contemporary artists include Nyein Chan Su and The Maw Naing. The Maw Naing's video *Off* is about experimentation with the video art medium itself, challenging the idea of motion nature in video. The artist said, "I just want to create a video artpiece without any movement or story." All elements in the dark are recorded as stills. "The door has been closed, the TV set was off, the switch was turned off, the computer was off, the washing machine was off, the fan was off[37]." The work may also refer to the frequent power cuts in Myanmar.

Another artist and filmmaker dealing with video experimentation is Ko Aung Ko. In his work *Light*, Ko Aung Ko aims to challenge the perception of the viewer. He said, "I have tried to get rapid shots by a harsh movement of camera[38]." The candle flame

in his video sways according to a rhythm of an emotion, like a dancing body. In reality, the flame was still and only the camera was moving.

III. The Rise of Local and International Audiences
Pioneers

For a few years now more contemporary artists such as Burmese artist Po Po[39] are able to participate in large international events such as the Kwangju Biennale or the Yokohama Triennale. The installation *Scream of the Dead* presented by Po Po at the Yokohama Triennial Exhibition in 2005 includes computerised images displayed on three computers, projections and sculptures, and dealt with the themes of documentary portraits and war history. Po Po says, "Called *Scream of the Dead*, it may help others to understand what is happening to us in Myanmar as well as in other communities. It is a metaphor for life in Myanmar and the world today[40]."

Kyi Wynn created the first interactive video installation in Myanmar called *Surveillance Six Video Screen Lives*[41] (2010). Using CCTV cameras and flat screens, the artist monitors the public visiting the exhibition. Kyi Wynn is seeking interaction with the public, and video is used as a tool for interactivity. The artist explains, "In contemporary art, the public and people must be included and participate in the art process. There is no definite identity of who the artist is but contemporary art is made through the participation of the audience[42]."

International Collaborations

Presented in Phnom Penh and Melbourne, *The Hawker's Song* is a collaborative project between two Cambodian artists, Meas Sokhorn and Srey Bandol and two Australian artists, Keith Deverell and Sue McCauley (p. 190). The full installation

Leang Seckon, *Heavy Skirt*, 2009. Courtesy of the artist. Nyein Chan Su (NCS), *Near Mandalay,* 2009. Courtesy of the artist.
Vattey Heang, *Talking Faces*, 2011. Courtesy of the artist and the French Cultural Center of Cambodia.
Blue Wind Multimedia Art Festival, 2010. Courtesy of Phyu Mon.

includes video works (by Keith Deverell and Sue McCauley), photos, performance (by Meas Sokhorn), sound and sculptures (by Srey Bandol).

Another international project is the 43-hour long audiovisual memory documentary/art installation *Voices of Khmer Rouge* consisting of 30 human stories, shown on 30 monitors, where 30 former ordinary Khmer Rouge soldiers tell about their personal life experiences during the Cambodian civil war: their upbringing, actions[43], battles, thoughts, beliefs, feelings, secrets, ideologies and values. It is an installation by Danish film directors Thomas Weber Carlsen and Jan Krogsgaard.

International Exhibitions

There are three notable local exhibitions that focus on international collaboration of video arts. Firstly, *Virtual Geometry* in 2010 presented video creations by students and young artists from the arts schools of Phnom Penh, Nantes, Caen, Lyon, Bourges, and Paris after a two-week workshop[44]. Secondly, *Digital Art Festival*, that took place in Yangon in November 2009 organised by the German Embassy and the Alliance Française. It involved eight artists of three nationalities (Burmese, German and French), who have been working together during four weeks of workshops in three disciplines: electronic art, video art and graphic art. The third event took place in September 2010 at the Dagaung Gallery in Bahan, Myanmar. The gallery hosted a multimedia art festival called *Blue*

Wind consisting of works by 58 women. The festival was organised by Burmese artist Phyu Mon, and comprised paintings, photographs, videos, documentary films, installations and sculptures. A series of talks by women artists, including Thai video artist Som Sutthirat Supaparinya and Burmese filmmaker Kyi Phyu Shin, was held n conjunction with the exhibition.

Speaking Alone: An Exhibition of Conceptual Art from Myanmar/Burma took place at the Thavibu Gallery in Bangkok in 2009. A video installation by Aye Ko, *Transfixed: Silent Escape*, included photographs and a 62-minute video showing images of the meditative gestures of the artist's body. The show displayed another video from Nyein Chan Su entitled *Goldfish* (2008) that expressed the artist's concern for his social environment though symbolic images.

The exhibition *plAy, Art From Myanmar Today*, held at the Osage Art Foundation in Singapore in 2010 presented a large collection of video works from young artists such as Ko Z (*Room*, 2009–2010); Min Thein Sung (*Restroom*, 2008–2010); Tun Win Aung (*The Train*, 2010); Wah Nu (*Aung Zeya Light Project No. 1*, 2004–2008); Zar Min Htike (*Portrait of an Artist as a Goblin*, 2009–2010).

Important platforms for exhibitions and residences like the Fukuoka Triennale, Yokohama Triennale, Bangladesh Biennale and Gwangju Biennale featured Cambodian and Burmese contemporary art including video works. Wah Nu's video *Tea Time in Spring* was presented in 2005 at the third Fukuoka Triennale. In the video, she explores the inner feelings of a woman indulging in dream/imagination, who is repeatedly awakened to reality by an image of a passing train[45].

Conclusion

It has been only a few years since Cambodia and Myanmar have been catching up on contemporary art trends. Video art is slowly emerging but a lot of effort is still needed in terms of providing training, information and exposure to the artists. Art spaces, galleries, collectors, museums to supp-

ort the contemporary art scene are also of vital importance. Video art, often seen as too intellectual or conceptual is still finding its place in the art market. In addition, both countries still carry the scars of wars and restrictions, and the expression of fear is visible in some of the artists' creations. Using the universal language of the image, video witnesses, creates, and shares a vision of Cambodia and Myanmar. This illustrates the concern about identity versus globalisation, as if artists wanted to slow down the rapid changes happening in their countries and to maintain some continuity.

1. The Socialist Republic of Burma officially adopted the name Myanmar (formally the Union of Myanmar) in 1989.
2. 'Art for art's sake', a slogan translated from the French '*l'art pour l'art*', which was coined in the early 19th century by French philosopher Victor Cousin. The phrase expresses the belief held by many writers and artists, especially those associated with aestheticism, that art needs no justification, that it need serve no political, didactic, or other end (*Encyclopædia Britannica*).
3. Turnbull, Robert, "Contemporary Art: After Troubled Past, New Expressions in Cambodian Art". In *Arts & Leisure: International Herald Tribune*, 5 July 2006.
4. Figures given by the Population Services International Myanmar (PSI).
5. See Nguyen Nhu Huy's essay, p. 39.
6. Phare Ponleu Selpak (PPS), which literally means 'the brightness of art', originated in 1986 in Site 2 Refugee Camp on the Thai border. The idea of a creative association, which would use art and expression to help young refugees overcome the trauma of war, emerged from drawing workshops held for children in the camps. This idea continued after the refugees returned to their homeland, and PPS was formally founded in 1994 by a group of former Site 2 children. http://www.phareps.org/.
7. http://www.bophana.org/.
8. In January 2007, German filmmaker Nicolaus Mesterharm and his Cambodian team opened Phnom Penh's Meta House in association with the International Academy at the Free University of Berlin. Meta House supports Cambodian artists and promotes the development of contemporary art in Cambodia through local and international exhibitions, workshops, community-based projects, artist exchange programmes and by fostering

links with Southeast Asian and international universities, galleries, curators, non-governmental and governmental organisations. http://www.meta-house.com/
9. The Yangon Film School (YFS), Association for the Promotion of Young Burmese Film and Video Artists, founded by Lindsay Merrison (UK). Since its inception in 2005, non-profit organisation YFS has brought together experienced filmmaking tutors from around the world and young Burmese men and women with some prior experience in the media for residential training in all aspects of filmmaking – from screenwriting to editing – with a particular focus on documentary. http://yangonfilmschool.org/.
10. Interview with Nicolaus Mesterharm, Phnom Penh, 16 September 2010.
11. Interview with Grace Swe Zin Htaik, Yangon, 10 August 2010.
12. Interview with Wah Nu, Yangon, 12 March 2009.
13. Reyum Institute of Arts and Cultures is a non-profit, non-governmental organisation dedicated to Cambodian arts and culture. Reyum was founded by Ly Daravuth and Ingrid Muan (1964–2005) in December 1998 to provide a forum for the research, preservation, and promotion of traditional and contemporary Cambodian arts and culture. http://www.reyum.org/.
14. Java Arts is run by Dana Langlois. http://javaarts.org/.
15. Exhibitions with video art components include *Carte blanche aux réalisateurs*, Meta House (2008); *I'm Pride*, Meta House (2009); *Géometries virtuelles*, Centre Culturel Français de Phnom Penh (2009).
16. http://www.cambodianlivingarts.org/about.
17. http://saklapel.org/.

18. http://www.newzeroartspace.com/.

19. Foundations: Prince Claus Fund, Netherlands; Asia Culture Council, USA; Heinrich Böll Foundation, Germany and Thailand; Freedom to Create, Singapore; Art Asia Network, Singapore; Japan Foundation, Japan; FOMA (Friends of Myanmar Art), USA. Art Organisations: Nipaf (Nippon International Performance Art Festival), Japan; Asiatopia International Performance Art Festival, Thailand; Cemeti Art House, Indonesia; TUPADA International Performance Art Festival, Philippines; Nha San Studio, Vietnam; Thavibu Gallery, Thailand; Antino Gallery, Singapore; Wina Gallery, Bali; Art hub, Shanghai, China; PAN ASIA, Performance Art Network Asia, Korea; Inya Art Gallery, Yangon, Myanmar; Studio Square, Yangon, Myanmar; Nan Nan Gallery, Yangon, Myanmar; Thargyi Gallery, Yangon, Myanmar.

20. *Cultures of Independence, An Introduction to Cambodian Arts and Culture in the 1950s and 1960s*. Phnom Penh: Reyum Publishing, 2001.

21. *Twin Diamond* is a 45-minute film about twin sisters, who were separated at birth and who struggle to investigate their mysterious past. Directed by Davy Chou and produced by Kon Khmer Koun Khmer along with 60 students from six universities in Phnom Penh.

22. Wah Nu's father, Maung Wunna and grandfather, U Tha Du, were famous film directors in Myanmar.

23. Wah Nu was born in Yangon in 1977, and launched her artistic career after graduating from the University of Culture, Yangon in 1998 where she majored in music. Since then she has developed a personal expression by mainly adopting painting and video as media.

24. Streitmatter-Tran, Richard, "Essay on Mapping the Mekong". In *6th Asia Pacific Triennial of Contemporary Art* (Brisbane: Queensland Art Gallery, 2009, p. 120–123).

25. Performance artist and singer, Leang Seckon was born in 1974 in Prey Veng province. He studied plastic arts from 1992 to 1997 and design from 1997 to 2002 at the Royal Academy of Fine Arts, Phnom Penh.

26. Interview with Leang Seckon, Phnom Penh 18 September 2010.

27. Svay Sareth was born in 1972 in Battambang province, and was a member of the small yet historic group of children who studied art in the Site 2 refugee camps with Véronique Decrop. Later, he co-founded Phare Ponleu Selpak, a private art school in Battambang. In 2002, he continued his studies in France, and earned the Diplôme National Supérieur des Beaux-Arts in 2009.

28. The exhibition, entitled *Tuesday* opened in March 2011 at the Arts Lounge of Siem Reap's Hôtel de la Paix and featured paintings, sculptures, and installations exploring ideas of survival and perseverance against the odds inspired by the 1719 Daniel Defoe novel *Robinson Crusoe*.

29. Article by Michael Sloan in the *Phnom Penh Post*, 4 March 2011.

30. Born in 1973 in Yangon, Nyein Chan Su (NCS) graduated from the State School of Fine Arts (Yangon). He attended the workshops on video art at the Alliance Française in Yangon. NCS started working in video art in 2002.

31. In the Taung Pyone Festival, the *nat* are worshipped and inspire a dance. The *nat* are believed to be spirits and in almost every Burmese home, there are miniature houses for the *nat*. Mandalay once used to be the capital of the last Burmese kingdom and today is the second largest city in Myanmar. In its vicinity the great Nat Festival is celebrated regularly. Belief in the *nat* is extremely widespread in Myanmar and it is to them that the people supplicate.

32. One of the most productive artists for video art in Myanmar, Nyien Chan Su's videos include *Who is?* (2004), *Opera #1, 2* (2006), *Gold Fish* (2006), *Red Circle* (2008), *Last Memory* (2010). http://www.nyeinchansu.com/videoart/.

33. http://www.transmediale.de/near-mandalay.

34. Interview with Wai Mar Nyunt, Yangon, 12 March 2009.

35. Interview with Wah Nu and Tun Win Aung, Yangon, 12 March 2009.

36. Yap, June, "You and I, We've Never Been So Far Apart". In *Videozone V: The 5th International Video Art Biennial in Israel* (Tel Aviv: The Center for Contemporary Art, 2010, p. 108).

37. *Opera # 1, 2, ...* and *Off, Flash Memory & Light*, Exhibition at Studio Square, Essay on Video Art Show by Aung Min, Yangon, 2007. http://studiosquaregallery.com/new-media.htm.

38. *Ibid*.

39. A self-taught artist, Po Po was born in 1957 in the Burmese district capital Pathein. Like other young artists from Myanmar today, he is trying to get round state repression and censorship in an experimental and interactive way. Po Po is widely regarded as Myanmar's first practitioner of performance art in the early 1990s.

40. Interview with Po Po, Yangon 7 August 2010.

41. *In Crossing Borders, Myanmar Contemporary Art Movement*, exhibition at the Lokanat Gallery, Yangon, 2010.

42. Interview with Kyi Wynn, Yangon, 7 August 2010.

43. One of the artists is Na Gyi, a video artist born in 1981 in Yangon. He studied digital filmmaking in London.

44. Artists from the Royal University of Phnom Penh include Chan Samonn, Tum Sakiny, May Sak, Meth Phearum, Vuth Sodavin, Meak Sophal, Heang Vattey, Mao Cheangleng, Sin Vuth Thoeun, Hong Bun Hak.

45. The artistic style of the video is evocative of contemporary music which repeats the same phrases. This device may be derived from the artist's career as a music teacher.

Apinan Poshyananda, *How to Explain Art to a Bangkok Cock*, 1985. Courtesy of the artist.

Video Art in Thailand

☐ Steven Pettifor

Thais have long had an obsession with the moving image. While the urban middle classes began owning television sets from the late 1960s, the agrarian majority socially congregated at newly built provincial picture houses, or at mobile cinemas touring the countryside. Dubbed *nang yai yaa*, or 'medicine movies', pharmaceutical distributors would erect a screen in villages showing dubbed mainstream Hollywood, Chinese, Indian, and locally produced flicks, with the ruse of peddling medicines to screen-sedated village folk.[1]

The popularity of films gained pace during the 1970s, dominated by B-grade movies packed with action and violence. However, television has supplanted film since the 1980s, propelled by a slew of formulaic soap operas that draw from the traditions of *lakhon* theatre as well as the great literary epic *Ramayana*. Brimming with restrained romance, the regurgitated plot lines typically focus on the hierarchy of the urban elite.[2]

Being raised on such a screen diet has proven inspirational to artists and filmmakers, none more so than director-artist Apichatpong Weerasethakul, and his occasional collaborator artist-actor Michael Shaowanasai. Weerasethakul's *Haunted Houses* (2001) is a parody of soap melodramas and their bias towards Bangkok's privileged set. In her slapstick video installation *Testosterone Paradise* (2008), Thai-British artist Tintin Cooper (b. 1982) juxtaposes classic Hollywood and Hong Kong action clips form absurd conversations.

Attached to the infrastructure of screen entertainment is the declining tradition of hand-painted movie billboards. Aside from traditional crafts and temple murals, billboard painting was one of the readily identifiable art forms people encountered beyond the capital. Such sensational craftsmanship germinated creativity for several artists, including Amrit Chusuwan (b. 1955) and Navin Rawanchaikul (b. 1971).

By the mid-1980s, home entertainment theatre had quickly become the leisure mainstay. Yet moving imagery had not permeated as a medium for visual artists. During the 20th century, artistic development in Thailand ostensibly emulated the modern movements set by Europe and America.

The establishment of a constitutional monarchy in the 1930s seeded an unyielding patriotism and nationalism, through the precepts of state, religion and monarchy. While progressive artists today expound upon societal critiques, gender delineations, and sexual identity among their subjects, conventional art is still underpinned by tributary renderings to these three tenets.

With its position as an exotic getaway historically independent from postcolonialism, Thailand has become reliant on tourism. Contrary to the country's rapid ascendency as a developing economy from the 1970s on, artists extol an Arcadian romanticism that a geographic and psychological return to the agrarian is the only way to save the nation from the psychosis and rot of modernisation, urbanism and consumerism.

Kamol Phaosavasdi, *Bon Voyage*, 2002. Courtesy of the artist.

Countering material magnetism, artists like Kamol Phaosavasdi (b. 1958) and Chusuwan have used video as an integral element to constructed environs, which like the guiding installations of Montien Boonma (1953–2000), perform as a 'temple of the mind'. Suspending the viewer from the vernacular in the hope of instilling a spiritual connection, they are driven by the Buddha's teachings.

Video first penetrated Thai art during the early to mid-1980s when graduate artist Apinan Poshyananda (b. 1956) returned from Edinburgh University after obtaining an MFA. At that juncture, the main path to domestic artistic recognition was the annual National Exhibition, which was primarily orchestrated by lecturers from the country's foremost arts institution, Silpakorn University.

The dominant university and annual award showcase were both established over half a century ago by the Florentine sculptor Corrado Feroci (1892–1962). Catalytic to the development of modern Thai art right through to his death in the 1960s, Feroci made Thailand his home from the 1920s, taking the adoptive title of Silpa Bhirasri. Rooted to canons of modernism, the Silpakorn institution could be deemed conservative to more experimental art. While international distinctions between video art and cinema increasingly blurred during the 1980s, such delineations were still pervasive in Thailand, with the medium considered peripheral.[3]

Poshyananda was instrumental to the foundation of the country's first multidisciplinary intermedia course at the state-run Chulalongkorn University. Influenced by European and American video artists Joseph Beuys, Bill Viola, and Nam

June Paik, Poshyananda also began experimenting with his family's then recently acquired VHS video camera to challenge reactionary attitudes in an entrenched art guard. As would be the case with subsequent artists utilising video, Poshyananda taught himself shooting and editing techniques.[4]

Preoccupied by the idea of reproduction and repetition, Poshyananda took on board the associated writings of Walter Benjamin as well as the pop-art iconography of Andy Warhol and Roy Lichtenstein. Interested in the degradation of an image, he appropriated da Vinci's *Mona Lisa* to construct a video sculpture incorporating a boxed television monitor and painted crates. Satirically titled after Beuys's 'action' performance *How to Explain Pictures to a Dead Hare* (1965), the 1985 *How to Explain Art to a Bangkok Cock* was a whimsical two-pronged critique, a post-modern questioning of authenticity and originality, layered with provocations to the art establishment.[5]

Today, there is a certain ironic hindsight attached to the contesting video, with Poshyananda considered an overlord of Thai art in his role as an international curator, and his current bureaucratic position as Director-General of Cultural Promotion at the Ministry of Culture (MoC).

It was during the same period of the late 1980s and early 1990s that Poshyananda's peers also began their own video experimentations. Fledgling artists returned from overseas art training: Kamol Phaosavasdi from Los Angeles, Chumpon Apisuk (b. 1948) from America and Hong Kong, and Amrit Chusuwan from Poland, bolstering a broader internationalism. Exposure to prevalent art mechanics enabled these artists to experiment with video, while home-nurtured artists still perceived video as an expensive medium geared towards commercial creativity. Approached primarily as documentation of performance works, socio-political artists Apisuk and the firebrand Vasan Sitthiket (b. 1957), began making provocative commentaries focusing on the body or self to challenge the conventions of a regimented society.

Returning from studying at Otis/Parsons Art Institute in Los Angeles in 1984, Kamol Phaosavasdi has spent over two decades steadily honing a reputation as one of Thailand's most capable electronic media artists. Experimenting with video while in the United States, Phaosavasdi visited the studio of Bruce Nauman, which proved instructive to subsequent incorporations of time-based video, sound, and participatory elements.

Exhibited in *Traditions/Tensions*, the groundbreaking 1996 international exposé on contemporary Asian art curated by Poshyananda at New York's Asia Society, Phaosavasdi first incorporated video in his installation *Mode of Moral Being*. Concerned with how the video monitor could be positioned within a larger installation, he inserted a television within the frame of a street-vendor's cart. Fringed by objects referential to the exoticisation and commodification of females in Thailand, the video featured documentary style interviews with several sex workers from Bangkok's red-light district.[6, 7]

While his work of the early 1990s highlighted environmental and political issues, at the end of the decade he was more in line with the anticipatory pre-millennial tension. In *Dilemma* (2001), *Bon Voyage* (2002) and *Memories Haunt* (2003), he is metaphysical and introspective in his attempts to unravel an individual's lifelong physical, psychological, and spiritual journey. Gravitating towards site-specific situational interactions and how audiences subjectively relate to the physicality of a space, he cites the light and space installations of American James Turrell as influential.[8]

Phaosavasdi's cerebral-therapeutic messaging was not dissimilar to other spiritually concerned Thai artists. Considering its centuries-old central role, Buddhism has long been pivotal to Thailand's cultural ideology. Aside from representations of the Buddha and his teachings, attempts to infuse modern referencing into traditional imagery have propelled the genre of Neo-Buddhism. Employing video art as a composite, Amrit Chusuwan is another artist preoccupied by Buddhist theology.

Gaining a BFA and MFA at Silpakorn University, Chusuwan studied in the late 1980s in Poland, where he regularly visited the studio of conceptual artist Tadeusz Kantor (1915–1990), who encouraged him to explore video art. Returning to Thailand at the start of the 1990s, Chusuwan created composite art installations that married conceptualism and Buddhism, evident in the Buddhist-focused video *Silent Communication* (2000). The 20-minute video shows Chusuwan intensely staring at a Buddha image and attempting to communicate by locking eyes – a simple yet potent juxtaposition of an earthbound mortal with a divine icon.

Exploring concerns over globalisation, in 2007 Chusuwan marked Thailand's third national entry at the Venice Biennale, by using malleable materials to enforce Buddhist notions of impermanence and the void of space. Installing a 2-tonne bed of sand that visitors stepped through barefoot, *Being Sand* was enhanced with ambient video wall projections of a solitary man and a dog wandering along a beach. Contradictions between the sanctuary-like cocoon and Venice's tourist crowds were heightened when exiting visitors encountered a screen showing live CCTV footage of a busy lane outside.[9]

Araya Rasdjarmrearnsook's (b. 1957) mortally engaged narratives avoid theological entrenchment. Since the latter 1990s, the Chiang Mai-based artist moved her main practice from gender-related print and sculptural installations to aesthetically arresting time-based video that have featured in numerous international showcases. A lecturer in Chiang Mai University's art faculty, Rasdjarmrearnsook received an MFA from Silpakorn University before further studies in Germany. While her art and poetry have a feminine sensibility, it is as much a provocative challenge to the accepted values in Thai art, delving into issues of dominance, religion, human relationships, origins and destiny.

While early video performances, like *Pond* (1998), were passive in delivery (Rasdjarmrearnsook recited poetry to a group of pickled cadavers floating in formaldehyde), the scholastic performance, *The Class* (2005), involved the artist directing a tutorial to a line of corpses. Engaging issues of death while highlighting differing religious and cultural attitudes to mortality, *The Class* was presented at the appropriate locale of a 13th-century church as a part of the Thai pavilion for the 51st Venice Biennale in 2005.[10]

In *Two Planets* (2007–08), Rasdjarmrearnsook reacted against the largely Western conventions to art viewing and appreciation, with four video vignettes that placed reproductions of familiar 19th-century masterpieces in front of villagers to record their responses (p. 224). Captured against rural backdrops, the anonymous gathering sit with backs to the camera, with the humorous responses from the unconditioned commentators revealing cultural nuances, as well as attitudes to race, gender roles and sex. Their sincerity and lack of pretension was a provocation towards the art-informed.[11]

Michael Shaowanasai, *Our Lady of the Low Countries*, 2008.
Courtesy of the artist.

Chiang Mai-based director Apichatpong Weerasethakul (b. 1970) propelled Asian cinema to new heights when he walked away with the 2010 Palme d'Or at the Cannes Film Festival. The winning film, *Uncle Boonmee Who Can Recall His Past Lives* (2009), is sensual in its impressions of dreams and memory, with underlying themes of ancestry, mortality and reincarnation.

Hailed as an auteur, Weerasethakul has technical mastery in all aspects of filmmaking. Delivered through languid atmospheric cinematography, nonlinear structures, and enhanced through a poetic aesthetic to space and geography, his emphasis is on rural heritage against modern urbanity, as well as sexuality and homoeroticism, animism and local folklore. He is inspired by the movies he watched as a child growing up in the impoverished north-eastern region of Isaan, by local soap operas, the live theatre tradition of *likay*, and experimental cinema à la Chris Marker.[12]

Having gained an MFA in Filmmaking, Weerasethakul is one part of the influential school of the Art Institute of Chicago graduates who returned to Thailand in the mid-1990s, making a significant contribution to Thai art. The gang includes one of the country's most respected curators, Gridthaya Gaweewong, and Michael Shaowanasai, who together initiated the non-profit arts platform of Project 304 (now defunct).

One of Thailand's only trained filmmakers to experiment in media art, Weerasethakul has explored the visual potentialities of shooting on a mobile phone for *Nokia Short* (2003) and the tsunami-resonant *Ghost of Asia* (2005), in which he invited three children to direct a solitary ghost character (pp. 160, 142).

Conscientiously attempting a more utopian approach to filmmaking, Weerasethakul recruits amateur actors in his improvisational films. One of his early collaborators, artist-actor Michael Shaowanasai (b. 1964) co-directed the camp B-movie spoof *The Adventures of Iron Pussy* (2003), in which Shaowanasai stars as the transvestite secret agent Iron Pussy.

Inspired by historical, art and film references, as well as mainstream pop culture, television and gay porn, the Thai-American multidisciplinary artist is recognised for his provocative video, photography and performances. Typically evolving from the artist dressing up in different but predomi-

59

Sudsiri Pui-Ock, *The Farmer*, 2009. Courtesy of the artist.

nantly female personas, he expresses notions of identity, celebrity and sexual orientation.

Dressed elegantly as a bejewelled society dame, in the 2008 video performance *Our Lady of the Low Countries*, Shaowanasai reinvented himself as a living public monument to explore symbols of feminine divinity. Despite any open confirmation, the female subject was interpreted as being Thailand's queen. Within the context of a patriarchal society and from the viewpoint of an openly gay male acknowledging role models as an impressionable child, the video homage explores the nature of ritualistic and/or institutionalised worship.[13]

Another artist to collaborate with Shaowanasai, and who has also been influenced by the pop aesthetic of the movie industry, is Chiang Mai-born Thai-Indian artist Navin Rawanchaikul. He is known for creating an imaginative and accessible brand of situational art that incorporates a diversity of media and collaborative characters to directly engage the community. Constructing narratives that blur reality with fiction and typically feature him as the leading player, Rawanchaikul bridges distinctions between high and mass art through the utilisation of Bollywood film and classic movie billboard painting.

A reconnection with his Indian heritage (Rawanchaikul is the son of Indian migrants) was the impetus behind his 2006 video *Navins of Bollywood*. Teaming up with Mumbai-based director Naren Mojidra, the mini-musical-style narrative evolves from his first journey back to his ancestral land. Full of humour, it is a personal quest for connection and community in an increasingly fragmented world.

The 2008 video installation *Hong Rub Khaek*, features candid documentary interviews with Chiang Mai residents of Indian origin. Discussing memories of their resettlement, aspects and boundaries of community are explored from a geo-cultural perspective, with cultural and racial implications of notions of belonging, immersion and acceptance.[14]

Raised in the digital era, the country's younger generation of multidisciplinary tech-savvy artists, like Sathit Sattarasart (b. 1979), Noraset Vaisayakul (b. 1975) and Prateep Suthathongthai (b. 1980), give greater consideration to technical aspects, such as camera-framing and editing, as well as the aesthetic architecture and ambiance of a video work. Saturated by the immediacy and intimacy of reality television and social networking sites, young artists tend to emphasise personal experiences using the self in relation to society.

A former student of Araya Rasdjarmrearnsook at Chiang Mai University, Sudsiri Pui-Ock (b. 1976) has great potential among Thailand's emergent generation of artists. Comfortably moving between photography, video performance, guerilla installations, and painting, her art has evolved to explore experiential detailing in relation to aspects of identity, immersion and acceptance within alien cultures.

Having completed several overseas residencies, Pui-Ock reveals personal thoughts on belonging, territory, and home. Such thoughts of isolation were present in the 2005 video performance *The Dinner*, in which she serves a banquet feast to invisible guests. Revealing in its emotional impact, the video is effective in conveying exclusion.[15]

Pui-Ock's first non-performative video, *The Farmer* (2009), is a time-based video of a farmer mechanically ploughing a paddy field. Framed from a high viewpoint, the film has a rhythmic and hypnotic aesthetic that invokes the cyclical nature of life, but also the increase of mechanisation against traditional farming, and the dichotomy of rural against urban.

The northern hub of Chiang Mai offers a more community-minded arts base for artists like Sutthirat Supaparinya (b. 1973), known for her video installations and interactive situational art. Incorporating reflective and transparent surfaces with pixilation distortions from advertising banners, her recent videoscapes have become increasingly politically and socially motivated as she examines the invasive saturation of media in the digital age.

Considering Thailand's underdeveloped collecting base which leans towards Neo-Buddhist imagery perpetuated through conventional media, video art has little domestic patronage. Only occasionally represented at commercial galleries, from the 1990s it has been Bangkok's university galleries, alongside rare non-commercial spaces like Project 304 and About Café/Studio (both defunct), that provided platforms for video screenings. Privately funded independent research spaces at the library of the Jim Thompson Foundation, and the small but popular Reading Room, are also sites where video art and experimental film are shown.

Unlike the fine art cadre, there appears better camaraderie among independent filmmakers and critics, as proven in the informal film bandings of Film Virus, the 3rd Class Citizens Group, and filmmaker Thunska Phansittivorakul's (b. 1973) initiated Thai Indie.[16]

Along with Weerasethakul, Gaweewong initiated the Bangkok Experimental Film Festival (BEFF) in 1996. Intended as a biannual showcase for fringe film and video art, the inaugural event screened around 50 films, most of which were foreign. For the fifth instalment in 2008, they recruited Australian curator David Teh to inject fresh perspective as it toured the provinces and overseas. An indication of the growing reputation of local filmmakers, the planned BEFF 6 in 2011 will feature over 400 films, with a significant proportion homegrown.[17]

In the context of visual art and the film industry, and against the persecutory fallout of the 2010 street protests, is the issue of censorship. In the past, occasional interventions by the Ministry of Culture as to what it deems visually appropriate for the public have seen works by Vasan Sitthiket and Michael Shaowanasai clamped or withdrawn. Yet within the visual arts, it is largely left to the galleries to pre-empt appropriate imagery or subject matter and self-censor anything potentially offensive to the status quo.

But in the more commercial world of cinema, morality surveillance towards acceptable standards is more rigorous. As a result, younger filmmakers have become more allegorical and layered to cloak potentially contentious subject matter. A critic of bureaucratic interference, Weerasekathul had his films *Blissfully Yours* (2002) and *Syndromes and a Century* (2006) tampered with, leading him to withhold the latter from domestic release.[18]

Reflecting the generally non-confrontational attitude of the populace, the majority of artists typically approach art from an apolitical viewpoint. But in the wake of the most recent coups of 1992 and 2006 – and recently evident in the deadly street protests of May 2010, artists have been incited to visualise dissent to the military putsches.

One of a number of artists who promptly responded to the violent political infraction of 2010 is Sakarin Krue-on (b. 1965), who employed literary allegory to indicate political dissatisfaction. An adaptation of a Thai folktale, his first video *Manorah and Best Friends of the Snake* (2010), mimics the sheen of early cinema through crude theatrics, camera work and editing. Yet his interpretation of the causes of the political impasse could be viewed as idealised, particularly in regard to moral waywardness a result of materialism and the media's manipulation of the masses.

Photographer Manit Sriwanichpoom (b. 1961) and his partner filmmaker Ing K. (b. 1959) are two of the only artists to regularly create visual commentaries against social and political injustices. Another artist to be clipped by censors, Ing K.'s satirical film *My Teacher Eats Biscuits* (1996) was banned by the Ministry of Education. The two collaborated on the 2008 political documentary *Citizen Juling* which examined Thailand's southern separatist issue. Their first feature *Shakespeare Must Die* (to be released in 2011) is a baroque-styled parody of Macbeth which denigrates the corrupt megalomania of Thai politics.[19]

The widespread availability of and familiarity to imaging technologies, along with web-based forums for viewing, offer greater democratic potential for today's video artists. Yet the forces of aesthetic resistance within the old art clique, commercial reluctance by galleries and collectors, funding constraints, and the constant threat of the censor's scissors, still present real challenges to the future trajectory of video art in Thailand.

1. Interview between the author and Gridthiya Gaweewong, 2010.

2. Cornwel-Smith, Philip, *Very Thai* (Bangkok: River Books, 2005), p. 238.

3. Pettifor, Steven, *Flavours – Thai Contemporary Art* (Bangkok: Thavibu Gallery, 2003), p. 10.

4. Silpasart, Chayanoot, *From Message to Media* (Bangkok: Bangkok University Gallery, 2007).

5. Interview between the author and Dr. Apinan Poshyananda, 2010.

6. Gaweewong, Gridthiya, *From Dead Art to Dilemma: Kamol Paosavasdi* (Bangkok: Thunkamol Press for Project 304, 2001), p. 17.

7. Interview between the author and Kamol Paosavasdi, 2010.

8. Pettifor, Steven, "Media Man with Conscience: Kamol Paosavasdi", *Asian Art News* 15(6), 2005.

9. Pettifor, Steven, "A Marriage of the Conceptual and Buddhism: Amrit Chusuwan", *Asian Art News* 20(3), 2010.

10. Pettifor, Steven, "Embracing Taboos: Araya Rasdjarmrearnsook", *Asian Art News* 16(4), 2006.

11. *Araya Rasdjarmrearnsook: In this circumstance, the sole object of attention should be the treachery of the moon*(Bangkok: Pimdee Printing for Ardel Gallery of Modern Art, 2009).

12. Quandt, James (ed.), *Apichatpong Weerasethakul* (Vienna: SYNEMA Publikationen, 2009).

13. Interview between the author and Michael Shaowanasai, 2010.

14. Interview between the author and Navin Rawanchaikul, 2010.

15. Pettifor, Steven, "Disturbing Narratives: Sudsiri Pui-Ock", *Asian Art News* 19(4), 2009.

16. Interview between the author and Narawan Pathomvat, Director of the Reading Room, 2010.

17. Interview between the author and David Teh, 2010.

18. "Apichatpong Weerasethakul: Agrarian Reincarnations of Cinema by HG Masters", *ArtAsiaPacific* Issue 70, Sep/Oct 2010.

19. "Journey into Film-making", *The Bangkok Post*, 11 December 2010, Muse section, pp. 8–9.

Liew Kung Yu, *A Passage Through Literacy*, 1989. Courtesy of the artist.

Languages and Locations:
Video in the Malaysian Art Context

☐ Adeline Ooi and Beverly Yong

In 1989, Liew Kung Yu exhibited a work called *A Passage Through Literacy* at the Young Contemporaries Competition show at the National Art Gallery. The work consisted of a sculpture of a broken egg on a low plinth, wrapped in strips of cloth stretching to the floor and ceiling, and embedded with a television monitor screening the documentation of a performance in which dancer Marion D'Cruz interacts with an audiovisual projection of random letters of the alphabet. This moment marked, if rather literally, the 'birth' of video as a medium in visual art practice in Malaysia.

Also in 1989, recently arrived American artist Ray Langenbach presented the synchronised video installation *The Language Lesson* in the inaugural exhibition of Galeri Luar Pusat at Universiti Sains Malaysia (USM), Penang. This featured a pair of 'talking heads' screened on two television monitors mounted on rattan torsos in what begins as a basic conversation between the English-speaking artist and a Malay-speaking woman, gradually broaching the contentious territories of cultural imperialism, racism, religion and politics in a 'dialogue' which never breaks the language barrier.

We can locate this emergence of video art in Malaysia in the context of a broader movement in the arts towards active experimentation and interdisciplinary approaches in the 1980s and early 1990s. Practitioners from the fields of literature, performance, film, music and the visual arts were seeking strategies to express a newfound criticality and awakening of social consciousness in an adolescent Malaysia coming to terms with the realities of rapid modernisation, the complexities and sensitivities of a multicultural society, and tumultuous local and global political events.[1] Concerns at the time centred around re-evaluating Malaysian postcolonial identity, and deconstructing the traditions of (Western) modernist influences to find a new 'language' of art to reflect the Malaysian perspective and experience. Emerging technologies offered new possibilities for creative media. Video signified a *tabula rasa* unconstrained by the weight of traditional media still dominant in the visual art scene, immediate and relevant to the (then) contemporary (techno pop) *zeitgeist*. The two 'pioneer' video installations by Liew and Langenbach nicely introduce the medium of video as a site of 'language learning', and within these works we see in embryo some of the many discourses which the medium would come to engage with, revolving around cross-disciplinary practice, the body in performance, the influence of new media technology, and cultural space and conflict.

Efforts to document the development of video art in Malaysia over the past 30 years since have shown this to be an elusive history, not easily bent to a linear reading of any specific tradition or discourse. Rather, video as a language has continued to prove an open and malleable medium within the scope of many different types of art practices, developing and expanding its reach in tandem with advances in video technology. The ubiquitous, democratic language of video at the same time operates as a creative and empowering medium in a much broader alternative Malaysian cultural discourse, which might include cultural documentation, experimental film, social advocacy and education projects, alternative media and other practices perhaps yet to be defined, sometimes blurring into concepts of video art.

Multilingual: Video in Interdisciplinary Practice

The collective Five Arts Centre[2] would prove instrumental in creating a platform for interdisciplinary practice in the 1980s and 1990s through its many projects bringing the streams of theatre, dance, music and visual arts together, often including video elements. Five Arts' multimedia performances such as *Skin Trilogy* (1995) and *Rama & Sita: Generasi Baru* (1996),[3] like labDNA's *To Catch A Cloud* (1996),[4] incorporated multi-channel video art, animation, live video feed, and video projections, and included visual artists among their collaborators.

Meanwhile, young artists spearheaded a move away from conventional visual art forms, calling for greater engagement with medium and concept, producing installations and mixed media work which incorporated video and performance. Wong Hoy Cheong's *Sook Ching* (1990) brought together an experimental video documentary based on interviews with survivors of the purges during the Japanese Occupation, an epic-scale painting and a collaborative performance. Liew Kung Yu's *Who Am I?* (1991) addressed issues of religious fanaticism, Chinese tradition and belief in an installation of Chinese prayer altars, and video work presented in a row of television monitors set on the floor, accompanied by a perform-

ance by the artist (breaking and throwing altar paraphernalia). Both works were shown at Alter Art, a presentation of six multimedia installations and performances at TheatreWorks in Singapore in 1991. These early examples were precursors to later installation works incorporating video by artists like Ahmad Fuad Osman, Masnoor bin Ramli, and Nur Hanim Khairuddin among many others.

In these different ways, video has established itself as part of the language of local interdisciplinary practice, of the arts event, at the same time absorbing into its own language those of theatre, performance, sound, literature, and spectacle. Today, this spirit of 'multilingual' collaboration continues in the work of young multimedia artists and groups experimenting with digital video feed, sound and performance such as Fairuz Sulaiman + Flica, Space Gambus Experiment, and Findars. 'VJ-ing', whereby artists/videographers mix and sample visual tracks as part of experimental performances combining electronic sounds and images, is gaining attention among a young niche audience.

New Coding: Video as New Media Art Practice

Concurrent with developments in the interdisciplinary arts scene in the 1990s were tentative efforts to introduce video and other electronic media – 'new media' – into local art education, whose mainstream focus from then until now has centred very much on plastic media (painting, sculpture, textiles, ceramics). By the end of the 1990s, new media, with video at its core, had found a firm place in the local art scene, as testified by the landmark *1st Electronic Art Show* at the National Art Gallery in 1997 and the resource E-Art ASEAN Online.[5] Competitions such as the National Art Gallery's Young Contemporaries Award pro-

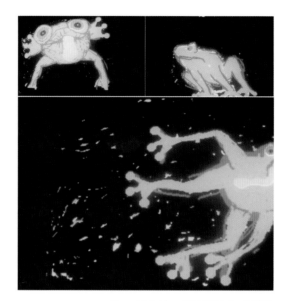

Hasnul J. Saidon, *Kdek! Kdek Ong!*, 1994.
© 1994 Hasnul J. Saidon.
Collection of the National Art Gallery of Malaysia.

vided exposure for local young talents eager to work with new media, as did events like the *SONY Video Art Festival* in 1994, and the annual *Malaysia Video Awards* (1994–2005).[6] Exhibitions such as *Flow-Arus: Electronic Media Art from Australia and Malaysia* (2000) and more recently *Malaysia-Japan Video Art Exchange* (MJVAX) (2010) have placed Malaysian artists in a larger network of video/new media art practice.

Ray Langenbach, who headed the Sculpture department at Universiti Sains Malaysia in Penang from 1988 to 1992, encouraged students to explore building robots, in part as a strategy to circumvent criticism about figurative representation from conservative Islamic quarters in the University at the time. Some of the works that emerged incorporated the use of video, notably Baharuddin Arus' installation in 1989 experimenting with perspective and reflexivity in relation to

an Islamic subject. Here an automaton affixed with a video camera encircled a television monitor on a black cuboid plinth, screening an image of the Ka'aba circumambulated by the crowds at Mecca montaged with footage of the room recorded by the video camera, as well as news and advertising images from television.[7]

Hasnul J. Saidon, a central pioneering figure in new media practice and education in Malaysia, returned from the United States with an MFA in Electronic Arts to teach at Institut Teknologi MARA in 1993, where he tried to introduce new ideas about process and methodology in its painting and drawing department in the face of some resistance. He went on to design a new curriculum in Integrated Art at Universiti Malaysia Sarawak (UNIMAS), and later to lecture in New Media at USM. He has initiated numerous programmes involving integrated media, both in collaboration with electronic art 'guru' Niranjan Rajah and more recently as director of USM's Muzium dan Galeri Tuanku Fauziah, where he has also incorporated new media including video works into its collection strategy.

For Hasnul, the virtual nature of video and other digital media marries well with Eastern philosophy and Islam, reflecting a concept of reality as illusion, as a coding of the mind. In a contemporary experience suffused with televisual information, engaging with video through art practice, theory and criticism is also an important means of "critique of the tools that define us". His work with video has mostly been a form of self-deconstruction. Initially formalist in approach, and playing off cultural and information theory, it has explored structure, montage, and the basic properties of video, integrating computer and sound processing, often making use of visual and linguistic/literary puns. Early works include the video installation *Kdek, Kdek Ong!* (1994) – in reference to the Malay saying '*seperti katak dibawah tempurung*' (like a frog under a coconut shell) – which describes his predicament as an artist who having ventured into new territories is unable to escape the limitations of his local situation, and *Mirror, Mirror on the Wall* (1994) which parodies the struggle of the modern Western artist-hero (here, a digital portrait of Vincent Van Gogh morphs into and out of an image of his angst-ridden self). Hasnul's work paved the way for other young artists in the 1990s from the fine arts, design and communications fields who began to explore and experiment with the nature of video as a medium.

A former lecturer at UNIMAS now based in Canada, Niranjan Rajah spearheaded the use of the Internet and computer technology as both an art medium and an art space in his practice which embraces the concept of virtual geography and participatory processes,[8] often incorporating and playing with video, most recently VJ-ing with footage from YouTube. *Video Reflux* (2007) "addresses the decline of the [figurative] power of video in the face of the sharing, recycling, appropriating and annotating of content over the Internet", a context which has shaped the way a new generation of Malaysian artists engages with video, as we will see at the end of this essay.

Video camera technology and the evolving role of the surveillance camera and live transmission have created avenues for physical dialogue between the viewer and the viewed,[9] as seen in Baharuddin Arus' work. Langenbach used the video camera to implicate his audience in *Framing War II* (1992) – as each viewer passed under the lens of the camera, his/her image would be labelled with the text 'Responsible for the war'. More recently, Lim Kok Yoong has used video and motion sensors in audience-participatory works. In the installation *When You Are Not Your Own Body* (2008), the artist sets out to displace viewers' awareness of their own presence and existence by using a digital video feed, transferring live images of viewers into another 'space' and 'body', forcing each person to confront his/her self as an 'other' image or subject.[10]

Reframing: Video as a Locus of Contending Discourses

The pervasiveness and influence of video in contemporary life as a source of information and a tool for commercial and political propaganda lends it a particular relevance and power as an alternative creative medium. Perhaps for those in the developing world especially, there is a will to reclaim video from mainstream broadcast, as a weapon of empowerment and criticism to document and create alternative narratives. In Malaysia, a culture of independent film, of video as a form of social advocacy, and of video as documentation of cultural practice has taken root, counter to a mainstream checked by restricted press freedom.

The complexity of Malaysia's social, political and religious make-up, and its self-positioning as a model of modern Islamic society as well as a model multi-racial country, have made video representation a hot locus of contending discourses and a powerful tool for visual artists addressing issues of power discourse, identity, social change and history.

Nur Hanim Khairuddin's work *Se(rang)ga* (2003) mounts a strong critique of Western mainstream media's projection of Islam, and more generally the power of images to influence perception. We are subjected to a barrage of the televisual and sound, an accelerating montage of images drawn from mainstream media: Osama and Bush, stereotypes of 'fundamentalist' Islam as well as of the 'licentious' West, war and devastation, to the soundtrack of war chants and electric grunge. The video begins with an image of the artist's face in alien green, shrouded by a headcloth (*hijab*), and the artist's statement in text, which quotes from Baudrillard and speaks of how "excessive disinformation, misconception and distortion deliberately manufactured by the media construct false realities". Pairs of eyes gradually swarm the portrait and fall away again like insects (*serangga*: insect; *serang*: attack, and *rangga*: label or status).

Wong Hoy Chong, within his larger multidisciplinary practice, has been investigating and exploiting the 'politics' of the video medium: the dynamics of the camera, object and audience,

and the malleability of authorial responsibility and audience reception. If *Sook Ching* sought to reclaim a forgotten, 'erased' chapter in Malaysian history using the language of video documentary, over a decade later the artist re-invents an entire political history in the mockumentary *Re: Looking*.[11] Adopting the format of historio-cultural documentary to re-imagine a postcolonial reality in which Austria is a former colony of the Malaysian empire, it neatly reverses media perceptions of economic and cultural hegemony while touching on issues such as migration, racial tension, social inequality, political imprisonment and historical revisionism, deconstructing the workings of television media on our reading of politics, culture and history. In later works, the artist attempts to surrender ownership of the camera to enable alternative viewpoints. *Trigger* imagines the experience of Roy Rogers' horse on his visit to Liverpool, an equine witness to Anglo-American relations in a five-channel projection shot from five cameras on a horse for the Liverpool Biennale (2004); in *Suburbia* (2006), the landscape of two Malaysian townships is tracked from cameras attached to a toy car and the feet of a wheelchair. In *Aman Sulukule, Canim Sulukule (Oh Sulukule, Darling Sulukule)* (2007), the camera is placed in the hands of Roma children in Istanbul, documenting their own everyday experiences in a work which also incorporates stopmotion footage of clay figurines made by the children – a story of hopes and dreams.

Video incorporating found photographic images has been used as a means of entering, altering and reclaiming the historical past. Ahmad Fuad Osman's *Recollections of Long Lost Memories #8* (2007) projects a succession of manipulated images in which a time-travelling long-haired artist gatecrashes key moments in Malay(si)an history.[12]

In Nadiah Bamadhaj's work, video, photographic imagery and authorial narrative come together to create a form of moving visual poetry. In *Not Talking to a Brick Wall* (2005), female members of the current generation of the artist's family walk into and survey the architecture of their ancestral home captured in old photographs. In *Beyond Recognition* (2006), excerpts from Joseph Conrad's short story *The Lagoon* set in the rainforest of 19th-century Malaya (or the Malay Archipelago) are written into a 'filmed' sequence of photographs of the landscape of the Faroe Islands, 'misplacing' received notions of colonial narratives and geography.

Location: Landscape and Architecture in Video

Hayati Mokhtar's practice uses the time-based nature of the video medium to address time, place and memory. *Near Intervisible Lines* (2006) made in collaboration with filmmaker Dain Said approaches landscape as an abstract understanding of place. The sand-spit in Setiu on the Malaysian east coast, an in-between, ambiguous space, is used to explore displacement and belonging – man's connection to his surrounding environment. New advances in video projection systems allow us to experience video art on a cinematic scale and *Near Intervisible Lines* is an epic presented on four

Wong Hoy Cheong, *RE: Looking*, 2002–2003. Courtesy of the artist.

large screens. Heavily influenced by the language of cinema, the images are rich in colour, detail and emotion, creating a physical experience as viewers 'enter' the work while the framing and the stillness of the panorama allude to the tradition of land-scape painting.[13] *Penawar* (2007) and *No. 55 Main Road* (2010), historical portraits of place, display a similar 'filmic' approach. *Penawar*, presented as a two-channel projection, records the packing up and closing of a stately home in Penang while *No. 55 Main Road*, a three-channel video projection, captures 87-year-old Uncle Chang in his home located south of Ipoh, which faces imminent demolition. In both, split screens juxtapose static

shots of the respective building exterior against slowtrack movements of interiors, creating time-based portraits of two vastly different buildings which are simultaneously historical/cultural land-marks and spaces of personal memories.

The aesthetics of place also figures prominent-ly in Malaysian independent films. From fishing villages to oil palm plantations or sleepy tin-mining towns where nothing much ever hap-pens, films such as Ho Yuhang's *Rain Dogs* (2006), Chris Chong's *Karaoke* (2009) and Bernard Chauly's *Goodbye Boys* (2006) are very much rooted in the concept of place, as each story is framed within the context of a particular environment and its relationship to its characters. Chris Chong's short film, *Block B* (2008) is a portrait of an apartment block and its residents who are mostly of the local Indian community and Indian expatriate workers. The fixed camera watches day turning into night across the courtyard at the building's façade, a stunning graphic network of horizontal and vertical lines, voyeur-like, as events unfold on various floors of the apartment complex to the soundtrack of residents' conversations. Conceived by the artist as a "living painting" or "a theatre performance through film using a 20-storey building as my stage, and using people's movements, clothing, fabrics, lights, and colours as my visual storytelling tools",[14] *Block B* straddles the independent film and visual art scenes, featuring in both international film circuits and museum presentations.

Private Space: Video as Performance Document

Performance and video have converged in a number of interdisciplinary installations and presentations, and video has also been used to document performance art works, allowing future and remote audiences to access what is usually a one-time presentation. *Lost Land* (1992) by Tan Chin Kuan and *Bernafas Dalam Lumpur (Breathing in Mud)* (1994) by Noor Azizan Paiman are early examples of video as performance document. Multidisciplinary artist Ahmad Fuad Osman, who consistently works with performance, employs video to document his work on identity and the body: *Hair Piece/Peace* (2004) which was performed during the artist's residency at Vermont Center Studios where members of the audience were invited to cut a length of the artist's hair, and *Some(one)* (2006) performed at Alternative Art Space LOOP in Seoul. Ray Langenbach's monumental Malay-

sian Video Archives project documents performing arts and performance art events in Malaysia from 1988 to 2006, a crucial initiative which also explores the role of artist as archivist.

For artists Au Sow Yee, Kok Siew Wai and Chan Seau Huvi, active members of SicKL (a studio for experimentation with various artistic disciplines), video is a potential alternative performance space, enabling a level of intimacy and the privacy to do things in front of a camera that they may not necessarily do in the presence of live audiences. Within the context of Malaysia where nudity and overt expressions of sexuality are considered taboo and may be read as offensive by Muslim audiences, video allows these women artists (Kok and Chan particularly) to express concerns relating to issues of body, gender and sexuality.

Popular Space: the New Demographics of Video

Current media and digital technologies have transformed and expanded artists' understanding of and approach to video. Video is now easily accessible, user-friendly and ubiquitous. It is no longer just a function of the video camera per se but also that of mobile phones, webcams, etc., allowing for new modes of practice which distance artists from the actual process of image creation in the conventional sense – the weight and preciousness of making a work. As a result, the engagement that younger Malaysian artists (who have grown up in the digital age) have with video tends towards the diverse, whimsical and casual. For them, video is perhaps one of the most immediate, 'natural' and relevant media for self-expression. Their grasp of the world is reflected in their visual surroundings dominated by moving images in the form of motion pictures, television,

Hayati Mokhtar, *Penawar*, 2007. Courtesy of the artist.

computer displays, computer games and virtual reality, surveillance television etc. on different media platforms and interfaces.

Artists commonly appropriate, co-opt and reinvent languages of image construction from cinema and television. In *Manglish for Beginners, Part 1!* (2007), Emil Goh returned to Malaysia and hit the streets of Kuala Lumpur to interview Malaysians about their favourite word in Manglish, a special mix of English and various local dialects that is adopted by all races in most urban centres. Presented in an 'on the ground' interview format, this work combines the styles of variety talk shows and language lesson programmes commonly seen on television. Vincent Leong 'borrows' Bruce Lee and Chuck Norris' ultimate fight scene at the Coliseum in Rome in *The Way of the Dragon*

(1972) in *How To Be Bruce* (2004). Here, Leong sets out to highlight Bruce Lee's graceful movements and masterful choreography by distilling the fight sequence into moving arrows and bouncing dots in blue (to signify Bruce Lee) and red (Chuck Norris), cutting the action into a sequence of codes. Meanwhile, Roslisham 'Ise' Ismail's *HI-S-TORY* (2008), a hilarious animated re-telling of the story of the legendary Hang Tuah's adventures in Malacca fuses footage from the original movie in Bahasa Malaysia with animation – raw and DIY – and voiceovers in a gibberish of Hakka, Mandarin, Bahasa Malaysia and English. Turning official text on its head, the work proposes the possibility that this national icon, the symbol of Malay bravery, may actually come from mainland China.

Emerging artist Chi Too's expositions of the personal and banal are often subtle parodies of art-making and satires of the personal-political. His video works reflect the artist's urban, media-savvy sensibility and are imbued with a sense of childlike wonder and longing (to engage). Characterised by repetitive (and at times futile) acts and gestures, works such as *Kafka Di America* (2008), *Watching Paint Dry* (2009), *The Way You Make Me Feel* (2009) and recently *Longing #3 a.k.a Longing is a Motherfucker* (2010) and *Longing # 5 Siapa Menang Dia Dapat* (2010) are irreverent and deliberately irritating.

Charming in its simplicity, *Making Night* (2006) by Sharon Chin and Iskandar Razak is based on the constellations of stars above three cities – Kuala Lumpur, Bangkok and Jerusalem – at 10pm on the first night of Ramadan in 2006. Filmed using a mobile phone placed in a shoebox with the lid shut, "night is made" by punching holes through the cardboard box, registered as points of light (or "stars") by the camera. Using micro to suggest macro, the simple action of punching holes in a shoebox is juxtaposed against the suggestion of an infinitely wide and complex, yet ultimately unifying, cosmos.

As the language of video – even its local patois – updates its vocabulary and redefines its syntax, so does its potential audience. The self is increasingly networked with others on various digital platforms. Sophisticated and instant channels of networking and communications have created different emotional and communication spaces previously unavailable in 'pre-Internet' video.

The brainchild of techno-preneurs, Hardesh Singh and Adam William, PopTeeVee is an Internet-based network which carries alternative programming with the primary objective "to engage with young Malaysians to help create a far more democratic media space". Programs like current issues talk show *The Fairly Current Show* and *That Effing Show*, satirical news programmes[15] have gained a large cult following, reflecting the evolution of video culture as "no longer an innocent play-thing of conceptual art. It has struggled to wean itself from the gallery and museum scene and developed its own community of co-operatives, festivals, academic programs, and independent production venues."[16] PopTeeVee programmes irreverently appropriate the styles of mainstream television and popular culture to engage with the current (apathetic and apolitical) 20-something audience, democratising access to and consumption of information and ideas with its "free for all" approach as programmes are filtered through Facebook, YouTube, Twitter or other social networking sites and personal blogs, breaking down traditional hierarchies of distribution. The way information is accessed becomes personality driven – dependent on who is sharing or recommending the link or programme, shifting audience attention away from the 'maker/author' towards more fluid ideas of creative participation.

Niranjan Rajah has proposed that "the sharing, recycling, appropriating, annotating and recontextualising of video has become both a disseminative and a dissipative force in contemporary visual culture".[17] From this survey of video in Malaysian art practice at least, we might find rather that artists are still constantly finding in video meaningful ways of engaging with that visual culture, and indeed finding new channels through which to infiltrate it.

1. Particularly Ops Lalang, a major crackdown on opposition leaders, social activists and the press by the Malaysian government in 1987 and the Gulf War in 1991–92.

2. Founded in 1984 by theatre directors Krishen Jit and Chin San Sooi as "a collective of artists and producers dedicated to generating alternative art forms and images in the Malaysian creative environment", Five Arts' scope of work includes theatre, dance, music, visual arts and young people's theatre.

3. Both were Five Arts productions, the latter in collaboration with Dramalab.

4. A collaboration between artist Yee I-Lann and architect Nani Kahar, produced by the latter's architectural practice, DNA.

5. Both are initiatives of Hasnul J. Saidon and Niranjan Rajah. E-Art ASEAN Online was a groundbreaking Internet database, journal and forum on new media art in the region set up in 1999 hosted by UNIMAS which has since been taken offline.

6. An initiative of post-production house VHQ and then MFX which included a category for experimental video, sponsored by the National Art Gallery. Past winners in this category have included artists and filmmakers such as Hasnul J. Saidon, Liew Kung Yu, Bernard Chauly, Nazim Esa, Sidney Tan, Ho Yuhang, Vincent Leong and Sherman Ong.

7. As described by Ray Langenbach in conversation, illustrated in the catalogue to *1st Electronic Art Show*, National Art Gallery, Kuala Lumpur, 1997.

8. As early as 1996, the artist made his first webwork *Failure of Marcel Duchamp*.

9. Krauss, Rosalind, "Video: The Aesthetics of Narcissism", *October* 1, Spring 1976, pp. 50–64.

10. Soon, Simon, *Bombay Sapphire Art Project 08: Lim Kok Yoong, When You Are Not Your Own Body* (Kuala Lumpur: Valentine Willie Fine Art, 2008).

11. This work is presented as an installation, the episode of the video mockumentary, *LUST & EMPIRE: The Discreet Rule of Malaysia in Austria 1683–1955* screened on a television set in a post-Empire Malaysian living room, where the audience can also access the broadcaster's website: http://www.relooking-mbc.com/. It was made in collaboration with Arifwaran Shaharudin for the video and Chimera Design for the website.

12. *Recollections of Long Lost Memories* is a body of work also including prints of the screened images and a series of paintings.

13. Interview with the artist via e-mail, 23 Jan 2006.

14. Interview with the artist via e-mail, 17 Nov 2010.

15. Produced by Mark Teh, *The Fairly Current Show* is hosted by Fahmi Fadzil and *That Effing Show* by Ezra Zaid.

16. Clarke, David, "The Ghost of an Exquisite Corpse". In Reinke, Steve and Tucker, Tom (eds.), *LUX: A Decade of Artists' Film and Video* (Toronto: YYZ Books, 2000).

17. Niranjan Rajah, quoted by Roopesh Sitaran in the exhibition thematic for *Relocations: Electronic Art of Hasnul Jamal Saidon & Niranjan Rajah*. Accessed 6 December 2010 from: http://www.12as12.com/relocations/.

Mohammad Akbar, *The Tubes*, 2008.
Courtesy of ruangrupa and OK. Video Festival, Jakarta, Indonesia.

Indonesian Video Art and New Media Culture

☐ Krisna Murti

Indonesian video art was not born out of a vacuum. Socio-culturally, it emerged in relation to the spread of new media culture in society. Television was the first media technology to shape media culture in Indonesia in the 1960s. In the decades that followed, this influence was accompanied by the emergence of video games, computers, mobile phones, CCTV, the Internet and its applications like YouTube. Media technology is practised – or more specifically, consumed – by the majority of people who use it as tools for their utilitarian, entertainment and lifestyle needs. This constitutes mainstream media culture. In the midst of this mainstream culture, awareness has arisen amongst individuals to use the same media to go beyond these functions. This is a cultural awareness which includes what we can call art: video art or new media art.

New Media: Television to the Internet

Media technology and information technology are basically neutral. But in practice, they become part of a struggle between political power, corporations and the public. When television first appeared in Indonesia (1962), the first president of Indonesia, Soekarno used it to arouse the spirit of nationalism. After that, under the authoritarian regime of Soeharto for 32 years (1966–1998), communication satellite technology, PALAPA, allowed people living across the thousands of islands to receive broadcasts of government programmes on TVRI (Televisi Republik Indonesia). TVRI with the slogan of *"persatuan dan kesatuan"* ("united and a unity")

was in fact more of a tool to centralise power and promote the mystification of Soeharto. For almost the entire period of Soeharto's reign, there was only one government television station in Indonesia. The people had no choice in televisual content. What is sad is that political propaganda certainly did construct reality, shaping the way an entire generation viewed the world around them.

In about the 1980s, shops renting entertainment videos began to offer films from Hollywood and Bollywood, as well as local films. Satellite dishes sprung up everywhere, but the information ministry at the time banned them. Nevertheless, technology made it possible for people to access alternative information from outside the territory. In 1997, shortly before Soeharto stepped down, the first private television station RCTI (Rajawali Citra Televisi Indonesia) appeared, offering an array of entertainment programmes. It was ironic because this station was owned by Soeharto's son, and almost immediately people could witness the reformation process towards political democratisation on their television screens. Packaged in the form of entertainment, news of *Reformasi* was automatically disseminated to every corner of the country. Private television continued to grow. Meanwhile talk shows, news and political debates offered alternatives to *sinetron* ("electronic cinema" or soap operas) which the wider public enjoyed. Profit-oriented corporate interests serving market tastes hence took over the power previously held by the political sector.

Tintin Wulia, *Slambangricketychuck*, 2002. Courtesy of the artist.

What was the position of the people in this struggle? Although the number was relatively small, intellectuals, university students, activists and others who used the Internet via cyberspace and through mailing lists such as *Apa Kabar* joined demonstrators marching in the streets to fight for *Reformasi*. It took place just moments before the transfer of power and evidenced the emergence of the people's awareness of the new media as a means of expressing their aspirations outside the existing information structure. John A. Walker explains that "the aim of the community arts and media movement is precisely to provide a decentralised form of media".[1]

The tradition of opposing flawed bureaucracy continued over the past two to three years. An example is the movement of 1 million Facebook users in 2009 calling for Prita to be acquitted from the charge of defaming a private hospital on the outskirts of Jakarta. What simply began as a housewife voicing her complaints on a blog was reported to the police by hospital authorities and the case was eventually brought to court. When the news was broadcast on television, it immediately drew attention and gained people's solidarity.

Obviously, the story of media culture is not only full of political nuance. There is also the tale of the young female lip-sync duet, Jojo-Sinta, which performed the *dangdut* song, *Keong Racun*.[2] Through YouTube, that video was downloaded by more than 4.7 million viewers. Jojo and Sinta went from complete unknowns to celebrities in advertisements and guest stars on talk shows. This is a brief anecdote on how the new media culture has changed behaviour, identity and even the system and power of information.

Video Art Interprets Media Culture

The power struggles of media culture have been mentioned earlier. Artists, while part of the public, form a small yet very significant group in terms of cultural attitudes. Here, a new awareness clearly emerged amongst individuals (and groups) to use media technology (including video) artistically as well as critically for cultural expression.

How should the relationship between art and this broader media culture be read? Let us look at a statement made by Christine Hill and quoted by Michael Rush: "… in order to have a critical relationship with a televisual society, you must primarily participate televisually".[3]

Televisual participation is expressed by Mohammad Akbar through the video installation *The Tubes* (2008), and it can be read as a conceptual statement. Three televisions show a video recording which throughout the duration presents the electronic components of the television itself. This means that "concept=content". Another case is Tintin Wulia. She criticises television programmes as being uniformly narrative and linear through a random visualisation video titled *Slambangricketychuck* (2002). This video really offers

Jompet Kuswidananto, *Neighbours*, 2000. Courtesy of the artist.

a new way of perceiving the language of moving pictures. Meanwhile, Jompet in his art television programme *Neighbours* (2000) shows that public participation is content. Television, as we know, is top-down, one-directional communication. Jompet breaks down the discourse on broadcast technology by facilitating the involvement of people living in a nearby neighbourhood to become equal participants: scriptwriters, cameramen, broadcasters and viewers at the same time. A possible entry point to understanding the piece by Jompet is Neil Postman's definition of media ecology: "Media ecology looks into the matter of how media of communication affect human perception, understanding, feeling, and value, and how our interaction with media facilitates or impedes our chances of survival. The word ecology implies the study of environments: their structure, content and impact on people."[4] However, an understanding through a study involving the structure, content and its influence on the public is not complete, because *Neighbours* is clearly a mediation on Postman's theme. Jompet's participative action of media ecology is actually an effort to facilitate the public in making social change happen.

This participatory character is explored by Wimo Bayang in an effort to question once again the hierarchical quality of CCTV that positions people as monitored objects. In his piece, *About Me About You* (2003), Wimo installed a CCTV camera and video on the head of a person walking through a city.

The principle of this CCTV piece deconstructs the distinction between actor and director, those being monitored and the one who monitors.

While Wimo is attracted to the technological aspect, Yusuf Ismail and Anggun Priambodo criticise the video genre. In the perspectives of Yusuf and Anggun, entertainment videos – local as well as global – dominate public life, and they are controlled by the entertainment industry. This has inspired the pair to create alternatives in the form of parodies. *Belah Duren Stranger* (2008) is a music video of puns by Yusuf on the sexy moves of American pop icon Madonna in the original music video for "Beautiful Stranger". In Yusuf's hands, it becomes a witty joke: Madonna mouths the lyrics in Indonesian of "lower class" *dangdut* music from the music video *Belah Duren*.[5] On the whole, this video still entertains, but because of the play – juxtaposition and collision – with cultural codes, semiotics and body gestures, it clearly pokes at the cultural construct residing in many people's minds.

Anggun's *Sinema Elektronik* (2009) is basically a lampoon of the video genre of commercial television in Indonesia. Soap operas are known as *sinetron* or 'electronic cinema' in Indonesia (*telenovela* in Latin America). Anggun's video actually imitates all the extravagant lifestyles stereotypically shown in *sinetron*: expensive homes, cars and swimming pools, as well as high fashion and snobbish behaviour. This lifestyle is of course diametrically opposed to the lives of most Indonesians. The video satirises it by exaggerating the extravagance and is intended to highlight the boundary between dream and reality, between that which is superficial and that which is not; it addresses what is usually masked by television culture as the myth of "reality". In the words of Sylvia Martin, "Television itself had meanwhile developed into a hybrid construct, in which one could only with difficulty distinguish between information and entertainment, documentary and fiction".[6]

Media, the Body and Performativity

Another trend which appears in Indonesian videos is the presence of the body (of the artist). From the perspective of performance art, the body is a concept, a context, and at the same time, an artistic process. This is almost parallel to the character of time, event, the ephemeral and immaterial in video (and other new media). As such, many artists (including performers) regard media as an extension of the body. This body-media synergy makes the intervention in social activities effective.

The performance video *Illumination* (2007) by Melati Suryodarmo can be read with this understanding. Artistically, this video borrows its visuals from television commercials for cosmetic products – but with a reversed logic. Melati's performativity[7] aims to provoke the viewers – directly – by slapping her face, over and over again. This is the opposite of what is seen in cosmetic commercials in which the body tends to be caressed. This pounding performance strategy is also used by Reza 'Asung' Afesina in his piece *What…* (2001). In a Foucouldian narrative, the body is disciplined, to become beautiful or handsome (according to a commercial vision), and that is essentially a process of torture. For Melati (and Asung), video

is a project of mapping and re-examining this cultural construct which is unfortunately mostly dominated by market logic.

The practice of torture through the misuse of media is "roughly" shown by Marzuki and the group Performance Fucktory in the multimedia performance *I'm Sorry I'm Fucking Sorry* (1999) in which Marzuki's body is hung and connected to electric cables. In a participatory way, the viewers are invited to press buttons that send electric currents to the performer's body, while a number of screens show a body being tortured. Here the viewers are not only witnesses but are actors/participants in the act of torture.

The effectiveness of the above described performance videos lies not only in their artistic quality, but their being shown repetitively (as a loop). A loop, according to Lev Manovich, is a new narrative form.[8] The loop in a performance video – especially in Melati's piece – is similar to the repetition of television commercials. Repetition is like a mantra, a visual piece able to present layers of mental explorations: impressions (first), understanding (second), knowledge (third), experience (fourth), extensions of the experience (fifth), and so forth.

Public Space: Physical and Virtual

An analysis of Indonesian video art as an art form should also be accompanied by examining where the works are shown and distributed. In contrast to conventional cinema which is limited by the concept of a dark space in a movie theatre or a "white cube" gallery, video can be viewed in any space. Moreover, the illumination technology of today's video projectors is very advanced. This provides the means for video to enter public spaces.[9] Even more than that, video is part of a struggle for public space in the context of influencing social life.

cellsOPEN: multimedia collaborative performance of Cellsbutton #01,
Yogyakarta International Media Art Festival, 2007, initiated and organised by HONF (ID). Courtesy of the artists.

Biosampler is a group of graphic designers and electronic musicians in Bandung. Their multimedia work involves sound, video, dance and performance, and they infiltrate spaces in discotheques, old buildings, beaches and music stages. House of Natural Fiber (HONF), an art community in Yogyakarta, has held a series of video and new media festivals, including *Cellsbutton*. In *Cellsbutton #1* (2007), HONF held an event in the electronics mall, Jogjatronik, combining sound, computer, video and dozens of television monitors. HONF (and also Biosampler) are involved in putting an end to the divisions between art disciplines. Most importantly, their events clearly transform commercial spaces into public and even cultural spaces.

To investigate this shift from commercial to public space, an event was also once held in the electronics mall of Bandung Electronics Centre (BEC) under the title, *Beyond Panopticon Art and Global Media Project* (2004). Video works were shown on about 200 television monitors, next to hundreds of televisions showing commercials for different brands of television sets, all vying to seduce the eye. The art of negotiating with the owners and managers of that mall was a cultural event in itself. Viewed as a whole, this event presents the paradox of the fierce fight for the influence of media culture.

We have discussed physical public space. What about virtual public space on the Internet? There are at least two main categories of video (new media) that operate in virtual space. The first is networking as a mode to distribute and store works. The second is networking as a medium:

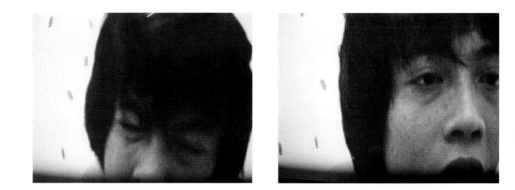

a creative process for distributing and storing. The earlier mentioned video *Sinema Elektronik* by Anggun Priyambodo belongs to the first group, as are several pieces by the group Tromarama, such as the music video *Serigala Militia* (2008). Both use YouTube (Broadcast yourself) to distribute their videos. Basically, this is not simply pragmatic; that video can be distributed across national boundaries and even across conventional (physical) art spaces such as museums and festivals has become something of an archaeological phenomenon.

The web art of Gustaff H. Iskandar, *Exotic-Erotic* (2002), may be the first example of new media to appear in Indonesia, using the media of networking of the second category. Gustaff's piece began with pornography sites on the Internet. He recycled them and then invited Internet users to interact with the work. This piece tested a number of issues: the boundaries between the legal and the illegal, the artist and the participant, and art and non-art, for example. Another hackitivism or hacking piece made by two artists with the monikers "Jack D2" and "Zeth" was shown at the new media art festival *Cellsbutton #1* (2007) at Own Café, Yogyakarta. The two of them manipulated the data and system of a world famous music site. In the event, a web designer Putu Hendra poured out his frustration at the ethics of information, and was even ready to

undertake counter-hacking. This event seemed to corroborate that the Internet network is a public space which is open and free. The debate, controversy, as well as solution, also took place directly in a virtual space, a new media culture previously unknown.

Interdisciplinary Tradition and Trajectory of Cultural Back and Forth

The relationship between video art and new media culture is closely tied to social human behaviour, behind which the artists operate. It is interesting to study, firstly that video artists come from diverse disciplines and backgrounds: Jompet (communication studies), Tintin Wulia (music and architecture), Mohammad Akbar (literature) and Reza 'Asung' and Hafiz (cinematography). Although some of the others come from visual art disciplines, such as Prilla (sculpture) and Wimo Bayang (photography), it is clear that video art in Indonesia is built upon diverse backgrounds of knowledge and practices linked to the artists' original disciplines. They have been united in a kind of "new media terminal," a home which is neutral and allows freedom of expression.

Secondly, this "terminal" not only provides an opportunity to go back and forth, but is also a safe atmosphere in which to share experiences and

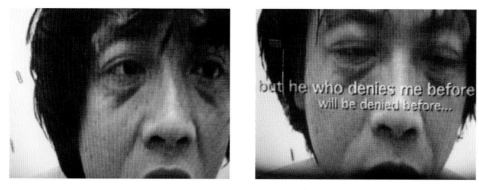

Reza 'Asung' Afesina, *What...*, 2001. Courtesy of the artist.

information – to cross breed even. With an inter-disciplinary tradition, it produces hybrids on the one hand, and helps to see mainstream culture more comprehensively and critically, because its explorations – political, social, environmental, media – become its strength.

Thirdly, these are artists born in the 1980s or even after. If we take another look at the history of commercial television in Indonesia at the end of the 1980s, it means that this generation has lived in a media-intensive environment since birth. It can even be said that they were "brought up" by television culture. Computers, games, handphones and the Internet next emerged, so that their media "upbringing" became intensified and more varied. Generally, it appears that this generation has difficulty keeping a distance from mainstream media culture. Luckily, some of them are not completely sucked in and they shuttle back and forth between the two cultures: they have no problem creating music videos or adverts for industrial products for commercial television, and making video art at other times. They also negotiate easily, ducking away into commercial spaces like malls and entertainment venues like discotheques. They are emancipated from the burden of differentiating "high art" from "low art."

Role of Artists' Initiative Groups

An important point to note is that the dynamics of Indonesian video art cannot be separated from the emergence of artists' initiatives or video and new media art communities such as ruangrupa (Jakarta), Forum Lenteng (Jakarta), Video-lab (Bandung), Videobabe (Bandung), Commonroom (Bandung), Ruangmes 56 (Yogyakarta), HONF (Yogyakarta) and Minikino (Denpasar, Bali). Their involvement with media culture is not limited to the production and distribution of works but is also significant as an organisational strength (or strengthening organisations). The weakness (absence?) of arts infrastructure in developing countries does not discourage this generation of new media artists to progress cultural growth. They take on the majority of roles that should be played by the state. Ade Darmawan is a new media artist, as well as the motor behind the alternative space ruangrupa which held an exhibition featuring artists from 20 alternative spaces and arts groups in Jakarta in 2010. In the catalogue, he explained: "The performance of the group of creative workers who are highly active in managing their ideas is not immediately affected by whether or not an art centre has existed previously in a certain city. This is possible because there has not been

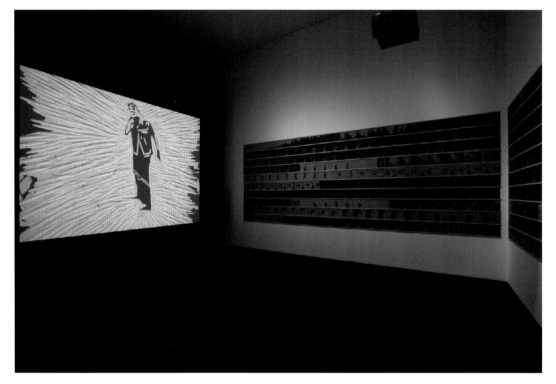

Tromarama, *Serigala Militia*, 2006. Courtesy of Mori Art Museum.

any link between one and the other that would enable them to influence each other. This also shows the failure of the art infrastructure that is not able to understand the movement of ideas in its surrounding."[10]

If that is how one positions oneself institutionally, what is the actual area of one's work? Ade continues to stress in the same text: "The work territory of these artists' organisations or groups then spreads across a range of functions, not only restricted to producing artistic works, but also helps them to have strong social functions through their programmes and activities with a strong public awareness. The range of activities include exhibi-

tions, workshops, festivals, artists' promotions, discussions, publications, film and video screenings, websites, archiving, and research."[11]

They work as networkers, building wide links in Indonesia and abroad. This cannot be separated from the role of the Internet, or the mobility of ideas, data, information and art products which is more flexible through the circulation of CDs or USB flash drives. It is not surprising that video and new media festivals on an international scale are continuously being held: *OK. Video* (ruangrupa, Jakarta), *Cellsbutton-New Media Art Festival* (HONF, Yogyakarta), and even *Video: WRK Surabaya International Video Festival 2009* in Surabaya which until recently was not on the map. This signals the self-confidence of this generation of digital artists: they do not wait to be invited to become international; they invite artists from abroad to take part in international festivals here in Indonesia. This is the opposite of previous generations of visual artists.

Conclusion

To close this essay, two points related to video art in Indonesia can be summarised. First, a country's people respond to the development of media technology to develop media culture. Political interests, pragmatism and fetishism influence this media culture, thus creating mainstream culture. In the history of new media in Indonesia – especially television, centralised politics was eventually met with decentralisation by the people. At the same time, video art seems to have taken a critical cultural distance from the mainstream. This criticism involves concepts, themes, content, distribution

and even intervention towards the system and (electronic) network data, as well as the struggle for public space. Secondly, there is the growth of an awareness amongst a generation of video workers that the struggles of media culture for a more balanced life is not just limited to the aesthetic or ideological plane with shifts in communication from "one-to-many" to "many-to-many"; it also extends to the building of arts infrastructures such as festivals, publications, archives, etc. through alternative spaces or arts communities. To make these efforts effective, they use new media technologies such as the Internet so that they are able to move across territories and avoid being trapped by the political structure of conventional information created by those in power. This then is the contribution of Indonesian new media and video art: not only to give meaning to today's visual culture dominated by media and Information technology, but also to express the intangible or hidden.

1. Walker, John A., *Art in the Age of Mass Media* (London: Pluto Press, 1990), p. 19.

2. Originally a *dangdut* song sung by Lisa and composed by Buy Akur, *Keong Racun* was actually not that well known. Ironically, Jojo and Sinta became famous through their music on YouTube and accessed by 4.7 million viewers and a "trending topic" for four days on the social network Twitter.

3. Rush, Michael, *New Media in Art* (London: Thames & Hudson, 2005), p. 82.

4. Postman, Neil, "The Reformed English Curriculum". In Eurich, Alvin C. (ed.), *High School 1980: The Shape of the Future in American Secondary Education* (New York: Pitman Publishing Corporation, 1970), p. 161.

5. *Belah Duren Stranger* actually consists of two music videos: *Belah Duren*, Indonesian *dangdut* music sung by the sexy singer Julia Perez and the music video *Stranger* by the sensual pop music icon Madonna. Yusuf Ismail found the video on a street seller's cart and regarded it as found footage. The juxtaposition is not only a strange experience, but is also funny as it pokes fun at two binary opposites: world pop and

local pop, the capitalism of world culture and the phenomenon of the local.

6. Martin, Sylvia, *Video Art* (Cologne: Taschen, 2006), p. 19.

7. Wikipedia: Performativity is an interdisiplinary term often used to name the capacity of speech and language in particular, but other forms of expressive but non verbal action as well, to intervene in the course of human events. RoseLee Goldberg in *Performance Art* (London: Thames & Hudson, 2001, p. 226) states that "performativity is used to describe the unmediated engagement of viewer and performer in art".

8. Manovich, Lev, *The Language of New Media* (Cambridge: MIT, 2001).

9. Wikipedia: Public space is a social space that is open and accessible to all, regardless of gender, race, ethnicity, age or socio-economic level.

10. Darmawan, Ade, "Fixing the Chain of the Cycles of Ideas". In *FIXER, Exhibition of Alternative Spaces and Art Groups in Indonesia*, (Jakarta: North Art Space, 2010), p. 16.

11. *Ibid.*

Monika Tichacek, *Lineage of the Divine*, 2002–2004.
Courtesy of the artist and Karen Woodbury Gallery, Melbourne.

Australian Video in Context

☐ **Jacqueline Millner**

Introduction

By the final decade of the 20th century, video art appeared to have come a long way from its counter-cultural origins over two decades earlier to occupy a place at the very heart of the institution of contemporary art. Primarily in its digital manifestations, video came to replace photography as art's platform of convergence, bringing together television and cinema, sculpture and painting, performance and music; video became the 'post-medium'[1] best suited to an age in which the moving image pervades every aspect of contemporary life. The discourse in which video art flowed broadened dramatically as the technology became cheaper and easier to use; practitioners who would not necessarily identify as 'video artists' began to regularly use the medium; and galleries and museums began to recognise the importance of video in their collections and exhibitions. And yet, I would like to suggest that despite the social, political and technological changes of the last four decades, the Australian experience evidences that there exist discernible continuities in some of the fundamental concerns of video art since the 1970s. At the beginning, video was integral to the development of performance art with its surgical scrutiny of the self, to the 'deconstruction' of television and the electronic image, and to early versions of the 'citizen-journalist' with their alternative narratives. Video art in Australia carried through these critical concerns into later decades.

This essay seeks to contextualise Australian video art in several ways so as to understand its roots, concerns and legacy (although it acknowledges that such overviews of practice are necessarily partial and never exhaustive, especially when it comes to a subject that has a somewhat patchy recorded history[2]). The essay undertakes a historical overview of video art practices, beginning with the early experimentation in the 1970s associated with conceptual art and performance and social activism, through to the full throttle image-appropriation of the 1980s, the installation and 'new media' practices of the 1990s, and finally the contemporary post-medium moment where video balances the aesthetics of painting with the impact of digital production and dissemination (including contemporary participatory practices with their increasing reliance on virtual networks). But the essay attempts to go beyond a survey by highlighting specific themes and concerns that have continued to shape video practice in Australia since its emergence in the 1970s.[3] These themes include: the interdependence of video and performance; the materiality of visual and textual language including a particular fascination with the 'found' image; and video's potential to create alternative spatial and narrative experiences. While these concerns may not be uniquely Australian, arguably Australia's particular geographic challenges – what historian Geoffrey Blainey has described as "the tyranny of distance"[4] – have disposed Australian artists exceptionally

87

well to "enunicating a meta-commentary about the cultural politics of identity and techno-representation"[5]. Such artists include Mike Parr, Peter Callas, Severed Heads, Tracey Moffatt, Monika Tichacek, Shaun Gladwell, Patricia Piccinini, Destiny Deacon, Daniel Crooks and David Rosetzky.

Activist Video and Performance: The 1970s and Beyond

As Hermine Freed once observed, the portable video camera arrived (in the late 1960s) just when artists needed it most: to release them from the *cul de sac* of formalism and studio-bound practice; to provide a solution to the ephemerality of performance and inaccessibility of land art; and to offer a means to confront the inescapable ascendancy of television in the popular consciousness.[6] The key attractions of the medium were its aesthetics of realism, together with its capacity for instantaneous recording and transmission, easy reproducibility and relative cheapness and ease of use that distinguished it from television and film. These attributes lent themselves readily to the aspirations of social transformation through activist and community-based art that marked the period, while also facilitating self-reflexive experimental work, meshing with explorations in performance, sound and visual effects.

The emergent video practice of Australia in the early 1970s reflected these two broad approaches. Video artists concerned with documenting communities and social issues were often associated with grassroots organisations and the video access centres established under the Whitlam government[7] – what video pioneer Peter Callas called "realist agit prop"[8] – and several began their work in the context of counter-cultural music festivals.[9] The video access network provided video facilities and production personnel to encourage communities to turn the camera on their own lives, demystify the medium, and tape their own news (rhetoric very similar to that surrounding the 21st-century phenomena of the 'citizen-journalist' and user-generated content). In the more radical practitioners, the desire for an alternative documentation of reality became tantamount to the "dis-assembly of TV – reverse engineering the code of the culture machine and uncovering its intentions".[10] Bush Video, a video collective and studio in Sydney, became the focus of innovation not only in activist video but also in electronic image experimentation, including the possibilities of feedback.[11] Members included founder Mick Glasheen, credited with producing the 'first' work of Australian video art, *Teleological Telecast from Spaceship Earth: On Board with Buckminster Fuller* (1970); Jeune Pritchard, whose collaboration with Luce Pellissier, *Queensland Dossier* (1977) examined civil rights abuses in that state during the 1970s; and Stephen Jones, who went on to play an important role in the music/video/performance innovations of the 1980s, including with the group Severed Heads.[12]

Video artists following more personal, experimental and 'apolitical'[13] approaches self-reflexively explored video image processing and synthesising, or engaged in performance, conceptual and emerging installation art, using video as an analogue or extension of performance. "Pure uses of the medium's reflexiveness and real time"[14] included works such as David Perry's *Interior with Views* (1976), and early experiments with the synthesised image by Ariel, Warren Burt and Stephen Jones. Some artists used video experimentally with music and dance, and explored the medium's potential to facilitate human and technological

Mike Parr, *Idea Demonstrations*, 23 May–10 June 1972.
Courtesy of the artist and Anna Schwartz Gallery, Melbourne and Sydney.

feedback. Philip Brophy's performance group Tsk Tsk Tsk foregrounded the aural capacities of video in their proto-multimedia performances, while Tim Burns' literally titled *Change of Plan-2 People in a Room-Closed Circuit TV Lent by Sony* (1973) – later described as 'Australia's first closed-circuit video installation'[15] – featured the real-time display of the everyday activities of a pair of naked actors, the monitor mounted outside the closed room in which they were.

"Probably the first use, in Australia, of video in a conceptual art context",[16] meanwhile, took place at Ihibodress, an artist-run space in Sydney established by Mike Parr, Peter Kennedy and Tim Johnson: it was Kennedy and Parr's video recordings of the performance of particular instructions, made in 1971 on an Akai ¼" Portapak and later shown as *Idea Demonstrations* (1972). Here the artists aimed to render the viewer complicit

in the often confronting physical ordeals of the artist, an aspiration which reached its apogee in *Cathartic Action/Social Gestus No. 5* (1977), during which Parr chopped off a life-like prosthetic arm with a tomahawk and proceeded to explain to an audience reeling in shock, the theoretical and ideological roots of his cathartic act. Parr's work, together with that of Stelarc, Ken Unsworth and Jill Scott, forms a key moment in the development of video art in Australia and its association with the body and performance.

This strain of personal experimentation and the focus on the self and body in video has carried through into contemporary practice, with artists who explore the relationship between the personal body and the body politic, the ethics of witnessing pain, and the construction of identity through the gaze. Parr himself has continued to use video not only to document performances, but also to heighten their effect and focus the viewers' attention on the ethics of watching; recent works where the artist subjects himself to privation and pain include *Water from the Mouth 1, 2 & 3* (1999) and *Kingdom Come and/or Punch Holes in the Body Politic* (2005). Artists of a later generation continue to mix video and performance to scrutinise the body of the artist and the role of video in regimes of surveillance. Tony Schwensen's videos feature a documentation of the artist following his own injunctions, which appear banal at first but grow monumental in their repetition and duration; an example is *Weighty Weight Wait* (2006) where the artist sat for 11 hours on the scales of the Art Gallery of NSW's loading bay while his ordeal was streamed live to the public gallery. Monika Tichacek's video works also betray elements of early endurance performances, as the artist dispassionately observes her own self-harm or bondage in a dark parody of the injunctions of conventional femininity, such as in *Lineage of the Divine* (2002–2004).

The Language of Video, the Found Image and Appropriation: The 1980s and Beyond

The self-reflexivity of video in the 1970s, with its structural analysis and unpacking of the mass media, developed further in the 1980s under the influence of postmodern critiques of the role of electronic media in constructing 'reality' in late capitalism.[17] The 1980s also saw the emergence of domestic VHS, video libraries and novel music and image synthesiser technologies which, together with the impact of MTV music video and the fresh legacy of punk DIY aesthetics, created the perfect conditions for the development of early remix culture.[18] Video proved particularly well-suited

to considering the creation of meaning and the positioning of the self in a media-saturated world, in works concerned with foregrounding the possibilities of what could be said via the electronic image, or exploring the relationship between the camera and the spectator. A key exponent of this approach was the group Severed Heads, electronic music and video pioneers who generated images through drum machines and bass synthesisers, and mounted interactive audio and video installations where audience movement triggered the production of images and sound, such as *Chasing Skirt* (1988).

But the parody and pastiche of film and broadcast material amongst Australian video artists in the 1980s must also be seen in the context of broader concerns in Australian visual art of the 1980s informed by postmodern ideas, in particular the critical power of appropriation and its specific relevance to a culture obsessed by its derivative, second-hand status – the fate of "the tyranny of distance".[19] Video proved apposite to artists inspired by critiques of originality and authenticity, not only in respect of art but also in respect of national culture.

Peter Callas pioneered an image synthesiser (the Fairlight CVI) and developed an innovative jump-cut technique able to compress a multitude of cultural signifiers, to generate videos now iconic of the image-overload of super-capitalism; works like *If Pigs Could Fly (The Media Machine)* (1987) powerfully foreground the role images play in constructing national identity. Randelli (Robert Randall and Frank Bendenelli) in works such as *A Taxi to Temptation* (1985) created overtly staged videos that appropriated the clichéd signifiers of commercial imagery to critique their vacuity.

The artists associated with Super8 Film Group

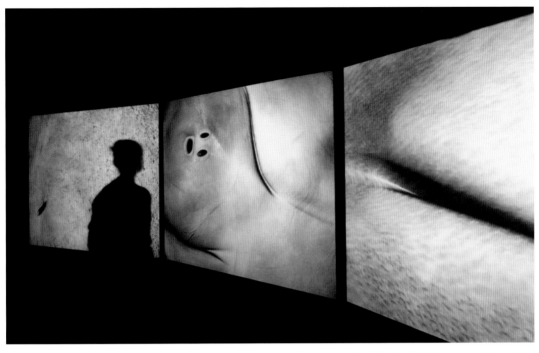

Patricia Piccinini, *The Breathing Room*, 2000.
Courtesy of the artist and Haunch of Venison Galleries.

and Metaphysical TV, including Mark Titmarsh and Gary Warner, explored the nature of television as a medium, making much of their work by "pulverising and reconstructing fragments from broadcast TV"[20]. Stephen Harrop's *Square Bashing* (1982), that blended motifs from Hollywood movies to create an eerie mediation on how such images structure our own psyches, remains a classic of this genre.

Appropriation of found imagery as a process for video creation continued into the 1990s and beyond. However, that the image was 'stolen', its source, and the form of the electronic language, became less important. Rather, due to video's ubiquity, the emphasis shifted to the video's content,[21] and increasingly to narrative. Tracey Moffatt's videos made in collaboration with film editor Gary Hillberg exemplify this trend. Beginning with *Lip* (1999), and going on to *Artist* (2000), *Love* (2003), *Doomed* (2007), and most recently

Other (2009), each video is a tightly edited series of scenes from mainstream films, set to a soundtrack and sequenced in a broad narrative arc. The result is a vivid enactment of how cinema creates cultural stereotypes – such as the black servant, romantic love, the exotic other – although the videos are also a fan's tribute. The compilation of personal favourite screen moments plundered from the near-infinite video archive has reached its apogee in the age of YouTube, vidding and mashups. Soda_Jerk (Dan and Dominique Angeloro), in works such as *Pixel Pirate II: Attack of the Astro Elvis Video Clone* (2007) edit renowned film and television characters into absurd narratives, challenging anachronistic copyright regimes but also having fun with the medium. Not even private archives are off-limits to the video pirate: Ms & Mr (Richard and Stephanie Nova-Milne), for example, draw on their own recorded family memories to fictional-

ise their pasts, providing a powerful metaphor of the contemporary self as mediated by electronic and digital media.

Installation, Spatially Fractured Narratives and Digital Media: The 1990s and Beyond

As evidenced by more recent work made by appropriating images, video art revised its earlier strategy of rejecting narrative altogether so as to craft an alternative visual language to television and film. Less concerned with its distinctive technical and formal aspects, video art embraced its ability to tell stories in the 1990s, coinciding with the turn away from appropriation in the visual arts in general,[22] and the emergence of identity politics. Yet video art did not abandon its quest to construct alternative ways of viewing the moving image: its narratives were often fractured through temporal and spatial disruptions in innovative

explorations of installation. At the same time, the 1990s witnessed the 'arrival' of 'new media', with its signature concepts of interaction, interface and immersion, concepts whose articulation, as media theorist Darren Tofts argues, had already begun in the early phase of video art.[23] Video in the 1990s was 'reframed' by digital technologies, and modulated into 'hybrid' works (another buzzword of the period).[24]

In the 1990s, Australian artists used video to explore traumatic historical and personal events, deploying narrative in different ways. Practice ranged from the low-tech personal stories of resistance in the satirical works of Destiny Deacon[25] such as *I Don't Want to be a Bludger* (1999) where the artist takes a humorous sledgehammer to stereotypes of Aboriginal identity, to the lugubrious imagery of Dennis del Favero's video testimonies of victims of war atrocities, such as *Motel Vilina Vlas* (1996).

Daniel Crooks, *On Perspective and Motion – Part II*, 2006.
Courtesy of the artist and Anna Schwartz Gallery, Melbourne and Sydney.

Its architectonic potential, meanwhile, saw video play an integral role in the consolidation of installation as the default form of contemporary art in the 1990s. Artists designed innovative and diverse physical spaces for the audience to encounter video imagery, such as multi-screen, immersive, or VR-like (virtual reality) environments, to disrupt conventional viewing conditions and heighten affective responses. Patricia Piccinini's *Plasticology* (1997) powerfully augments the effect of the computer-generated eco-system represented on the screen by dispersing monitors throughout the space, while *Breathing Room* (2000) integrates videos of digitally constructed skin into a self-contained cubicle with a vibrating floor, which rumbles in synch with the skin's dilating orifices to create a stultifying simulation of a panic attack. In complex installations such as *From the Darwin Translations* (1994–2000), Lyndal Jones also pioneered the spatial fragmentation of

video, an approach continued by numerous artists in the following decade. Daniel von Sturmer enlists video installation to playfully dismantle the conventions of viewing art in works such as *The Truth Effect* (2003), while the fractured narratives of David Rosetzky, including *Untouchable* (2003), rely on the physical platforms and layout of video images to drive home the deadening lack of intimacy among his contemporary cast of characters.

By the mid-1990s, digital technologies had become integral to many video works, yet, recalling earlier electronic image experiments, some were literally only possible due to the computer's capacity to produce radically new images. In Jon McCormack's *Turbulence* (1994), an artificial life program developed by the artist generates "a menagerie of synthesised forms" that riff on the impact of philosophies of evolution on contemporary thought.[26] The beautiful digital video imagery projected onto hand-held bowls in Lynette Wallworth's *Hold Vessel 1* (2001) could only be recorded by the highest-end digital telescopes and deep-sea cameras, while Daniel Crooks' mesmerising *Time Slice* works (from 2002 on), such as *On Perspective and Motion – Part II*, that realign Melbourne's urban landscape in alternative spatio-temporal representations, rely on precision motion control combined with sophisticated digital processing.[27]

The Postmedium Condition: Aesthetics and Participation

A sure sign of the postmedium condition is the recent embrace by certain video artists of the aesthetics of painting, given video's beginnings as an anti-establishment riposte to the commodity form par excellence, and its self-reflexive tradition whereby works consistently called attention to the conditions of their own making. Even when relying on digital effects, some artists mask over their works' technical underpinnings for aesthetic effect. Both Shaun Gladwell's *Storm Sequence* (2000) and Susan Norrie's *Undertow* (2002) use a single large-scale projection and radically slowed footage to represent the forces of nature in the manner of the sublime landscapes of the Romantics, the same landscape tradition that also informs the wondrous videos of David Haines and Joyce Hinterding, such as *The Blinds and the Shutters* (2001).

Yet, the postmedium condition also allows other contemporary artists to jettison aesthetics altogether, to embrace instead digital media's capacity for wide and instant dissemination and social networking. The Perth-based 'tactical arts group' PVI (led by Kelli McCluskey, Steve Bull and Ofa Fotu) blend video, mobile communications technologies and performance to engage communities in public interventions. Recent works include *Reform* (2007), "a radical vision of community-watch gone awry",[28] where performers in the guise of local concerned citizens patrol a city precinct for anti-social behaviour, and *Transumer* (2010), "a site-specific intervention that encourages audiences to clandestinely take over their city in preparation for an anti-consumerist uprising".[29] Video-hosting networking sites provide the means to realise global participatory projects of unprecedented scale, such as Deborah Kelly's *Tank Man Tango* (2009), a synchronised dance performance that paid tribute to the humble figure who, shopping bags in hand, stood his ground against the tanks in Tiananmen Square twenty years earlier, on 5 June 1989.

Conclusion

Throughout the last four decades, Australian video art has ceaselessly explored its intrinsic qualities and its relationship to the broader world: the world of mass media images, the world of art, and the world where real people live. Against the contrary claims of theorists like Fredric Jameson, cultural historian Nicholas Zurbrugg (who for much of his career was based in Australia) passionately argued for video art's criticality: video art allows for self-analysis and for the critical examination of culture, disorienting viewers and compelling them to think about their own processes of perception and cognition.[30] By consistently exploring performance and the body, the language of film, television and digital media, and the implications of spatial disruptions to the viewing experience, Australian video art has aimed to fulfil this expectation.

1. A description attributed to American art theorist Rosalind Krauss in *A Voyage to the North Sea: Art in the Age of the Post-Medium Condition* (London: Thames and Hudson, 1999).

2. Most commentators, including John Conomos, Peter Callas, and Daniel Palmer agree that Australian video art has not received the historical attention it deserves: see Palmer, Daniel, "Medium without a memory: Australian video art", *Broadsheet* 33(3), Sept–Nov 2004: 20–21. This 'amnesia' has prompted such recent initiatives as the Australian Video Art Archive, (see http://www.videoartchive.org.au/) with an associated touring exhibition and symposium (2010) and publication (2011).

3. While Australian video art as conventionally understood emerges in the 1970s, there were important antecedents in the 1960s such as innovations in electronic image generation and experimental film. Stephen Jones explores this 'pre-history' of video art in "Participation TV: notes on early Australian video art". In *Video Logic* (Sydney: Museum of Contemporary Art, 2008), pp. 84–88. Notable figures include Stanislaus Ostoja-Kotkowski who experimented with disassembling televisions to produce synthetic images, and the experimental film groups Ubu Films (including David Perry, Albie Thoms and Aggie Read), and Arthur and Corinne Cantrill.

4. Blainey, Geoffrey, *The Tyranny of Distance* (1966, 1982 and 2001). Blainey's account of how Australia's geographical remoteness has been central to shaping its history and identity has become a classic.

5. Conomos, John, "Framing Australian video art". In *Mutant Media: Essays on Cinema, Video Art and New Media* (Sydney: Artspace and Power Publications, 2007), p. 110.

6. Freed, Hermine, "Where do we come from? Where are we? Where are we going?". In Schneider, Ira and Korot, Beryl (eds.), *Video Art: An Anthology* (New York: Harcourt Brace Jovanovich, 1976).

7. In 1973, 13 free Video Access Centres were set up around Australia, funded by the Whitlam government and modelled on the Canadian Challenge for Change project in which video was used for community negotiation and dispute resolution.

8. Callas, Peter, "Australian video art and Australian identity: a personal view". In *Continuum '83*, (Tokyo, 1983).

9. For example, the Odyssey Rock Festival (Wallacia, 1971) and the Aquarius Arts Festival (Nimbin, 1973).

10. Jones, *op. cit.*, 2008, p. 84. An early Australian example of a video work literally de-constructing the television is David Perry's *Mad Mesh*, 1968.

11. See Jones, *op. cit.*, 2008, pp. 88–94.

12. Other members of Bush Video included Ariel, Philipa Cullen, Joseph El Khourey, John Kirk, Jon Lewis and Ann Kelly.

13. "Peter Callas interviewed by Nicholas Zurbrugg". In Zurbrugg, Nicholas (ed.), *Electronic Arts in Australia Continuum* 8(1), 1994: 94.

14. Murphy, Bernice, "Towards a history of Australian video". In Scott, Jill and Couacaud, Sally (eds.), *The Australian Video Festival 1986* (Sydney, 1986).

15. Jones, *op. cit.*, 2008, p. 96.

16. Jones Stephen, "Some notes on the early history of the independent video scene in Australia". In Scott and Couacaud, *op. cit.*, p. 23.

17. Key theorists include Jean Baudrillard, Paul Virilio and Fredric Jameson.

18. Haig, Ian, "Australian video in the 1980s", unpublished paper presented at the Video Void symposium, Contemporary Centre for Photography, Melbourne, November 2010.

19. See Butler, Rex (ed.), *What is Appropriation? An Anthology of Critical Writing on Australian Art in the 80s and 90s* (Sydney: Power and Brisbane; IMA, 1996).

20. As described by fellow Super 8 member Mark Titmarsh in *SynCity* (Sydney: d/Lux/MediaArts, 2006), p. 11.

21. Koop, Stuart and Delany, Max, *Screen Life: Videos from Australia* (Madrid: Reina Sofia Museum, 2002).

22. What American art theorist Hal Foster termed "the return of the real": *The Return of the Real: Art and theory at the end of the century* (Cambridge:MIT Press, 1996).

23. Tofts, Darren, *Interzone: Media arts in Australia* (Melbourne: Craftsman House, 2005), p. 33. This point is reiterated by Andrew Frost in his account of the work of the Sydney Super 8 Film scene in the 1980s, whose image collage Frost claims evolved into the sample culture of contemporary video art: Frost, Andrew, "Intelligent Dolphins: From Metaphysical TV to Remix Culture". In *SynCity* (Sydney: Australian Centre for Photography, 2006), p. 28.

24. Tofts, Darren, "Australian Video in the 1990s", unpublished paper presented at the Video Void symposium, Contemporary Centre fo r Photography, Melbourne, November 2010.

25. Deacon worked collaboratively with Michael Riley and Virginia Fraser.

26. Jon McCormack's artist statement: http://www.csse.monash.edu.au/~jonmc/, accessed 25 January 2011.

27. Daniel Crooks' artist statement: http://danielcrooks.com/, accessed 25 January 2011.

28. PVI artist statement: http://www.pvicollective.com/, accessed 25 January 2011.

29. Biennale of Sydney 2010 website: http://www.biennaleofsydney.com.au/, accessed 25 January 2011.

30. Zurbrugg, Nicholas. "Jameson's complaint: Video art and the intertextual Time-Wall", *Screen* 32, Spring 1991.

TOP ROW, LEFT TO RIGHT: Lee Wen, *World Class Society*, 1999, © Singapore Art Museum collection; Toshio Matsumoto, *Ki or Breathing*,1980, © Coll. Centre Pompidou, courtesy of the artist; Liu Wei, *A Day to Remember*, 2005, © Coll. Centre Pompidou, photo Georges Meguerditchian, courtesy of the artist; Richard Streitmatter-Tran, *Missed Connections*, 2004, © Singapore Art Museum collection.
MIDDLE ROW, LEFT TO RIGHT: The Propeller Group, *Uh...*, 2007, © Singapore Art Museum collection; Ko Nakajima, *Mount Fuji*, 1984, © Coll. Centre Pompidou, photo Brigitte Rodoreda, courtesy of the artist; Isaac Julien, *Baltimore*, 2003, © Coll. Centre Pompidou; Keith Deverell, Sue McCauley, Meas Sokhorn and Srey Bandol, *The Hawker's Song*, 2010, © Singapore Art Museum collection.
BOTTOM ROW, LEFT TO RIGHT: Tun Win Aung and Wah Nu, *Kekeke! Kebalaba!*, 2009, © Singapore Art Museum collection; Trinh T. Minh-ha, *The Fourth Dimension*, 2001, © Coll. Centre Pompidou, courtesy of the artist and Moongift Films; Nam June Paik, *Moon is the Oldest T.V.*, 1965–92, © Coll. Centre Pompidou, photo Peter Moore/VAGA, New York; Jun Nguyen-Hatsushiba, *Memorial Project Nha Trang, Vietnam: Towards the Complex – For the Courageous, the Curious and the Cowards*, 2001, © Jun Nguyen-Hatsushiba. Coll. Centre Pompidou. Courtesy of Mizuma Art Gallery, Tokyo, Lehmann Maupin Gallery, New York.

Video Ecologies – Asian and European Dialogues in Artists' Moving-Image Work

☐ **Mark Nash**

Video art is a global art form, which evolved in parallel with the neo-liberal economies that drove the internationalisation of the world's economies and movements of peoples known as globalisation. Video art also developed in tandem with the apparatus of television and the analogue and then digital video cameras. Artists often use video as a form of social critique, as well as to explore the possibilities of this new electronic medium. Artists associated with the international Fluxus movement, concerned to question art's relation to its public, the market and society, were associated with the development of early video. In the notes that follow I explore several interrelated questions. Is there a distinctive Asian, European or North American video aesthetic? How do the works on display in this exhibition reflect the post-Cold War politics that so affected the Asian region and so on?

Context

The new media works in the Centre Pompidou and Singapore Art Museum collections are intended to represent innovative works in the medium. It will be useful for a fuller understanding of the works themselves to consider something of the political and social changes the Asian region has undergone. Asia has been marked by a number of tectonic political shifts in the post-war period. The Allied defeat of Japan marked the end of Japanese colonial occupation of Korea, Taiwan, Malaysia, Singapore and the Philippines. Movements of

liberation and independence from British, Dutch and French colonial rule developed swiftly – Indonesia declared independence in 1946,[1] India became independent in 1947, Malaysia in 1963 and Singapore in 1965, to give some key examples. The 1949 victory of the Chinese Communist Party in the Chinese civil war meant that Asia became a second front for the Cold War that had already drawn an "Iron Curtain" through Europe. This Asian curtain divided Vietnam and Korea and separated Taiwan from mainland China.

The political, ideological, cultural and economic power of the United States began to bear down in the region, prompting some countries to attempt to detach themselves from the great power struggles of the Cold War and set up the Non-Aligned Movement in 1961.[2] The US-led fight against communism suffered some major setbacks in Asia, most notably their defeat in the Vietnam War. However the non-communist regions in Asia began to prosper economically when they adopted a US-friendly approach, developing a highly educated (and low-paid) workforce to promote export-led growth in financial services and high-tech industries. The four centres for this economic growth (Hong Kong, Singapore, Taiwan and South Korea) were known as the "Four Asian Tigers".[3] They were followed in the 1980s by the "tiger cub" economies of Indonesia, Malaysia, Philippines and Thailand pursuing a similar strategy. Despite the setbacks of the 1997 Asian Financial Crisis and the recent global economic meltdown, the region now has a vibrant cultural and artistic scene which is increasingly independent of the former colonial patterns of cultural patronage, while at the same time able to draw on a rich and complex cultural history. The financial success of these emerging economies is reflected in their development of cultural infrastructure (e.g. the art cinemas of Taiwan, South Korea, of Hong Kong or the biennales of Singapore, Taiwan or South Korea).

Mythological First Steps

Video art is often regarded as beginning at the moment when Nam June Paik bought a prototype Sony Portapak video recorder in New York in 1965[4] and shot footage of Pope Pius VI's motorcade, playing it back the same day to friends in a neighbourhood café. Paik was a refugee from the Korean War and had studied both art and music history at Tokyo University before travelling to West Germany in 1956 to continue his studies. There he met Karlheinz Stockhausen and John Cage, and also worked with Joseph Beuys and Wolf Vostell[5] already involved in the Fluxus movement. In 1963 at the Galerie Parnass, Wuppertal, Paik created one of his first installation works featuring television sets altered by using magnets to distort their images, *Exposition of Music-Electronic Television*.[6] *Moon is the Oldest T.V.* (1965) shown in this exhibition is similar (p. 108).

In 1964, Paik moved to New York but travelled regularly to Japan to collaborate with electronic engineer Shuya Abe to produce the first video synthesiser, mixing live channel television. From its inception, video was an international, indeed global medium, and Paik one of the first generations of artists to really promote its potential. The title of Paik's 1973 work *Global Groove*, in which multiple channels of television news and docu-

mentary are mixed with earlier works by Paik himself, as well as those by other artists and friends, encapsulates this concept (p. 114).

Video of course was not the first global art form. Film deserves that designation – from 1896 Pathé news cameramen relayed images from around the world to cinemas in metropolitan centres. Film, unlike video, was not instantaneous: it needed developing, editing and printing. Being exhibited in public, it was open to censorship. Legislation was enacted to regulate theatres or censor films before they could be shown.[7] Video, however embodied a principle of instant feedback – recorded images could be immediately played back through a monitor or suitably adapted television set. Instant feedback facilitated work that played with this property of the medium, though it was regarded by some, such as influential art historian Rosalind Krauss, as inherently narcissistic.[8] Vito Acconci's *Turn On* (1974) shown in this exhibition plays with this dynamic by frustrating the viewers' expectation of an intimate dialogue by showing his head rather than his face for almost the whole duration of the piece (p. 126). "No more waiting for the perfect love, all I want is to fuck with you": both sexual provocation as well as a description of his aesthetic strategy. Leo Castelli was one of the first gallerists to purchase video equipment for his artists; Acconci uses his gallerist's camera to attack the art world establishment – "No more galleries, no more museums"!

The cross-currents of social, cultural and political history referred to above can be seen in Nam June Paik's *Guadalcanal Requiem* (1979) (p. 196). This is an exceptional work, combining as it does Paik's by then now signature mixing of documentary and fiction films, interviews with Solomon Islanders and cello performances by Charlotte Moorman on key sites of the 1942 battle between Allied and Japanese troops. Paik's work presents the defeat of the Empire of Japan and its replacement by that of the United States as a victory for television and global communications. Though they had just been introduced to television, Solomon Islanders in the late 1970s already have the afros and flared jeans of their "brothers and sisters" in the USA. Paik's 'mash up' puts Moorman's eulogies on Red Beach or Henderson field on the same level as newsreel footage of the Allied landings and air battles, or interviews with the men who rescued Jack Kennedy the future US president, and creates a fascinating if somewhat seductive vision of post-war global harmony.

1989–1968, Incident and Event

There is a comparable understatement between the French use of the term "*événement*", (to refer to the popular uprising of students and workers in France as in the events of May 1968) and the official Chinese term 'incident' to refer to the 1989 Democracy movement that resulted in the Tiananmen massacre of peaceful student protesters.[9]

This exhibition presents several artists who are foundational for the video medium. However, curator Christine Van Assche is concerned to stretch the concept and the possibilities of the medium by presenting work by filmmakers Jean-Luc Godard and Chris Marker who have worked with art and political cinema, as well as the newer media of video and in the case of Chris Marker the CD-ROM *Immemory* (1996) (p. 234).

Marker's *Sans Soleil* (1982) has the global ambition of Nam June Paik (p. 198). It travels from Iceland, through Africa to Japan (with a diversion to the San Francisco of Alfred Hitchcock's *Vertigo* (1958). It is a personal and poetic documentary

film, in which the narrator searches for images that "quicken the heart"[10]: a group of fair-haired children on a road in Iceland; a woman waiting for a boat at the dock in Cape Verde, Amilcar and his brother Luis Cabral with guerillas in the jungle of Guinea-Bissau, and long passages documenting everyday rituals in Japanese contemporary life, with particular emphasis on Marker's totemic animal, the cat. Film for Marker is a memory system, and the film slides elegantly between personal and political narratives.

Liu Wei's *Floating Memory* (2001) and *A Day to Remember* (2005) represent his attempt to preserve the memory of the hopes and ambitions of a generation of younger people that were dashed in the 1989 Tiananmen protests (pp. 208, 218). In the first piece, using simple video-mixing techniques, he superimposes photographs that he shot during the 1989 protests (and kept hidden in his Beijing apartment for more than a decade) onto present-day footage of the square, empty except for tourists and the militia. A young boy traces a chalk line along the brick wall of a *hutong*. In one sequence, these images of dissent are inserted into the bas-relief panels at the base of the Monument to the People's Heroes, an imposing 10-storey obelisk in the middle of the square which commemorates political martyrs in the struggle for Chinese independence, thereby linking the Tiananmen protests of 4 June with this heroic past. By the end of the piece the image turns to negative; these people have become ghosts. In the second work, Liu Wei visits Beijing University on 4 June 2005 and asks students leaving the campus what day it is. Some profess ignorance, others say they know but cannot speak on camera, and one or two ask not to be filmed or go so far as to mention the name of this problematic event: the June 4th Incident (as it is referred to in Chinese).

As already mentioned, the Vietnam War profoundly reshaped East Asia. It produced an anti-war movement that was foundational for many Western artists at the time. For an older generation, such as Jean-Luc Godard and Chris Marker, the Vietnam War also prompted reflection on fiction, narration and issues of representation. They both participated in a compendium film *Loin du Vietnam* (1967)[11] protesting about the war. Contributions ranged from documentary footage shot in Vietnam itself (Joris Ivens was one of the few directors to shoot on the North Vietnamese side, contributing footage from Hanoi) to Godard's "home thoughts from abroad" reworking material from his film *La Chinoise* (1967) about five Maoist university students discussing ideological and political struggle from within a Parisian apartment. The film preceded by only a few months the 1968 Tet Offensive in which the North Vietnamese began to win the ideological battle with the Western public.

One of the paradoxes of the post-war anti-colonial struggles was that artists found themselves encased in a socialist-realist aesthetic intended to support political struggle and guerrilla warfare, and after independence, to create images that would contribute to the formation of new national identities. Vietnamese artists for many years were constrained by this necessity. Indeed this restriction remains true for North Korea even today! In recent years, however, a younger generation of expatriates have returned to support the art scene that is developing, particularly in Ho Chi Minh City, the former Saigon, in the south of the country.[12] This artist diaspora (referred to as *Viet Kieu*, or overseas Vietnamese) is mostly American-born and/or educated, and includes Trinh T. Minh-ha whose digital video film *The Fourth*

Dimension (2001) is showing in this exhibition (p. 210), probably the best known of the first generation of expatriates, Jun Nguyen-Hatsushiba, Dinh Q. Lê, Richard Streitmatter-Tran, Tuan Andrew Nguyen and The Propeller Group all of whom are represented in this exhibition. They helped found and support independent spaces in Ho Chi Minh City. The Propeller Group's *Uh…* (2008) superimposes a New York style graffiti image on tracking shots in Ho Chi Minh City to comment on this grafting of West and East (p. 184). Keith Deverell. Sue McCauley, Meas Sokhorn and Srey Bandol's installation *The Hawker's Song* (2010) is a focused account of social mobility with its graphic images of hawkers – dragging sandals made of old tyres behind them on pink twine, their damaged faces in close-up as they sing their wares (p. 190).

Dinh Q. Lê's 2006 *The Farmers and the Helicopters* is a three-screen installation that takes the memory of the war and attempts to work it into something more constructive (p. 220). The work starts with a haunting Vietnamese song over beneficent images of clouds of dragonflies. This segues into archive footage of US helicopters on combat missions in Vietnam, machines in formation firing on people or settlements, with present-day interviews with people who were children, farmers, or soldiers during the war. Interviewees describe how to deal with a helicopter when it is observing you ("behave calmly, don't run away"), how helicopters would land and abduct any Vietnamese without papers, and how they would attempt to bring helicopters down with small arms fire and so on. Some Vietnamese are still frightened of these machines today; others admire their adaptability and usefulness in peacetime. Towards the end, a younger interviewee confesses to his fascination with helicopters:

like the peasant-designers of flying machines in Cai Guo-Qiang's *Peasant Da Vincis* (2010), he has made his own machine and dreams of helicopters returning to a more constructive use now they are no longer instruments of terror.

Jun Nguyen-Hatsushiba, like Nam June Paik, has a diasporic biography. Born in Tokyo in 1968, the son of a Vietnamese father and Japanese mother, he spent the first 10 years of his life in Vietnam and Japan before moving to the United States and studying fine art. This exhibition presents his first installation *Memorial Project Nha Trang, Vietnam: Towards the Complex – For the Courageous, the Curious and the Cowards* commissioned for the 2001 Yokohama Triennial 2001 (p. 178): three teams of two men push and pull three cycle rickshaws (cyclos) – under water! The young men struggle with the yellow sand and boulders on the seabed which impede their task, returning from time to time to the surface for air before diving back to continue with their Sisyphean task. At the end they swim off-screen left and our gaze is concentrated on a series of white undersea tent-like structures.

This is one of several of Nguyen-Hatsushiba's "alternative histories" or memorial projects that seek to metaphorically represent the experience of Vietnamese people who tried to escape from the country following the communist victory.[13] However, in the vibrant life and energy of their attempt at underwater life, it also acts as a metaphor for the challenges of life in present-day Vietnam. His ongoing project, *Breathing is Free: 12,756.3* is both a performance and video installation (p. 188). In a series of video works, he documents a series of physical runs he makes in various cities around the world in which he will attempt to cover the diameter of the earth. Cities covered

to date include Ho Chi Minh City, Singapore, Tai Chung, Taipei, Tokyo, Shanghai and Phoenix. Each run is filmed differently depending on the artist's feeling about the particular location. In Shanghai for example, video dissolves have Nguyen-Hatsushiba almost running on the spot, whereas in Tai Chung the impression is much freer. In this work he literally enacts a representation of the artist's freedom to travel around the world and at the same time makes reference to the migration and movement of diasporic and exilic populations who do not have the same freedoms.

Narrative and Fiction

Jean-Luc Godard and Chris Marker provide very different heuristic models for understanding oppositional film and art practice as it developed in the shadow of 1968. Marker was more poetic, lyrical, using first-person fictional narration to link East and West as already mentioned. Godard's work develops a series of increasingly oppositional critiques – the Nouvelle Vague's cinephilic appropriation of Hollywood; the denunciation of the cinematic spectacle of Hollywood-Mosfilm and the institution of the family in works such as *Numéro Deux* (1975) which uses television as a form of critique. A similar approach is developed in Mako Idemitsu's *Yoji, What's Wrong With You* (1987) in this exhibition (p. 120). Here an oversized television set dominates a series of soap opera exchanges between a young man Yoji and his mother.

In Godard's work, fiction and documentary become increasingly intertwined with the history of cinema and that of the 20th century. His film presented here, *Scénario du Film Passion* (1982), is one of his more radical television works, unpacking as it does the conditions for film spectatorship at the end of the 20th century (p. 232). Godard dis-

101

trusted the traditional narrative script – regarding it as the invention of cost accountants – and preferred to improvise. *Scénario du Film Passion* shows him using video as a sketch pad, trying out ideas with video before shooting in film. Godard sits at an editing table in front of a white film screen, narrating, philosophising and lecturing the viewers as he makes and unmakes his scenario.

Although Godard's work is foundational for an understanding of film, video and television, his cultural frame of reference is deeply European. Although his earlier works reference the Vietnam War, Godard is not interested in engaging with 'other' perspectives. The chinoiserie of *La Chinoise* represents an ambivalent identification with Western Maoism as well as a critique of it as a Western fiction.[14]

In relation to the dualism I have just been sketching, Isaac Julien's work represents an engagement with images of others rather than their incorporation into a pre-existing narrative. His installation *Baltimore* (2003), showing in this exhibition, presents an engagement with narration and image in black popular culture – in this case the blaxploitation film, which his recent installation *Ten Thousand Waves* (2010) extends to Chinese narratives and images (p. 246). Similarly, Yang Fudong's *Backyard - Hey! Sun is Rising* (2001) is one of his first engagements with the conventions of Chinese and Western art cinema (p. 242). In this narrative, four men improvise various rituals, marching around the city streets brandishing toy swords, or yawning and fighting in the bedroom – an echo of early American silent film comedy or René Claire's surrealist *Entr'acte* (1924).

Araya Rasdjarmrearnsook's installation *Two Planets* (2010) concerns narration and the place from which the artist speaks and the audience engages (p. 224). In this project, she films groups of Thai peasants out in the countryside looking at classical works of European realist and post-impressionist work: Millet's *Les Glaneures* (1857) or Manet's *Déjeuner sur L'Herbe* (1863). Seated in a bamboo grove, as if in a cinema, they comment knowledgeably on the works presented to them. "This isn't our landscape, but it's like the old-time [Thai] landscape" they say of the Courbet. The two planets she refers to in the title are a whole series of worlds which connect and disconnect the Asian peasant from the European – worlds of city/country, East/West, then/now and so on. The complicity of the audience is also alluded to in works by Valie Export's *Facing a Family* (1971) and Bill Viola's *Reverse Television/Portraits of Viewers* (1983–1984) where the video camera interrogates the viewer (pp. 112, 118). Rasdjarmrearnsook is more concerned with pedagogy, in impossible or bizarre locations, such as her earlier pieces where her audience is a class of dead bodies.

One of the key points this exhibition makes is that conventional histories of video art need to be rewritten and that there are the resources to do so in the Centre Pompidou (and Singapore Art Museum) collection. Not only has there been a network of globally connected diasporic artists such as Nam June Paik working between East and West, but from the beginning there have been locally based artists, particularly in Japan working with new technologies – in *Mount Fuji* (1984), Ko Nakajima takes video footage of the iconic image of Mount Fuji and plays with different compositional possibilities – dividing it vertically to allude to the Japanese hanging scroll as well as creating moving sculptural forms composed of multiplications of the image, similar to the early experience of colour and space of the De Stijl group (p. 174). Toshio Matsumoto similarly explores the technical possibilities of the medium: in *Ki or Breathing* (1980), he divides an image of landscape vertically and then inserts into vertical scrolls or fans, to make video landscape paintings along traditional formats (p. 166). A score by Tore Takemitsu, experimental music composer who was very influenced by John Cage, points to the cross currents which linked Cage and Fluxus with Asia and Japan in particular.

Bill Viola's early video works such as *Chott ed-Djerid* (1979) celebrates the potential of video to capture the changing appearance of landscape and the impermanence of vision in real time. In the early 1980s, American artists were encouraged to visit Japan through grants and collaborations with television stations such as WNET Channel 13. Viola continues his exploration of visual atmosphere by filming a wide range of Japanese country- and cityscapes. *Hatsu Yume (First Dream)* begins at sunrise and ends at night with beams of light tracing on the video image through a bamboo forest (p. 170). He explores abstract reflections such as the colours of koi, shapes of clouds, lines of fishing nets. Panning shots through fields and forests recall another great North American artist, Michael Snow and his earlier *La Region Centrale* (1971). Images of waves cut to city streets then to abstract colours of brightly lit lanterns. Viola's video has no voice-over, and just uses natural sounds in the soundtrack. This work is less about the representation and the fascination of the East for the Westerner but rather an attempt to escape the West through contact with Eastern, specifically Shinto spirituality – also a key point of reference for Chris Marker's *Sans Soleil*.

Lee Wen is an established Singaporean performance artist who like Nam June Paik also works globally. In a series of performances such as *Journey of a Yellow Man No 3: Desire* (1993) per-

formed at the Substation, Singapore, he shackles himself in chains like a prisoner, performs a ritual in a shopping mall, or carries a bird cage full of books down a Singapore street (p. 204). He might be carrying a cello (a reference perhaps to Nam June Paik's work with Charlotte Moorman) or burning some books recalling the burning Cambodian incense houses in Than Sok's installation *Negligence Leads to Loss; Attention Preserves* (2009) (as well of course as those millions of houses set on fire during the Vietnam War) (p. 226). Lee has presented his "Yellow Man" performances throughout Asia – India, Thailand, Singapore, Australia and elsewhere. In his mobility as an artist, his performances create a link between these regions, helping transmit the codes and conventions of performance art. By literalising the racial stereotypes of Asian peoples, his performances also draw attention to their/Lee's overseas Chinese ethnicity. Other performance works are more straightforwardly conceptual: moving a series of chairs; sitting on block of ice; exchanging photocopies of zloty notes for the real thing in a performance in Poland; or speaking directly to the camera in the manner of Vito Acconci so that 'world-class' is the only permissible adjective, satirising Singaporean ambitions for their city-state: "We have a world-class art biennale, world-class food, a world-class public transport system" and so on (p. 136).

In these notes I have only been able to refer to a small cross section of works on display. In *Video, an Art, a History 1965–2010*, Singapore indeed has a world-class exhibition, one which hopefully Lee Wen will also join in celebrating as it introduces key moments in video history, presents new directions in artists' moving-image work while at the same time serving as an inspiration for Singaporean artists, students and the general public.

1. Although it was only recognised by the Dutch colonists in 1949.

2. The Non-Aligned Movement was set up by Yugoslavia, India, Egypt and Indonesia at a conference in Belgrade. It was preceded by the first Afro-Asian Conference in Bandung, Indonesia in 1955 dedicated to opposing colonialism, neocolonialism and imperialism.

3. 'Little dragons' is the literal translation from Mandarin.

4. The Portapack was only made commercially available in 1967.

5. Vostell had also made an installation using television sets at the Smolin Gallery in New York in 1963.

6. This was not the first use of a television set in an artwork. In 1959 Wolf Vostell had incorporated a television set into Deutscher Ausblik.

7. For example in Malaya, The Theatres Enactment 1910, Ordinance 200 (Cinematographic Film) 1923 and The Cinematograph Films (Control) Enactment 1927.

8. Krauss, Rosalind, "Video: The Aesthetics of Narcissism", *October* 1, Spring 1976.

9. There is some irony in the fact that a building designed to democratise access to the arts in France and develop a new concept of the museum as library, resource and production centre should take the name of the politician credited for restoring order in 1968 by breaking the alliance of students and workers: Georges Pompidou.

10. Based on Sei Shonagon's *The Pillow Book* (1001): a "list of things that quicken the heart".

11. Agnès Varda, Joris Ivens, William Klein, Claude Lelouch, Jean-Luc Godard and Alain Resnais, co-ordinated by Chris Marker.

12. I am particularly indebted to Yung Yuen Ma's "The Tales of Three Cities: The Emergence of Performance Art from Hanoi, Ho Chi Minh City and Yangon", MA dissertation, Curating Contemporary Art, Royal College of Art, London, 2011.

13. This was one of the earliest uses of the phrase 'boat people', to describe the 2 million people who left Vietnam by boat, many of whom, up to half a million, lost their lives in the process.

14. A similar point could be made of Roland Barthes *L'Empire des Signes* (1970), or indeed of Chris Marker's *Sans Soleil*.

TOP ROW, LEFT TO RIGHT: Lee Wen, *Journey of a Yellow Man No. 3: Desire*, 1993, © Singapore Art Museum collection;
Jean-Luc Godard, *Scénario du Film Passion*, 1982, © Coll. Centre Pompidou, courtesy of the artist;
Tony Oursler, *SWITCH*, 1996, © Coll. Centre Pompidou, photo Jean-Claude Planchet;
Tun Win Aung and Wah Nu, *Kekeke! Kebalaba!*, 2009, © Singapore Art Museum collection.
MIDDLE ROW, LEFT TO RIGHT: Keith Deverell, Sue McCauley, Meas Sokhorn and Srey Bandol, *The Hawker's Song*, 2010,
© Singapore Art Museum collection; Nam June Paik, *Guadalcanal Requiem*, 1979,
© Coll. Centre Pompidou, courtesy of Electronic Arts Intermix (EAI), New York;
Nam June Paik, *Global Groove*, 1973, © Coll. Centre Pompidou, courtesy of Electronic Arts Intermix (EAI), New York;
Jun Nguyen-Hatsushiba, *Breathing is Free:12,756.3*, 2008–2009, © Singapore Art Museum collection.
BOTTOM ROW, LEFT TO RIGHT: Dinh Q. Lê, *The Farmers and the Helicopters*, 2006, © Singapore Art Museum collection;
Yang Fudong, *Backyard - Hey! Sun is Rising*, 2001, © Coll. Centre Pompidou, courtesy of the artist and ShanghART Gallery;
Isaac Julien, *Baltimore*, 2003, © Coll. Centre Pompidou; Lee Wen, *World Class Society*, 1999, © Singapore Art Museum collection.

Utopia and Critique of Television

Video was born in the 1960s into two contexts: those of the fine arts – performance art in particular – and television production and broadcasting.

The first section of the exhibition presents works which explore the processes of television production, the political and social influence of the media, as well as the role of the viewer. Television here appears as the key subject of the works and the medium of production and broadcasting. Video is thus shared between television and artistic creation.

At first, some artists explored the television set as an object by placing it within the artistic context and displaying it in exhibitions. The first to do so was Korean artist Nam June Paik who made use of the signal emitted by television sets. He manipulated it in a very minimalist way in the installation *Moon is the Oldest T.V.* realised in 1965, and later in the video *Global Groove* produced for the New York television channel WNET in 1973.

Other artists like Valie Export in Austria in 1971 and Bill Viola in the United States in 1983–84 question the role of television audiences and adopt an ethnological approach to this 'new population of spectators'. The screen becomes a mirror reflecting the attitude of this new 'ethnic group'.

Some other artists examine television programmes from a more critical angle, studying their strengths, powers of attraction and flaws. In the works of Sonia Andrade and Mako Idemitsu, video deflects television broadcasts to serve critical purposes, analysing semiologically their content in the 1970s and 1980s.

Nam June Paik

Since it was first produced in 1965, this work by Nam June Paik has appeared in different versions, in particular substituting colour television sets for the dozen black-and-white monitors used at the start. However, to this day the monitors are still being displayed in a room plunged into darkness and silence, which also contains a magnet placed on a cathode tube which interferes with the electronic signal before every transmission of the recorded images, which show differing stages of the progression of light and darkness on the moon's surface, as seen from Earth. In its physical form, forever advancing and evolving, the installation is a response to the different lunar phases that are presented to us, as if following a cycle of differences and repetitions.

It is worth stressing that Paik has not, in the meantime, chosen to show images of the hidden side of the moon, which we have known about since 1959 thanks to retransmissions carried out by space probes; rather he makes do with what we can observe with the naked eye. Ever since the earliest ancient writings that have come down to us, observers had already noted that this side of the moon looked like a visage, a human face, which has inspired and excited the imagination of many painters, illustrators and narrators, not forgetting the first filmmakers, such as Georges Méliès. Insomuch as the moon is presented in a form that resembles us vaguely, it is still a constructed image. If we see this image as a product of light thrown on a surface, a phenomenon readily comprehensible after the invention of film, it is easy to think of it as the projection of such an image on this part of the Earth's satellite. The moon is a kind of screen on which an image is projected in the endless darkness of an endless cinema auditorium. In other words, according to Paik, it is the "oldest T.V.".

The context of the period in which Paik produced this installation is very clearly characterised by the invention of television in the 1940s in the United States, followed by its rapid spread to other parts of the world from the 1950s onwards, as with the mass culture which it helped to disseminate to households on a large scale. This was also the period when Marshall McLuhan delivered many a pertinent reflection on television in *Understanding the Media* (1964), and also when men had been preparing, since 1960, to journey to the moon, although the actual moon landing did not take place until 1969 with Apollo XI. Whether as a mass medium or a mass consumer product, television and television sets are not understood as such by Paik. He may be one of the very first artists to make use of the possibilities of this medium and what it represents as an object, but Paik immediately took a salutary step back, in a way worthy of an Oriental sage. He prefers silence, quietness and slowness to noises, sounds and speed; he contrasts the spectacular, the narrative, and multiplication to what is evident, what is pure vision, and the passing of what is eternal. The moon has been there forever, and once its image is obliterated it starts all over again. It recounts nothing or, perhaps, recounts nothing other than the passing of time.

Paik actually pushes the limits of his rejection of the various parameters associated with this medium even further – live broadcasting, recording, repeats, an ongoing flood of every manner of imagery, among other things – because in reality the alleged images of the moon's phases are non-existent. The shapes that we may take for the various progressive stages of the lunar waxing are in fact obtained by the placement of magnets on the cathode tube, thus making it possible to obtain, without any prerecorded image or image captured live, a supposed lunar image stemming more from an imagination rather than from any real vision. For the image has clearly origi-

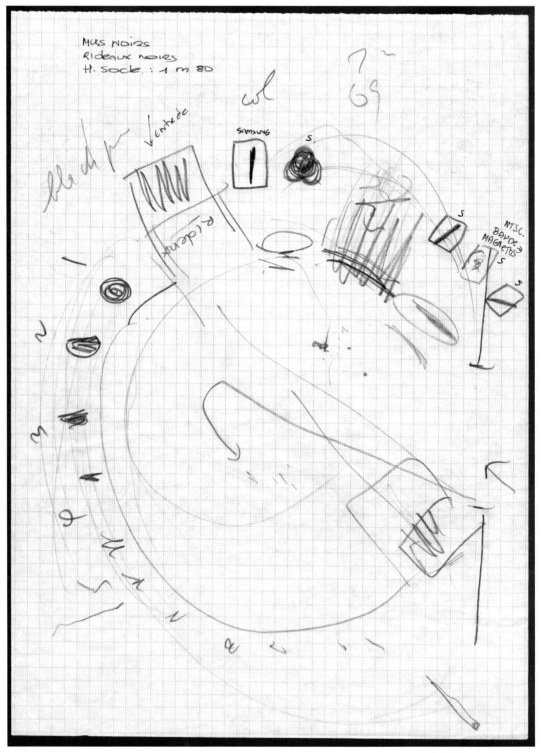

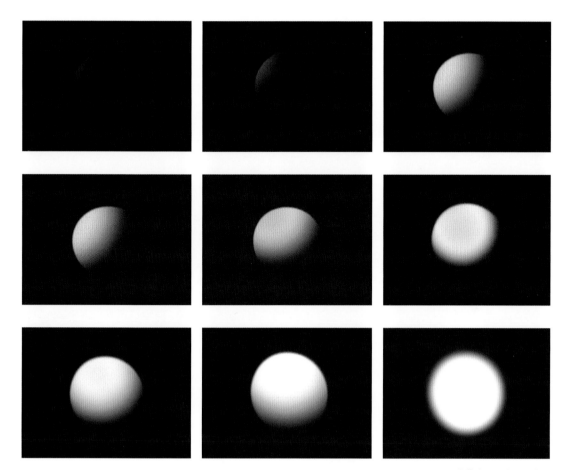

© Coll. Centre Pompidou.

nated from our imagination, even though it is likewise based on a phenomenon hyped by the media. As an odd mixture of the ways in which we really perceive the moon and of the different images transmitted by media such as photography, television and film, these projections are not really diversions or appropriations, but rather, manipulations of an apparently acquired imagery, acquired because it is indexed to the image of the real moon. Likewise all the many memories, accumulation of manufactured images, scientific and otherwise, and direct, live visions when we turn our eye towards the sky, as if to check the permanence of the celestial reality above our heads. The moon is always there – it waxes and wanes indefinitely and the schematic diagrams that we make of its cycle are so simple that even any ordinary old television set contains, so to speak, this image. And if the moon is, in this sense, the oldest television, the title seems to be turned inside out, because television also becomes an original form, present well before man was able to look at it as a natural phenomenon and as an image.

Jacinto Lageira
Translated by Simon Pleasance

Facing a Family, 1971

Facing a Family is the only video by Valie Export to have been screened on Austrian television. To understand this work, it is important to re-situate it within its context of production and presentation. *Facing a Family* is a televised programme that was made for the programme *Kontakte*, which was broadcast in 1971. The video was not originally conceived to be projected in a museum but to be screened on television in private and home settings.

The five-minute re-screening of this video on a public television channel affirms the artist's wish to propose a different style of presentation and reception from those of her other works. Indeed, since the beginning, Export has sought to depart from the classical framework of the museum and an initiated public. After spending a part of her childhood in a convent, she trained in textiles in Linz before leaving for Vienna where she majored in design. In 1968, she met Peter Weibel with whom she had a long partnerhip in works such as *Aus des Mappe des Hundigkeit* (1968) and *Tapp- und Tastkino* (1968). She also joined the circle of Viennese actionists consisting of Otto Mühl, Günter Brus and Hermann Nitsch. These artists primarily performed actions on their bodies which could be violent or simply symbolic, with the aim of liberating Austrian society from its framework of reactionary thought.

However, Export broke away from the actionists by casting herself in performances conceived for the public space instead of a space reserved for art. "Very soon I made a choice to use the streets and commonplace surroundings. I did not want to act in a museum or a gallery because these sites were too conservative for me and when I perform there, I would only receive conventional responses to experimental works. It was important for me to present my works to the public, in public, in public spaces … I needed a different reception which could only be found outside the museum."

In showing *Facing a Family* on Austrian television, she is reaching out to a greater audience and seeking new ways of communication. She had already highlighted these issues through her experiments in *Expanded Cinema* (literally the extension of film into the streets): "In the 1960s, *Expanded Cinema* began the deconstruction of the predominant reality in order to make new forms of communication accessible and to establish new ways of communication."

The video of *Facing a Family* consists of a static shot of a common scene from a family's daily life: two parents and two children finish their meals in front of the television. They seem unaware that they are being filmed. The only indication that the video is helmed by Export is the manipulation of the flow of images with mute intervals and freeze frames. Export describes the device of *Facing a Family* as two families facing each other, one in the television and the other in the apartment. She sums up the project, "Invisible programme, imaginary screen, two families watch each other."

Instead of presenting a transmission or a programme as we normally see on television, the video confronts the viewer with a situation of reception. Two families watch the same screen in a startling mirror effect; it is what Export calls "a closed-circuit communication" (*Geschlossene Kommunikationskreis*). Through this experience, Export questions the consumption of television as family entertainment by confronting Austrians with their own behaviour as viewers. Furthermore, the muted intervals and freeze frames created by the artist aim to break the usually uninterrupted television transmission that the viewer is used to. In *Facing a Family*, the artist seems to question the notion of the television viewer by the *mise en abyme* contained in the formula: "the television in the family, the family in the television".

Diane-Sophie Girin
Translated by Yin Ker

113

Nam June Paik

Global Groove, 1973

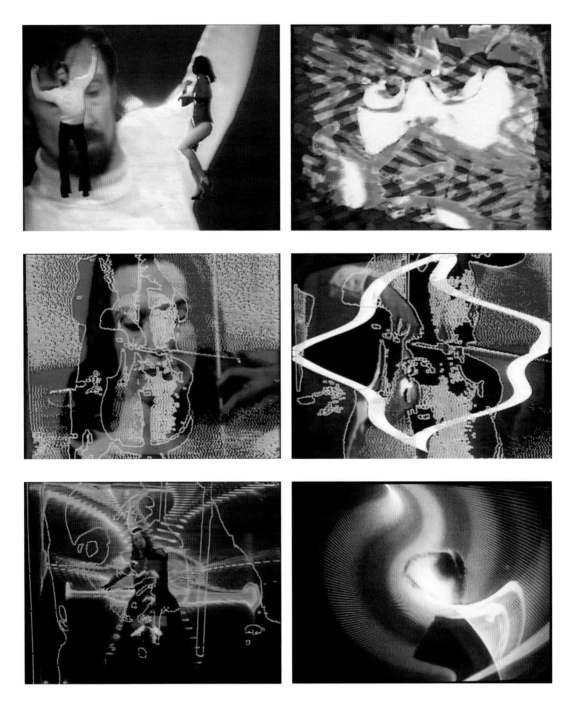

Global Groove is certainly the most well-known video by Nam June Paik, who anticipated the globalisation of the media and changing behaviour in a consumer society. It dates from 1973 and was produced in the studios of public television station Channel 13, in New York.

The action unfolds with the electronic images of a sun-drenched landscape, followed by the close-up of a television guide. The sound recording announces the artist's concerns with regard to new media, which television is certainly part of: "This is a glimpse of tomorrow's video landscape, when you will be able to switch to any TV station on the Earth, and the TV guide will be as thick as the Manhattan telephone book."

The rest of the video is structured as a flux of sequences, whose disparate elements Paik coalesces: fragments of television broadcasts from different countries around the world with extracts of interviews with artists he frequented during that period, or videos of his own performances and installations. As such, the frenetic images of two dancers moving to a worldwide hit like "Devil with the Blue Dress On" comes just before Allen Ginsberg's very refined concert; a documentary excerpt in which John Cage relates electronic sound to the nervous system and blood circulation is alternated with traditional Korean choreographies.

In each sequence, through either the intermediary of synthesisers designed by the artist or the effect produced by a magnet on the television's cathode ray tube, the image is constantly deformed and rendered unstable. The contours are accentuated, the colours saturated, and the forms flee and disappear. Paik also employs overlay techniques to multiply the images ad infinitum, to cut out and to divide figures into halves – parts of which he reflects in the background. The set's plot is transposed from the studio environment where it was recorded, to a new universe whose characteristics, configurations and boundaries are henceforth defined by the aesthetic potential of this new media, video. On the whole, while each sequence composing the flux takes into account the results of Paik's artistic experimentation conducted in the 1960s – especially the then novel possibilities in artistic form offered by video and the electronic image during this period, the work appears to zap ahead of its time. The synthesis of the artist's research allows him to elaborate on a new critical economy of the image in Global Groove; he decomposes and recomposes the language employed and still used by television – a mastered and controlled language adapted to the wonts of consumer society, in other words. Paik liberates it from its imposed forms and denounces the alienation and exploitation of the media by and for the market's needs.

Yekhan Pinarligil
Translated by Yin Ker

Sonia Andrade

In *Rio de Janeiro, Sans Titre 2*, the second video produced by Sonia Andrade since 1974, the artist films herself in a fixed sequence shot on the terrace of an apartment, eating a traditional Brazilian meal: a plate of black beans with some bread and a guarana soft drink. She faces the camera with her back to a television set featuring an American television series, *Tarzan* (1966–1968), followed by commercials. Shortly, this ordinary meal transforms itself into a regressive scene, as the artist plunges both hands into the cooking pot and compulsively covers her face and body with food, before directing her gestures to the camera, throwing the food at it until the field of vision has been completely covered.

Parts of Andrade's early videos address the intrusive and subjugating power of television. Her protean oeuvre also uses other techniques. In this film, the artist does not look at the camera. The private space of the meal is entirely controlled by the televisual image: by the artist's recording on the one hand, capturing an everyday scene, and by the broadcast image on the other, which hammers home the values of consumer society. The viewers themselves are brutalised, firstly by the visual competition that they experience between the banal action of the meal and the attraction of the television screen in the background; then by the hysterical turn of events, in which the violence of an obliterating gesture dominates – the obliteration of the filmed subject and the blinding of the gaze directed towards her. Colonial discourse on televisual entertainment also resonates, and the cultural identity that the artist heavily underlines here provokes an ethnological gaze through to the sudden 'barbaric' change in the action.

Marcella Lista
Translated by Yves Tixier and Anna Knight

Reverse Television/Portraits of Viewers was originally a television clip created by Bill Viola in 1983 for an experimental programme on the public television channel WGBH-TV in Boston, the United States. Like Channel 13 in New York, WGBH-TV had set up a research unit dedicated to experimentation with video images in the late 1960s. The results of the research were broadcast on the channel as weekly episodes created by their own producers.

For this show, Viola produced 44 video portraits of randomly chosen residents from around Boston. He asked them to sit wherever they liked in their apartment and to look into a camera placed right before them, at the same level as the television screen. The camera angle was fixed and frontal, and a very sensitive sound receiver captured any background noise.

The artist had intended for each portrait to be shown for one minute between two television programmes, at approximately every hour; the clips were supposed to appear in the interval set aside for commercials, with neither trailer nor credits, and to be simply followed by the next programme, ending in the same way without any indication. This method of transmission devised by Viola would have created an effect of disruption on the routine flow of programmes on the channel when "[the viewer] is the most relaxed" – meaning the moment when the latter lets his or her attention wander and is prepared to see an advertising clip. But as Viola reminds us, "Everything has to be framed on television; it is essentially an art of conditioning"; the channel refused to bow to the artist's specifications. Eventually, the videos were only shown for 30 seconds at the rate of five portraits per day, and with a short credits section at the end, whereby only the name of the author and the date of the work appear.

Reverse Television/Portraits of Viewers draws attention to the immobility of the viewer before his or her screen, which is contrasted against the extreme mobility of the flux of images imposed on them by the power of their structure; the viewer is subjected to them and finds himself or herself in a passive position. By confronting him or her with the image of another person watching the television – whom he or she finds to be in a similar position to his or her own – the video provokes an awareness of this state in the viewer, who thus realises his or her own inertia before the images. This work denounces the sightlessness induced in the viewer by the television system: "… as if there were a sheet covering something, and that from time to time, through an opening, it parts to allow a glimpse of this ground or field, which is always there, just beneath."

The video *Reverse Television/Portraits of Viewers* is a compilation of these portraits. It was created by Viola as an video that can be shown on its own outside the framework of television broadcasting.

Yekhan Pinarligil
Translated by Yin Ker

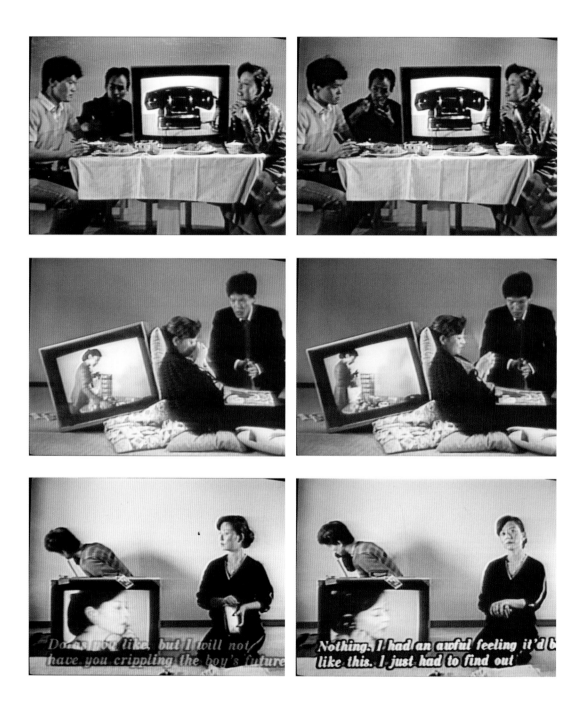

The video *Yoji, What's Wrong with You?* from 1987 is inscribed in Mako Idemitsu's video works from the beginning of the 1970s. It explores the theme of the mother-and-son relationship in a method similar to that employed in another video, *The Marriage of Yasushi* (1986).

Idemitsu was born in Tokyo in 1940 to a traditional patriarchal Japanese family. After marrying Sam Francis (an abstract expressionist painter), she settled in California where she had two children. Torn between the roles of a woman and a mother, she next went through a phase of identity crisis. Seeking means to express her doubts, she acquired an 8mm camera and began filming the feminine condition within feminist circles. In 1973, she decided to return to Japan where she continued to work on feminist issues, incorporating a critique of the Japanese family at the same time. She has since become a pioneer of feminist art in her country of origin.

In time, the videographer established her own "Mako Style" characterised by the projection of the characters' interiority on television monitors that are integrated into the video settings. It was while enhancing the videos' quality when Idemitsu first had the idea of inserting monitors into the frame. In her opinion, as video is the best medium for information, the monitors have an important narrative role. By revealing to the viewers the characters' thoughts and past events in their lives, the monitors add depth to the plot.

Yoji, What's Wrong with You? explores numerous questions which are inherent in Idemitsu's analysis of Japanese society since her beginnings as a videographer. Marriage, family, womanhood and motherhood are the major themes in her work. The mother-and-son relationship is at the heart of *Yoji, What's Wrong with You?*: Mama had everything planned out for Yoji way before he was born, and neither her husband who left her, nor her beloved son could turn her away from her aspirations. Maternal manipulation thus collides with the son's desire to live his own life.

Idemitsu's style is evident here in the way images on the monitors play a decisive narrative role, informing the viewer on the mother's psychology and the son's dilemmas. We learn that Mama's husband cheated on her, that he did not keep his promise to make her happy. Terrified of losing her son one day, she makes Yoji vow to satisfy her unfulfilled wish. In liberating herself from marital dependency, she succumbs to maternal obsession. Having no identity apart from the maternal role she plays, Mama condemns Yoji to remain a son and not a man.

On the overall, Idemitsu's oeuvre takes interest in the feminine condition in contemporary society and, in particular, Japanese society. With *Yoji, What's Wrong with You?*, the videographer appears to ask: in accomplishing motherhood, is the woman reduced to become a seductress?

Diane-Sophie Girin
Translated by Yin Ker

II.

Identity Issues

In the 1970s, video art entered a period of social and political revival marked by student movements, the rise of feminism, and pacifist and anti-racist demonstrations.

Following Joseph Beuys' idea that "every man is an artist", the human body became a piece of artistic and aesthetic material. In this context, video registers, deconstructs and recreates performances by artists, whether in public or alone in their studio. In the latter case, the camera becomes the only witness to artistic expression.

The human body – the artists and actionists' primary instrument – most often expresses feelings of pain, violence (Vito Acconci) and desire, but also objectified physical experience which transforms the body in analogical codes, such as in Toshio Matsumoto's work. In 1988, Jean Baudrillard posed this question: "Am I a man or a machine?"

Valie Export belongs to the first generation of women artists who challenged a patriarchal media society, using the female body to combat fossilised stereotypes. As for Sonia Khurana, by showing her denuded body, she attacks clichés about conventional ideals of beauty.

The integration of the public into performances or as a participant in video installations leads to an interactive reflection on the role of the individual in our society, as in Lee Wen and Joan Logue's works. In 1996, Tony Oursler conceives the installation *SWITCH*, a circuit of *mise en abyme* within the museum itself, which incorporates the visitor in an imaginary narrative throughout his or her visit using 'talking heads' and surveillance cameras, while at the same time questioning our contemporary world populated with cameras and surveillance systems.

Valie Export

The video *Space Seeing/Space Hearing* originates from Valie Export's performance in 1974 for the exhibition *Art Remains Art: Aspect of International Art in the Early 1970s* at the Cologne Kunstverein.

This performance follows earlier works on the perception of space that Export began in the early 1970s. In the series *Body Configurations,* started in 1972, she questions in particular the adaptation of the body to its cultural environment and has already addressed the question of spatial perception. The minimalism of *Space Seeing/Space Hearing* ensues from a montage of sound and images following a quasi-mathematical logic. The result aims to be a basic demonstration of the movement of the body and of sound in space.

In this public performance, Export is standing still in the middle of one of the museum's empty rooms. Four cameras are aimed at her, presenting still shots of her on four monitors. These monitors show six different images of the artist: on the left or the right of the screen, in the foreground or the background, in full-length or close-up. The video begins with a musical note produced by a synthesiser. Each position is characterised by a change – be it in volume, the interval of the repetition or the pitch of the sound. The end result is shown on a fifth monitor equipped with a split-screen device, which is capable of synchronising both sound and image. While spectators present at the performance can observe Export as a fixed reference point in the white room, the visual combinations superposed with the sound combinations in the video give the impression that the artist is moving to the left and right, as well as back and forth.

Export describes this experience with the equation: "music + sculpture = melody". Indeed, contingent on the combination and assembly of screened still shots, sound is transformed into a meditative melody. This melody is supposed to help the spectator experience a sense of movement with just the combination of sound and images.

Diane-Sophie Girin
Translated by Yin Ker

Vito Acconci

■ *Turn On*, 1974

Turn On is in the same style as Vito Acconci's other autobiographical works, such as *Face Off* (1972) and *See Through* (1970). These are actions in which he plays the protagonist, using his body to engage the viewer. His oeuvre is founded upon the poverty of materials and the simplicity of composition, similar to the work of conceptual and body art artists. The way he manipulates images of himself in his performances opens up a new field of thought in the use of video in art. Using this method, Acconci constructs a confrontational relationship with the viewer that is pushed to its climax in *Turn On*. This work is characterised by its introspectiveness since it is more a presentation of his status as an artist, his work and of the reception he expects from the public. Instead of employing an intimate tone of speech, Acconci challenges the viewer with an aggressive and insistent manner. Hence, the title of *Turn On* is explored in all its senses since the term means to agitate, as well as to excite.

The video begins with a very long shot of the back of Acconci's head. The setting is bare and stripped of any superfluous detail, and the artist's head takes up the entire space. He hums softly, swaying his head lightly in rhythm. This movement becomes more and more insistent, furious and almost autistic. His singing then accelerates and amplifies, becoming more violent and aggressive. He creates the expectation of action, of a dénouement while provoking a certain malaise. After a while, he turns around abruptly to face the lens, his face filling the whole frame. Out of breath, he addresses the viewer, "Now! I have to face you now. Reveal myself … But you can't take it yet. I have to wait." In addressing the viewer directly, he thus presents the main point of his video: the will to expose and to create an anticipated and geared-up meeting between him, his work and the public.

After the furious attack of this first phase, he returns to his original position and continues his frenetic humming. He repeats the movements at irregular rhythms and makes several declarations. Thereby, later in the video, he says, "I've waited for the perfect time, for the perfect piece, I'm tired of waiting … but no, you want me to have something ready for you, something prepared." These challenges before the camera allow him to express his expectations, to address aspects of his work and relationship with the public. "I can talk about her, but maybe you've heard me talk too much about women." Acconci's rapport with the viewer is contingent upon a balance between independence and dependence – the viewer representing motivation in a way and above all the validation of his work, but also fear of repetition in the event of success. While the artist is free to create, he seeks response and recognition from the viewer. He does not hesitate in going back on his artistic choices either: "I've been too abstract, now I can be concrete, no more galleries, no more museums. It's me. I have no conviction anymore. I can't find any reason to do art." There is no intermediary, only a direct confrontation. He even evokes his doubts.

The work becomes a balance sheet. After having rebuked the viewer for a while, he goes as far as to discredit him in a paradoxical manner: "I'm waiting for you … not to be there." Like a fantasy of a form of art raw, pure and emancipated from all commercial pressures, *Turn On* is one of Acconci's most dramatic works. It stages a tense confrontation with the viewer that goes as far as to provoke a sense of guilt.

It is one of Acconci's last autobiographical videos, whose work deeply evolved after the 1970s. In *Face of the Earth* (1974), he also uses a close-up of his face but introduces a different speech addressing the notions of history and cultural dentity. This discourse is similar to *Body Building in the Great Northwest* (1975–1993), in which objects and documents from daily life are projected in a small, enclosed room reconstituting a traditional way of life in an exaggerated way. The shift in the style of his works from autobiographic theme to questions of social representations, where *Turn On* marks the turning point, continues with the tripartite video *The Red Tapes* (1976), where Acconci is more concerned about creating a cultural and social, rather than personal, space.

Priscilia Marques
Translated by Yin Ker

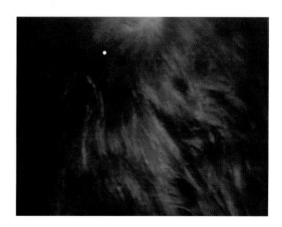

Joan Logue

Through an intimate and sensitive use of video, Joan Logue has developed the art of making video portraits. After training in painting and photography at the Mount St. Mary College of Los Angeles, she became interested in video in the late 1960s during the commercialisation of the first portable video camera, the Portapak by Sony.

In 1979, she experimented with a new format of very short video portraits entitled *30 Second Spots*. It was a series of concise video portraits defined by the artist as commercials for artists and their work. With an economy of means, each artist engages in an action, often close-up and facing the camera. Through this very short format, she brings forth a sense of intimacy with the artist, a brief shared moment with a visage that is usually overlooked. This project was executed in the cities of New York, Paris and San Francisco. In *30 Second Spots New York*, Logue offers a dynamic presentation of about 20 artists from art, literature and dance. Amongst them is composer John Cage, whose humour is highlighted – he opens a notepad and reads, "Dad says, 'Remember, your mother's always right.'" He next removes his spectacles and smiles, "Even when she's wrong."

Of great visual impact is artist Tony Ramos spinning on himself: a close-up of his face divided into two parts, one white and the other black. The rotation increases in speed, creating the optical effect of a face blending two colours together. The image is technically accelerated to accentuate the effect. In his portrait, Nam June Paik is seated before a piano. He prepares his hands like a pianist and closes his eyes in concentration. He hesitates to place his fingers on the keyboard, thinks and then has a change of heart. Eventually, he plunges his head on the keys and plays it as would a pianist with fingers.

As for Laurie Anderson, she uses her body to make sounds. In close-up, she uses her fist to knock on her temple and skull to create a rhythm whose sound is accentuated by Logue. Gradually, she turns to face the camera while continuing these rhythmic movements. At the end, she clatters her teeth three times to produce a curt sound that is heightened by the effect of echo. The study in sound is likewise present in the portrait of musician Yoshi Wada. The frame is a close-up of his foot acting on a pump. He creates a rhythmic breathing that accompanies a piece of electronic music inspired by Buddhist throat-singing.

Focusing on movement, Logue proposes a portrait of dancer Lucinda Childs who appears on the screen against a black background. Her movements, which are repeated and accelerated stroboscopically, blur her figure. Using tracking, her silhouette is imprinted on the screen. The dancer appears again, clearer, and executes a series of pirouettes with an effect of echo on the image. In *30 Second Spots Paris*, Logue offers another portrait of a dancer-choreographer, Ushio Amagatsu. Through a play on the lighting, she aestheticises the artist's body.

Thus, while they are an experiment with new video techniques, these video portraits are also a concise means of crystallising the artistic and intellectual panorama of a city's cultural life in the 1980s.

Priscilia Marques
Translated by Yin Ker

LEFT TO RIGHT: John Cage; Tony Ramos; Laurie Anderson; Yoshi Wada; Lucinda Childs; Nam June Paik.

© Coll. Centre Pompidou. Photo Brigitte Rodoreda.
Courtesy of Electronic Arts Intermix (EAI), New York.

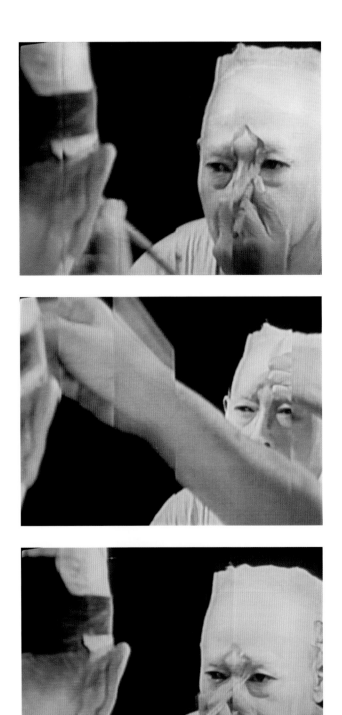

Formation exemplifies the geometric scission of images recurrent in Toshio Matsumoto's work. The video exhibits various ways of slicing the image, of moving the equal parts vertically or horizontally and rotating each fragment within the overall frame of the image. The entire video is made up of close-ups of the visage of renowned Japanese *kabuki* actor Uzaemon Ichimura who is seen carefully putting on make-up in a conventional manner by outlining the muscle features on the face with bold colour lines. The title *Formation* thus takes on a double meaning: it refers to the transformation process of both the images and of the appearance and character of the protagonist who will be endowed with a different personality on stage.

The beginning of the video provides a complete view of the actor's face and gradually reveals itself to be the reflection of the face in a mirror. The double nature of the image will subsequently become multiplied as the entire image is sliced into strips that are slightly dislocated in relation to one another or simply desynchronised. Another way of multiplication reproduces a certain detail of the image so that the identical fragments, gradually revealing slight differences in their framing, are seen covering the whole screen. The process of visual disintegration, addition and multiplication is parallely enhanced with sound realised by the artist himself (according to Nanako Tsukidate in an interview conducted in January 2011). Originally, a haunting music soundtrack accompanies the ritual action of the actor making up his face. As the image gradually becomes a composite of autonomous fragments, a minimalist soundtrack resounds, acting as the counterpoint to the music. Contrary to the first soundtrack composed of sparse sounds, the minimalist soundtrack brings forth regular beats and sounds which evoke a sense of volume. A few brief moments of silence add

tension and dynamism to the layered soundscape.

Having been making experimental films since the 1960s, Matsumoto represents the first generation of Japanese experimental filmmakers. As much as he forged his own approaches to the image without being influenced by Western filmmakers or artists (as he affirms), works like *Formation* can be compared to certain works in the Western avant-garde tradition, especially Fernand Léger's *Ballet mécanique* (1924), which shows a fragmented image of a woman's face, or Hans Richter's abstract films in which geometric forms move in different directions and patterns inside the frame. Such abstract works of moving images take abstract or cubist painting – genres which challenge the illusion of perspective and of depth – as their model of reference. Just as in *Formation*, the image in constant disintegration and reproduction renders its representation unstable and points to – by means of the geometric play – the platitude of the image and echoes the indefinite character of the theatrical persona.

Sylvie Lin

S*WITCH* is an installation made of eight parts scattered in the presentation area. It is a sort of theatricalisation of the contemporary subject torn between practice and theory, as suggested by the work's subtitle, *Theory vs. Everyday Experience*. The English term "versus" emphasises the combative style of this strange encounter between the characters, as well as with the spectators who discover them and start to listen to their strange quibblings. The word "switch" is sufficiently vague for us to be able to interpret it as a change, a permutation, an exchange, a diversion, or alternatively as the fact of turning off or turning on some switch. By gradually discovering the characters, it is of course possible to understand that what is happening is a change or a shift from one theoretical and/or practical model to another, with each one behaving differently – moreover without any hierarchy being established between them, or any order of appearance. Because the artist takes into account the architectural specificity of the place, using here the threshold spaces of the museum which artists usually do not make use of (such as walls, floors, white cubes, black boxes), it is only after having encountered all the characters in this little theatre, hidden here and there, that it is possible to get a more precise idea – but one that remains ambiguous – of what they are and what they are doing, both in theory and in practice.

The doll called "Emotions" expresses various emotions solely by way of onomatopoeia, from laughter to contentment, fear to anger, not to say general ease of being, disgust, anxiety or even pleasure. Contrary to their name, the "Talking Lights" (two bulbs which are synchronised with sound) do not really talk to one another, but rather let loose their monologue, even if the exchange can exist to all intents and purposes, as if by complementarity, because the red, associated with a man's voice, defends the negative vision of the "ego", whereas the green, associated with a woman's voice, defends a positive vision of it. The "Director" gives instructions to a crew we do not see, unless we ourselves are involved in it – a sensation strengthened by certain sentences like, "You're all there at the same time, in the same space," or, "Hey you! You with the face, I can see you moving!" The "Simulacrum" for its part is interactive, since the spectator can, through the doll, via which he is able to manipulate the device made up of a camera and a microphone, thanks to a surveillance station with monitor, microphone and lever, be in contact with another place in the exhibition venue, and thus move about with a false body. The "Philosophers" (the same character duplicated or with a twin) also carry on monologues alternating between banalities (such as how to treat flu, for example) and much more serious questions concerning judgement, conscience, necessity and the value of the truth of propositions. In the "Wall Projection", a hidden surveillance camera captures people who happen to be outside the museum, and projects their image inside, transforming times and spaces, as well as their functions. Lastly, "The Eye", an impressive socket which we first of all think is keeping an eye on us, is, in reality, watching the television, feverishly channel-hopping from one programme to another, something attested to by the reflections we can make out in the iris, and the different voices of the presenters and actors coming from the set.

Several readings are open to us – all of them plausible: each character is in fact the metaphor of a single person split into several egos, having as many forms of existence, attitudes, emotions and reflections as he does by offering technologies which he manipulates or which manipulate him, which he makes use of or which make use of him, which are a part of him or which he quite simply uses. The characters are subjected to this omnipotent and omniscient eye which seems to control everything, steered by its sole and powerful gaze, cast at any given moment on the tiniest detail, movement, word or expression. The eye inevitably calls to mind the eye of Big Brother in George Orwell's *1984*. Or it is just the opposite: the characters control the eye, for the programmes which intrigue the latter are perhaps the theatrical presentations made for us by Oursler, unveiled and laid bare. All kinds of media dominate us and fracture the ego that we are, cleave it and fracture it the better to distil their commercial and instrumental ideology. What "The Philosophers" are actually talking about (starting, among other things, with extracts of writings by Roland Barthes, Michel Foucault, Gottfred Wilhelm Leibniz, Immanuel Kant, Philip Kitcher): what is to be done, how are we to act, and should we judge things thus? But a more attentive ear and a liaison with the other characters lead us back to the initial question: are all these theoretical words which do not seem to culminate in anything concrete, practical or applicable, or any action which might change the course of things? Are they thought through for us by the media, by the characters we are listening to? Or are we not, in our turn, characters conceived by the objects we make and think we have mastery of? If the installation as a whole can be understood as a narrative relating metaphorically to the cinematographic system, we might also understand that we have become part of a film in which we are at once viewers and actors, subject to the orders of the director.

Jacinto Lageira

Translated by Simon Pleasance

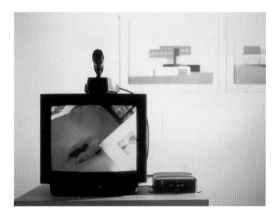

© Coll. Centre Pompidou.
Photo Jean-Claude Planchet.

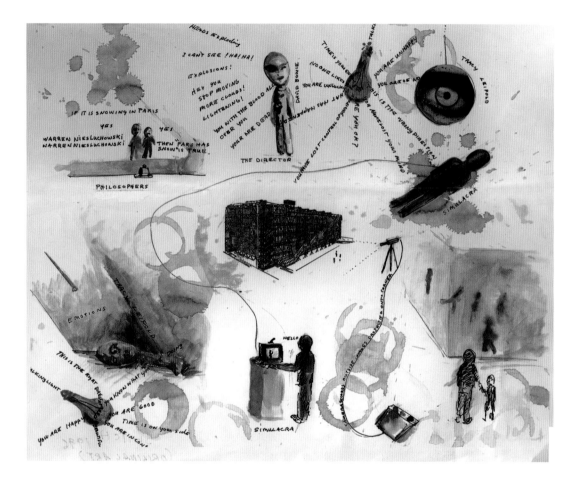

© Coll. Centre Pompidou. Photo Jean-Claude Planchet.
TOP LEFT AND BOTTOM: Courtesy of RMN.

"Be a World-Class Citizen. Fill in a questionnaire, pin it on the wall and get a free World-Class Badge." These are ostensibly Lee Wen's simple and uncomplicated terms and conditions in exchange for a 'free' world-class badge – and status – bearing the insignia of a winged globe. A sample of the object of desire rests on a stuffed white star, enshrined in a glass case, and placed near a desk where aspiring world-class citizens respond to a survey on the definition of a world-class society. Everything is stark white in *World Class Society*: white walls, white pedestals, white papers, a stuffed white winged globe suspended from the ceiling, and a white cloth tube that floats like a soft sculpture across the room. One at a time, the museum visitor watches the artist – bespectacled and sporting a tie – in close-up, delivering an emphatic speech on "world-class artists with world-class directors and actors", "world-class facilities, infrastructures, roads", "world-class food", etc, in loop, at a safe distance from the screen. It is a spotless and shielded space – only the absence of padded walls sets it apart from a psychiatric ward.

What is the import of this video installation, first shown at *Nokia Art Singapore 1999*, "a spectacular national showcase of visual art trends in Singapore", jointly organised by the National Arts Council and National Heritage Board and named after the corporate sponsor? What is so sensitive about this topic of world-class society that has caused the work to be shrouded in polemics? There is nothing politically contentious about the context of the work's debut, and the mantra of 'world class' is not Lee's invention either. For several years it has been a staple of the local government's discourse. In the National Day Dinner Speech of 1997, then Prime Minister Goh Chok Tong asserted, "to be a world-class business centre we must seek out world-class foreign talent … to make Singapore a world-class city". Citizens,

permanent residents and foreign workers alike from diverse sectors have been responding in their own way to this call. *World Class Society* can be seen as the response of Lee, winner of Singapore's highest cultural award, the Cultural Medallion, in 2005, to this national aspiration, in his characteristic manner, melding wit and humour as an artist.

Lee acknowledges the drive to make the island nation world class and attempts at least two things. First, through the language of installation, he presents the mechanisms that set the campaign in motion in a materialistic society; second, he invites reflection on what truly constitutes a world-class society. In a carrot-and-stick culture, action hinges on the promise of reward, which takes the form of the badge conferring world-class status; it is Lee's way of inducing the visitor to pen their thoughts on the meaning of 'world-class society'. While the white-shrouded monitor blasts a monologue on world-class prizes on one hand, the visitor is urged to remove him or herself from its influence – not without a carrot – while on the other hand, to reflect on the monologue's content. Hence, Lee subsumes parody into his course of action, intensifying the irony within *World Class Society*, which is far from being a didactic piece of work. It is, above all, an invitation to pause and think: is becoming world class a purely mechanical process?

As nations join the race to become First World, the space for thought is often banished. The individual is easily rendered apathetic by the satisfaction of material comfort and becomes unthinking. In fact, unthinkingness is often an essential condition for efficient integration into any competitive capitalistic society; even art and culture must become co-opted to serve capital accumulation. Here, Lee warns against the fixation with material achievements and their trappings and, if they must remain

© Singapore Art Museum collection.

the priority, then it is at least important to be aware of their price. *World Class Society* is the mirror the artist holds up to all societies committed to progress and a better tomorrow. Beneath the irony there is, first and foremost, faith in humankind's capacity for good greater than mere material enhancement.

Yin Ker

Sonia Khurana

Sonia Khurana created *Bird* in 1999 for her degree at the Royal College of Arts in London. In this short black-and-white video, the artist stands naked on a pedestal – a metaphor of a perch from which she attempts to fly. She stands on tiptoe, struggles to find her balance, tries to flap her wings, leaps but falls to the ground every time. The editing and instability of the camera which follows her body at close range accentuates the sense of movement. This graphics and video montage gives one the idea of derision, of the absurd even, given how improbable it is for this body to take flight like a bird, which gives the work its title.

Khurana was born in 1968 in India and currently works in New Delhi in various media, such as video, photography, text, installations and encounters with the public. Through performances using her own body, she addresses the themes of interiority and identity. Therefore she concentrates more on experience rather than representation.

While *Bird* was presented in London as part of her degree, Khurana wanted above all to show her work in India, where the message of this short video assumes full relevance. In her attempts to take off in flight, the artist wants to show how difficult it is to be liberated from her own condition. Literally, the body is at odds with its own flesh and the laws of gravity; similarly as a metaphor, it is difficult for a woman to be free from the rules imposed on her by society. *Bird* therefore puts forward a critique of the condition of womanhood, showing both the oppression and violence done unto women, as well as the impossibility of being divested of a feminine identity predefined by patriarchal society.

Also, the fact that she presented a nude female body which does not conform to the canons of beauty (notably that of slimness) was interpreted as a provocation in her country of origin. The artist was accused of pornography for displaying the obscenity of an undesired body form.

In Europe, the reception of this work was very different and it allowed her to gain ground as an integral part of the emerging generation of Indian artists. After two years at the Rijksakademie in Amsterdam, she exhibited in Europe, and in the United States at the exhibition *Global Feminisms* in Brooklyn in 2007. She has also organised workshops in Cameroon. Khurana is clearly in the company of other female artists who create works with their own bodies to better question the idea of sexual difference as well as representations of femininity.

Diane-Sophie Girin
Translated by Yin Ker

Apichatpong Weerasethakul and Christelle Lheureux

■ *Ghost of Asia*, 2005

142

A collaboration between two artists working in video and installation as well as cinematographic composition, *Ghost of Asia* films children playing at issuing orders to a man on the beach of a Thai island. Partners in crime for several years, Apichatpong Weerasethakul and Christelle Lheureux were on the island to shoot a film on the tsunami that swept through the area on Boxing Day in 2004, when their encounter with a group of children evolved into a game: the children direct the cinematographic action.

This video installation consists of a double projection on two opposing screens. On one side, the children are shown in quick shots interjected by blackouts. One only gets to hear their instructions, which begin in the flavour of Antoine de Saint Exupéry's *The Little Prince* with requests for drawings and evolve to become more authoritarian orders, a succession of actions with no specific aim ("drink milk", "catch a lizard", etc.). The children finally laugh when one tells the man to defecate. On the other screen, the man complies with all their demands in good humour, acting them out with a surprising adroitness that is accentuated by an accelerated montage which adds a touch of the burlesque to the scene.

The title *Ghost of Asia* stems from the belief in ghosts that is entrenched in Thai culture and is a recurring theme in Weerasethakul's films where the living and the dead rub shoulders in an ambiance of geniality. Here the children play at taming a ghost which is in no way terrifying, but which evokes the many bodies that littered the paradisiacal beaches following the tsunami. In the video, trauma is forgotten and the children regain authority over the actions of errant spirits through make-believe. At the end, the music stops and one hears the sounds of the earlier setting again: waves and conversations, guitars and singing, soothing the atmosphere which resonates with children's laughter.

Even though both artists did not intervene in the shooting and remained withdrawn from the action – as is often the case in Lheureux's work – the framing and assembly assert a very strong point of view which structures how the scene is perceived. Shot within the same space and time, the choice of using two projections creates an interregnum between the two. While the man is filmed in wide shot and is thus inserted within a festive and touristic atmosphere, the children are framed in medium shots and close-ups, isolated and their faces bathed in a beautiful lighting which intensifies the asperity of their expressions. Their appearances alternated with the succession of black screens create a sense of frustration and a sentiment of the unreal and the uncanny.

Seated between the two screens, the spectator has to summon the dynamism of visual perception to keep up with the very rapid tempo of the two screens. Immersed in darkness, captivated by the images and a very rhythmic and repetitive soundtrack, he finds himself in turn manipulated, breathless and plunged into the heart of a childhood vision, a world which is a little mad and where the boundaries between make-believe, reverie and reality become blurred.

Mathilde Roman
Translated by Yin Ker

III.

From Videotape to Interactive Installation

The 1960s and 1970s were conducive to research in phenomenology, parapsychology, conceptualisation and technology. In art, the emergence of video coincided with the acceptance of performance art and the arrival of installations.

This section examines representations of the self and the other, especially through the placement of the body in space. Artists began by documenting their performances on videotape (Bruce Nauman) before delegating the role of the performer to the viewer who is also bound by the conditions of museum space. In the age of minimalism and conceptual art, artists like Martial Raysse, Peter Campus, Dan Graham and Bruce Nauman transformed the visitor into an active and indispensable parameter of the artwork which cannot otherwise function. This is seen in Raysse's picture, Graham's mirror and Nauman's white cube (in connection with the works of author and playwright Samuel Beckett).

Most of the works in this section employ the closed circuit (a video camera linked to a monitor) or the surveillance circuit. The screen is likened to a window or a mirror, and the camera to the human eye. The visitor is often filmed unbeknown and his or her image is reversed, delayed or displaced several metres away in a meticulously designed space.

Martial Raysse

W hile Wolf Vostell and Nam June Paik were experimenting in the early 1960s, in Germany and the United States respectively, with video in the form of installations, it was not until 1968, and in a different context, that video started to be developed in France, with the works produced by Jean-Christophe Averty with the ORTF (Office de Radiodiffusion-Télévision Française; the French national broadcasting agency from 1964 to 1974), the television activities of Fred Forest, and the post-May 1968 tracts of Chris Marker and Jean-Luc Godard. Independent of this development, the composition entitled *Identité, maintenant vous êtes un Martial Raysse* was shown in April–May 1967 in the exhibition *5 tableaux, 1 sculpture* at the Alexandre Iolas Gallery in Paris. Chronologically speaking, this work was one of the first video installations made in France, and definitely the first closed-circuit piece. However, if it could be considered as a forerunner of video art, it was in spite of itself – for neither the context for the emergence of video in France nor the issues dealt with in Raysse's work are able to explain it.

Identité … is an installation made of a black plywood structure representing, in a simplified way, the oval shape of a hollowed woman's face standing out against a white background within which a video monitor is embedded. Based on a preparatory sketch made prior to the installation, dated 1965, the work was originally to have been called *Tableau à géométrie variable*. The presence of the video monitor seems here to be more of an opportunity for the artist to replace the customary painting with an animated image than to develop his film research work embarked upon with *Jésus Cola* or *L'Hygiène de la vision* (1966–67) and *Portrait électro machin chose* (1967), made with the ORTF. At a formal level, the installation is actually more akin to his previous works

incorporating a projection screen in the composition, such as *Suzanna Suzanna* (1964) and *A Propos de New York en peinturama* (1965). The picture remains, but the representation painted has here vanished, making way for the video image of the spectator.

The female oval motif, borrowed from advertising stereotypes, crops up regularly in Raysse's works of the 1960s and 1970s. As early as in 1964, in *Tableau métallique: portrait à géométrie convexe*, the artist had pared down the details of a face, and retained just the outline of the hair, a form which he would use in many works and object-pictures with free forms. Here, though, unlike the colourful environments borrowed from display cases from the world of consumerism, which hallmarked Raysse's work alongside the Nouveaux Réalistes, the artist simplified the forms as much as possible, and kept just an abstract outline in order to maintain a clean look.

When the visitor gets nearer to *Identité* …, he finds himself in front of a video monitor which transmits back to him his own image filmed by a surveillance camera, from behind and from a high angle, with a lapse of a few seconds. Unlike the primary function of video – simultaneous recording and broadcasting of an image – a slightly delayed action is enough, here, to create a time lapse. *Identité…* is a specific experiment with – and experience of – time and space. As its title indicates, the spectator is projected into the work, him- or herself becoming a Martial Raysse. The device makes him/her an onlooker in the Duchampian sense of the term ("It's the spectators who make pictures."). By announcing the artist's subsequent research work dealing with interactivity, the picture is no longer an opaque canvas to be contemplated and looked at, but an interface referring the spectator to his own image, yet without tallying this with his reflection in a mirror. The present image, on the other hand, is a vision from

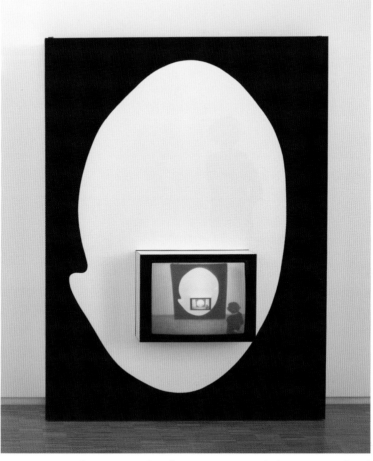

© Coll. Centre Pompidou. Photo Georges Meguerditchian. Courtesy of RMN.

behind and sidelong, capable of making him think about his own role as a spectator.

In her essay entitled, "Video: the Aesthetics of Narcissism", which was published in the first issue of *October* in 1976, Rosalind Krauss points out the feeling of frustration experienced by the person viewing a closed-circuit video installation, which unsettles his or her awareness of time and the perception he or she has of him- or herself as subject: "The self is a projected object, whose frustration issues from its own ensnaredness by this object, an object with which he can never really overlap." By his use of a closed circuit and delayed action, typical factors in the earliest video machines, it is in this respect that *Identité* … can be compared with other installations in the Centre Pompidou collection, such as *Interface* (1972) by Peter Campus and *Present Continuous Past(s)* (1974) by Dan Graham. But unlike his contemporaries, for whom the video machine was a way of specifically putting into perspective issues likely to go hand in hand with the theoretical debate about identity, which was in vogue at the end of the 20th century, this aspect of video seems to be something of an exception with Raysse, who would make a swift return to figurative painting steeped in mythological references.

Marianne Lanavère
Translated by Simon Pleasance

147

In her article "PheNAUMANology" in 1970, curator and critic Marcia Tucker wrote that Bruce Nauman's work "is so varied that it has been briefly categorised as 'Eccentric Abstraction' (1966), 'funk' (1967), 'body art' (1968), 'Anti-Form' (1969), 'process art' (1970) and 'Conceptual Art' (1971)." This usefully points to the eclectic modes of expression Nauman uses. Working with rubber, fibreglass and neon, as well as his own body, photography and film, he fundamentally questioned artistic practice or what an artist should do. More concerned with the ideas behind the artwork or the process of making art, he wondered about the validity of producing any object of art. Indeed significantly, in 1969, his work was included in Harald Szeemann's ground-breaking exhibition *When Attitudes Become Form* at the Kunsthalle in Bern, Switzerland.

Nauman graduated from the University of California at Davis in 1966 and lived in San Francisco and Mill Valley until he moved temporarily to Southampton, New York, in 1968. The gallerist Leo Castelli included him in a group show that year and bought video equipment that was shared by Nauman, Keith Sonnier and Richard Serra. Sony had only just released the Portapak portable camera in 1967; this technology was in its infancy, but already a new medium for experimentation by artists like Nam June Paik and Andy Warhol.

Around this time, Nauman made a series of performative single-screen videos in the enclosed private space of his Southampton studio. In *Stamping in the Studio*, the fixed camera is installed high up, rather like a closed-circuit television (CCTV) surveillance system, and flipped so that the image is upside-down for the viewer. Nauman records himself for the entire 60-minute duration of the tape doing exactly what he had indicated in the title. What we observe, therefore, is one continuous take of the artist walking around in circles, lines or other configurations in and out of the frame of the monitor. A mysterious artistic ritual is cap-tured. Action with no clear object that generally occurs offstage, like a preparatory sketch, is made manifest.

Fascinated by human behaviour and art-world phenomena, Nauman performs the activity of the artist in his workplace. Here "stamping" can be considered in the sense of marking territory or making a mark. He presents a solitary repetitive action, searching for inspiration, obsessively working out intent. The movements appear to be purposeless and nearly absurd. Rather like in Paul McCarthy's video *Painter* (1995, also in the Centre Pompidou collection), the creative process is art in itself.

Minimalist music by the likes of Philip Glass and Steve Reich was a great influence for Nauman. Sound – here the quasi-mechanical stomping of his feet on the floor – is an essential element in this video to the extent that it nearly becomes a complex percussion piece in itself. The ascending and descending volume and rhythms of his footwork vary and each sequence is repeated methodically several times. Time and space converge through sound and movement.

The same year, in 1968, Merce Cunningham's piece *Walkaround Time* was based on Marcel Duchamp's *Large Glass*. Bay Area artists like Nauman in the 1960s had strong connections with the humour and absurdities of the Dada artists from the beginning of the 20th century. Encounters with dancers, such as Cunningham and Meredith Monk, informed Nauman's interest in cross-disciplinary experiments. *Stamping in the Studio* integrates body art, performance and dance. His upright body with dangling arms is a material. By monitoring an occupation, occupying space and appropriating the studio, Nauman is practically a living sculpture.

Vladimir: That passed the time.
Estragon: It would have passed in any case.
Vladimir: Yes, but not so rapidly.
(Samuel Beckett, *Waiting for Godot*, 1952.)

Caroline Hancock

Bruce Nauman ◼ *Going Around the Corner Piece*, 1970

I t is pretty much a given these days to expect a museum visitor to actively approach the exhibits on display – to look at them, examine them, walk around them, and perhaps even touch them. In a word, the visitor usually masters the 'art observation code'. However, there are artworks which unseat certain societal preconceptions and challenge the visitor's own beliefs, though in a constructive way.

Art must strike the visitor like a blow to the nape of the neck, Bruce Nauman declared once, with an intensity that seizes the onlooker's whole being – body and mind alike. And it is a fact that even frequent visitors to museums are often caught unawares when they suddenly find themselves standing in front of a simple white box which they absolutely cannot enter. What are they supposed to do with it?

Going Around the Corner Piece is a closed rectangle, twice as long as it is high. At the very top of the four white walls hang four cameras, like vultures keeping an eye on their prey. And we, the visitors, are precisely that fresh carcass. Once digested (our black-and-white image as seen from behind), the 'prey' ends up in front of us on the floor, at the end of the wall – you can see it on the four monitors there. Samuel Beckett, whom Nauman held in high esteem, once described the eye of the camera with its aggressive stare as the 'Eye of Prey'. In so doing, he wanted to express not only the unavoidable but also the destructive facets of self-observation. When visitors catch a fleeting glimpse of this experimental installation, they are seized by a slight yet unmistakable sense of disquiet – a malaise which Beckett calls the 'Agony of Perceivedness' in his film *Film* (1964). Even with the stark spatial constellation constructed by Nauman with the cameras, monitors and white walls being as aggressive and striking, the participation of the person viewing it

still plays a significant role in realising the intended experience of the installation.

In spite of its slightly menacing look, the work is seductive and the visitor assumes his actor's role, drawn to it as if by magic. Self-defence may well be a powerful driving force in man, but curiosity is another such force, and every bit as strong. And curiosity is as powerful as the need to cavort in front of a mirror or a camera – which, with Nauman, is readily put on the same level in his closed-circuit works. The artist is interested in models of human behaviour, and is well aware of the fascination that everyone feels in front of their reflected self. He accordingly draws the onlooker into his work like a painter, while at the same time hugely limiting his possibilities of action. By the very construction of the installation, the visitor-cum-investigator is guided by the artist who, in fact, leaves him no other choice than to follow the track he has traced for him along the walls. From then on, the camera – that 'Eye of Prey' – pursues him, and he is forever seeing himself from behind going round the next corner. The visitor thus feels directly, in his own skin, what it is to be an artist: the disturbing feeling of being barred from his usual experience of self, and chasing after himself without any hope of being able to catch up with himself. This amazingly simple immediacy is an unpleasant experience, and it is definitely not coincidental if the visitor recalls Beckett's *Film* (1964). In it we see character O (Buster Keaton from the rear) being closely watched for 22 minutes by the eye of a camera (E), which Keaton eventually looks straight in the eye at the very last reverse shot, and in that gesture, shows that he is exactly the same as that eye. Man is both hunter and hunted by his own self, hence creating a vicious circle. As in Nauman's other works, what is involved here are themes such as the futile flight from self and the quest for self – themes already outlined in 19th-century novels about the doppelgänger (the ghostly double or other self) as a loss of existential reference.

In *Going Around the Corner Piece*, Nauman casts the spectator in a role which he himself played in his early pieces about body and movement – pieces like *Dance or Exercise on the Perimeter of a Square*, *1967–68*; *Slow Angle Walk (Beckett Walk)*, *1968*. In these works, he put life into the sculptural space by means of original and almost ritual bodily motor functions. At the time, he no longer regarded art as a finished product but as a continuous process of self-creation. Like a series of sequential movements which evaporate at the very moment in which they are made, but which, by its continual repetition, become part and parcel of the physical, bodily memory, as it is with dancers. Nauman was obviously putting the works in the context of dance studies, which undoubtedly was influenced by his friendship with choreographers Meredith Monk and Merce Cunningham. But his works are also studies in human empathy: Nauman observes how his own physical tension is transmitted to the spectator in the form of muscular tension. Ideally, as he used to say then, he would like the endless sequence of those movements to be a continuous loop. Where content is concerned, the loop does indeed signify the freeze frame and frozen time, but this does not necessarily conjure up boredom: the body's monotonous and endless to-ing and fro-ing in a limited range of movement also relaxes the mind and opens up the inner stage. Nauman has observed that during their passage through the works belonging to the 'corridors' series, to which this 'corner piece' belongs, many things pass through people's minds. The outer space of the 'corner piece' which is strictly geometric also leads into the visitor's labyrinthine self. And this is not something awful and hopeless because,

as Jorge Luis Borges puts it: "In a labyrinth, you don't get lost / In a labyrinth you find yourself".

Gaby Hartel
Translated by Simon Pleasance

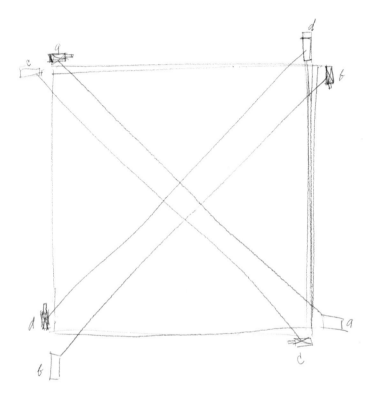

20'×20' 18'high – 4 T.V. cameras, 4 monitors on diagonal connections
–going around the camera piece.

B. Nauman Jan. 70

© Coll. Centre Pompidou. Photo Georges Meguerditchian.

Peter Campus

■ *Interface*, 1972

Peter Campus came up with the idea for the installation *Interface* in 1972. This work was the artist's second closed-circuit installation and was exhibited for the first time in Europe in 1979 at the Kölnischer Kunstverein, Cologne. The main component of *Interface* is a sheet of glass in the shape of a screen, set towards the back of a dimly lit room. A video camera is placed behind the glass and aimed towards it. On the other side of the glass and facing it is a video projector. The camera and the video projector are placed diagonally opposite each other across the sheet of glass and linked by a cable, applying the technical principle of the closed circuit. The projector is designed to retransmit, live, what the camera records – in this case an image of the spectator in the exhibition area, rebroadcast in real time. The visitor, who is part of the installation, is in fact invited to move about in the space in front of the sheet of glass. The role of the latter in this set-up is twofold: it is designed on the one hand to reflect the image of the spectator like a mirror, and on the other, acts as a screen, enabling the visitor to see an image of himself as recorded by the camera. So, by means of the glass, the visitor who enters the interface environment is confronted simultaneously by two images of himself, one positive – the video image – and the other negative, the image reflected by the glass. While the glass sends back a colour image with clearly defined outlines, the taped indirect image projected in black and white, and "ghost-like", seeming more fragile, as if floating in space. When the visitor moves about in front of the glass, he is led to determine the exact place at which his two images overlap. It is from this precise point that the visitor can then visualise the progressive duplication of his image.

Interface is an example of the minimalist-type approaches of the 1960s and 1970s, aimed at questioning – here by way of video as a medium – notions of space and perception, through the involvement of the subject in the work and the exhibition area. Put more specifically, it is the principles which construct the physical and mental identity of the subject that are involved in *Interface*, through the presentation of the spectator's body as subjected to performance and combined with the manipulation of his image. Campus systematically uses this principle which alters the image of the spectator in the 18 closed-circuit installations that he produced between 1970 and 1978. Because of different technical procedures associated with objects arranged in space at very specific distances and angles (mirrors in *Kiva*, 1971; glass in *Interface*; prisms in *Statis*, 1973; etc.), the artist creates a display which places the spectator opposite his fragmented, duplicated, distorted and inverted image – so many ways of translating the complexity of self-perception and challenging the foundations of identity construction. These effects are thus aimed not only at describing, in a system of phenomenological logic, the perception which the individual has of his own body in space, but also at visualising the notion of the psychic fragmentation of the subject, between essence and appearance. It is in this sense that Campus defines video as a "function of reality", that is to say, a medium encouraging a questioning of the subject/object, interior/exterior, conscious/unconscious categories, which have interested him ever since his studies in experimental psychology in the late 1950s. These research projects are, incidentally, inseparable from the technical possibilities offered by video. From this viewpoint, Campus' work comes across like an investigation of the capacities of this burgeoning art medium.

Frédérique Baumgartner
Translated by Simon Pleasance

Dan Graham

The year 1974 was a particularly fruitful one for Dan Graham in terms of video production, for he produced some 10 installations known collectively as *Time Delay Room*, all of which are designed to show live recorded images which are then re-transmitted on monitors with a slight time lag using different devices. *Present Continuous Past(s)*, first exhibited in Cologne, is the first work in the genre and, more importantly, the model on which most later works presenting space-time interpenetrations in rooms partly lined with mirrors would be based, in which the spectator is simultaneously the subject and object of perception. Graham's own description for *Present Continuous Past(s)* can in no way replace the spectator's proprio-perceptive experience. It does nevertheless help to grasp the problem set involved here: "The mirrors reflect present time. The video camera tapes what is immediately in front of it and the entire reflection on the opposite mirrored wall. The image seen by the camera (reflecting everything in the room) appears eight seconds later in the video monitor … If a spectator's body does not directly obscure the lens' view of the facing mirror the camera is taping the reflection of the room and the reflected image of the monitor … A person viewing the monitor sees both the image of himself or herself of eight seconds earlier, and what was reflected on the mirror from the monitor eight seconds prior to that – 16 seconds in the past … An infinite regress of time continuums within time continuums (always separated by eight-second intervals) within time continuums is created."

The work's title suggests different interpretations with regard to past and present temporal overlaps: what may be involved is a continually past present, or a continually present past or pasts, or alternatively a continually present present in the past or a continually past past or past(s) in the present. All

this is made perfectly possible if we bear in mind that the images retransmitted with their permanent and successive lapses are perceived in present time by the onlooker, that the latter is reflected in present time in the mirrors, but that, at the same time, much of what he perceives already no longer exists. More precisely, it is already no longer present in the sense that the image is retransmitted, but present all the same at the very moment when its viewing takes place, because this always takes place now.

The device developed by the artist does not, incidentally, contain all the possible space-time arrangements, because the spectator's memory, no matter how infinitesimal or elementary it may be, likewise contributes to the composition and recomposition of his experience of space and time. One might think that the only things changing are the sense of the duration of time and the fleeting memory of time past or passing; this is to forget that the system of capture is capable of recording ad infinitum all future presence, which will be immediately reintroduced into a present, and then a past. Once an approximately complete system of capture or harnessing has been assimilated, any spectator may forecast, project into the future, as it were, the underlying principle of the arrangement. On the other hand, what he cannot imagine or

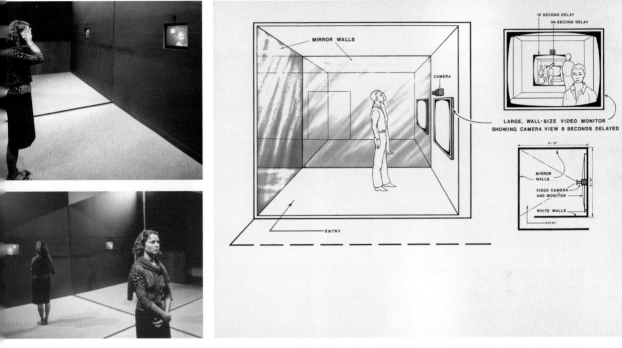

Labels within diagram:
MIRROR WALLS
CAMERA
ENTRY
16 SECOND DELAY
24 SECOND DELAY
LARGE, WALL-SIZE VIDEO MONITOR
SHOWING CAMERA VIEW 8 SECONDS DELAYED
MIRROR WALLS
VIDEO CAMERA AND MONITOR
WHITE WALLS
ENTRY

FACING PAGE AND ABOVE RIGHT: © Dan Graham. Photo Harry Shunk. Courtesy of John Gibson Gallery, New York.
LEFT ABOVE AND BELOW: © Coll. Centre Pompidou. Photo Philippe Migeat.

recollect is precisely the present experience of present time, which only has any consistency when we are caught in the interplay of images and reflections of the room, and when we are physically included in its space.

Without denying the playful, and somewhat spectacular and theatrical, or even – for some spectators – upsetting features of *Present Continuous Past(s)* still at work today and which are also part and parcel of the work, the latter subtly sheds light on a phenomenon that is almost always hidden by our everyday preoccupations, namely the space-time experience of self. The fact that we are living in space and time is obvious, but we pay no heed to it as far as it concerns our time and our space. Above all, we are in no way accustomed to seeing this virtually elusive time and space unfolding before and with us in a concrete way, as here in Graham's

work. For *Present Continuous Past(s)* does not show us just an infinity of perceptive forms of the time and space of an object – the installation properly so-called, but essentially our space-time experience as lived, as if we were entering into another one-self. The experience undergone is none other than the experience of ourselves which nobody else can have. In this work, and other similar works, Graham does not just offer us the chance to be the subject of our own experience; he pushes us in a way – felt by some as relative physical and psychic violence – towards the exploration of other ways of seeing ourselves and learning about ourselves as subjects. Graham shows us that what we are or think we are is never closed and defined, but rather, always shifting and unfinished.

Jacinto Lageira
Translated by Simon Pleasance

Samuel Beckett

■ *Arena Quad I + II*, 1981

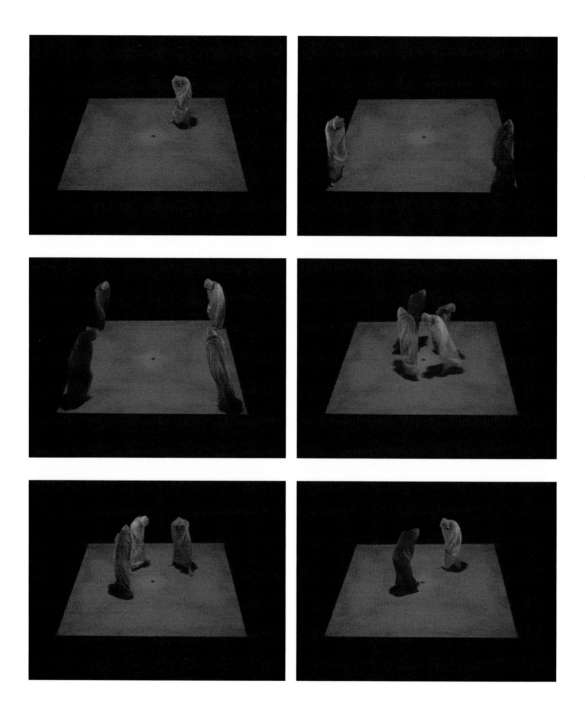

© Coll. Centre Pompidou. Courtesy of the estate of Samuel Beckett.

Arena Quad I + II, a play for television written in 1980, was staged by Samuel Beckett in 1981 for German television. *Arena Quad* presents a fixed cinematographic shot and theatrical setting whose stability is disrupted by the successive entrances of four ghostly walkers at the four corners of the square. As often in Beckett, the "performers" exhaust logical series by combining all possible trajectories: one by one, one after the other, appearing in a tunic, hooded, head down, face hidden. There is minimal dramatisation, without any event other than the appearance/disappearance of the bodies and their obligation to avoid the "danger zone" in the centre with an abrupt lopsided walk.

The idea is to understand how the decomposition at work in *Arena Quad* provides a rhythm for a new type of ritual (spatial decomposition, but one that is also, in *Arena Quad I*, audio and visual, with a specific percussive sound for each dancer and the allocation of a primary colour). The closed, repetitive structure effectively evokes the dance of a pagan ritual, the redemptive and poignant walk of monks in their cloister, or the comic and troubling movement of a nameless curse: thus, Beckett had cited Dante's *Inferno* concerning the movement of the walk of the damned who "always go left into Hell (the direction of the damned)".

The bodies themselves appear to be dissociated and independent of any desire to move. Instead, the speed of their walk is governed by automatism, lending a mechanised, inhuman, systematic aspect to their dance, situated between life and death, humanity and inhumanity, mechanical automatism and the autonomy of the living, thus reflecting their uncanniness.

Guillaume Gesvret
Translated by Yves Tixier and Anna Knight

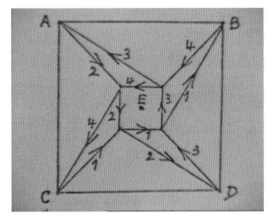

© Coll. Centre Pompidou.
Courtesy of the estate of Samuel Beckett.

Apichatpong Weerasethakul

Shot on a mobile phone, *Nokia Short* is a brief immersion in a dulcet reverie. An act of spontaneity that is no doubt gratifying for Apichatpong Weerasethakul who is used to the economic constraints of cinematographic productions, whereby the period between screenplay and shooting can be very long and laborious, this video is representative of the formal liberty offered by the medium. The images radiate a light and joyful atmosphere: shot live on a beach, they film exposed bodies, legs and faces in very tight shots that come close to abstraction. The video's low definition is played up by the pixels' pictorial substance, and the tinted filters distance the gaze from a quest for realism to submerse it in a dream world. This is precisely the point of videos shot on mobilephones: one is liberated from compositional concerns to embrace handshot images whose jerky movements bring on effects of interference. One loses the clarity of vision and struggles to locate oneself, to link the diffuse impressions to a specific representation. Laughter and voices simply evoke good humour, a moment of the daily life or an evening by the sea. While there is no structured narrative built upon the images, the montage does provide some clues for interpretation through its emphasis on certain images: the eye in close-up which is shown repeatedly or the alarm clock indicating "8:06", for example. In the festive general atmosphere punctuated by singing, shouting and bodies underwater, this alarm clock appears, as if it were an effort to suppress nocturnal languor.

In using the mobile phone as a means of filming, Weerasethakul manipulates a poor practice which allows him to break away from the constraints of cinematographic production, as well as to explore another form of image. Indeed, he does not seek to obtain the best possible aesthetic quality from his Nokia as the idea is not to produce a video with other means. On the contrary, the aim is to experiment with a new territory of moving image through

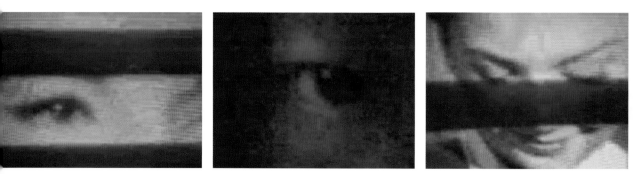

emphasis on its technical penury. The title hence designates the medium of production and not the content to show that the departure point lies in the appropriation of a new film technique. He uses his mobile phone as a means of proposing a state of perception which flirts with 'non-mastery', accident and a form of confusion. This praxis is similar to works filming the intimate, the banal and the day-to-day since the beginning of video art, whereby artists assert to work in spontaneity and to be on a quest for forms of the ordinary. The ensuing poetry is that of small things, of fleeting impressions. *Nokia Short* also comes close to the filmed diary and one of its key figures, Jonas Mekas for example. As in *Walden* (1968), one finds in this video a penchant for movement, the inconstant subjectivity of the gaze and the importance accorded to auditory substance. What takes shape is another state of the visible – at times unrecognisable – which expresses the elusive ephemerality of life and allows the evocation of hidden forms. In the work of Weerasethakul, such states of perception are in reference to the personal vagabondages linked to the quest for the supernatural and the invisible which traverses his films and videos. The filter of the phone allows the unveiling of the diffuse and the expression of sensations, in the same way that the photographic act allows the son in Weerasethakul's 2010 film *Uncle Boonmee Who Can Recall His Past Lives* to meet ghosts.

This video will be presented on mobile phone screens in the exhibition space. This avoids the aesthetisation produced by large projections and plays on the element of surprise brought about by the work's intrusion into the visitor's private space via a personal object with which one often nurses a coalescent kind of relationship.

Mathilde Roman
Translated by Yin Ker

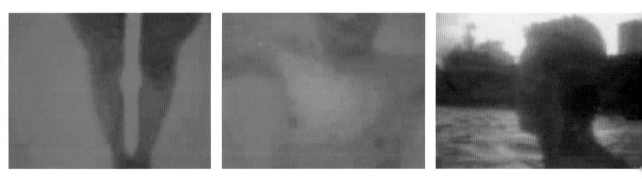

© Coll. Centre Pompidou.
Courtesy of the artist and Kick the Machine Films.

Pipilotti Rist

"I'm not really interested in unrealised work. I want people to take part in my creation, and if they can't, I feel I have failed."

A la belle étoile (*Under the Sky*) is a showpiece projected onto the ground that invites the public to penetrate the mental space conjured up by Pipilotti Rist. The work to be presented at SAM at 8Q is adapted from the larger original presentation shown at the Centre Georges Pompidou in Paris in 2007 for the Centre's 30th anniversary. The projection can be seen from various levels: from the piazza itself or from the passageways on each floor of the building. Visitors on the piazza will be engulfed by the artist's surrealist images and in turn, participate in the audiovisual installation. Meanwhile, the video can be seen in its entirety from the surrounding passageways overlooking the piazza.

Rist was born in 1962 in Grabs, Switzerland and works as a videographer and musician in Zurich. Her works result from a montage of sounds and images of which she is simultaneously producer, director and, quite often, the protagonist as well.

The major themes in Rist's videos are the differences between the sexes, identity and femininity, yet they do not necessarily advance a clear feminist message: "I am grateful for feminism. But women did it once so I don't have to go back to what they did". She expresses great interest in the culture of entertainment and in particular television, which she considers to be the cornerstone of popular culture. She cites Nam June Paik amongst her influences: "[What] Paik's work and mine have in common [is] that we both try to draw the viewer inside it. At first you look at the box, at the screen or projection, but when you concentrate on the sequences you feel as if you're inside the box, behind the glass, within the wall. You forget everything around you and concentrate completely on the box: you're swallowed."

Under the Sky encapsulates this idea as it welcomes the visitor into the heart of the image and places him in strange environments. The sequences carry the characters of Chris and Ewelina, as well as the spectators, away into nature, the cosmos and the city. Via a *mise en abyme* of images, the spectator plunges into Ewelina's mouth and finds himself carried off by lava flow. The high-angle and low-angle shots create confusion in perspective and scale, and give the spectator an impression of weightlessness and flutter. This feeling of lightness is further accentuated by the seagull camera style and the soundtrack composed by the artist. Rist hopes the spectator will arrive at a state of mental flux, in which almost anything seems possible.

Diane-Sophie Girin
Translated by Yin Ker

TOP: © Coll. Centre Pompidou.
BOTTOM: © Pipilotti Rist. Courtesy of Hauser & Wirth, Zürich.

163

IV.

Landscape Dreams

The Chinese concept of landscape (*shanshui*) has two basic elements, mountain (*shan*) and water (*shui*), and has inspired countless poets and painters. Using ink and brush, China's greatest artists strived to transcribe their contemplations on paper or silk. In this artistic practice, which is one of the noblest, the quest for the Way (*Dao*) and breath resonance (*qiyun*) unites the artist and nature through meditation (Toshio Matsumoto).

The mountain is also the land of myths and legends, feared at times, venerated at others and sometimes even deified. In Asia, Mount Wutai in China and Mount Fuji in Japan attest to this (Ko Nakajima). After sojourning in Japan, artists living in the United States (Bill Viola) and in France (Thierry Kuntzel) have expressed interest in landscape as a metaphor for time and space. Both of these artists, who filmed in Japan, present man with the infinity of the landscape in their exhibited works.

The urban landscape has become a recurrent theme in contemporary video art. With the largest number of megalopolises in the world today, Asia's transformation over the last few years has been rapid and dramatic. Urban dynamics (Louidgi Beltrame), population influxes (Jun Nguyen-Hatsushiba), architectural renewal (Rachel Reupke), as well as the effects of globalisation (The Propeller Group), and the loss of natural spaces or local patrimony (Keith Deverell, Sue McCauley, Meas Sokhorn, Srey Bandol) preoccupy the artists in their video works.

The natural landscape – the field of meditation and contemplation – confronts the urban landscape, the theatre of a passive and apprehensive observation.

Toshio Matsumoto ▦ *Ki or Breathing*, 1980

Based on a structural and materialist approach towards the image, the experimental works of Toshio Matsumoto are based on the processes of encrustation, split, stratification or interlocking of close-ups, whereby the images seem to be disintegrated, fragmented and recombined under ceaseless modulations in their frames, forms and colours. Though apparently related to the Western structuralist method of image-making, these works are characterised by Oriental thought which emphasises the harmony between Man and Nature, in contrast to the Western view based largely on the presumed division between Man and Nature. Such an integral vision from the East is seen incarnated in the cosmic dimension recurrent in several of the artist's experimental pieces which elaborate upon the perceptual and sensual aspects of images and sounds involving elements such as water and air and is best represented in *Ki or Breathing*.

The Japanese word *ki* means air and breath, the basic element for the existence of all creatures. In Oriental thought, there exists also a kind of air within the entire universe; it circulates and sets the cosmos in motion. *Ki or Breathing* begins precisely with the image of a rotating planet covered with layered colours representing the layers of atmospheres. Throughout the video, we see various modalities of splitting images linked by close-ups and occasionally with pans. It is often a miniature view which shifts into a full-screen vision, like at the beginning of the first chapter of the video: a zoom-in closes in on the square at the centre, showing a misty mountainous landscape accompanied by a soundtrack of flute and sporadic sounds of bells, adding to the mysterious ambiance. What follows is a split-screen scene composed of two identical landscape views, yet the nuances of the flow of the fog indicate that the images are actually slightly desynchronised.

The second chapter takes on a relatively impressionist tone, in comparison to the geometric play of the first. After a few landscape scenes in full-screen, then in encrustation, whereby the same image in different sizes are set one within another, several close-ups focus on archaic stone figures of a somewhat disquieting character, stressing on the wide-open mouths of certain sculptures in their apparent immobility, thus creating a surreal effect. The stone figures are then shown juxtaposed in strips of almost identical images, filling the whole screen. The juxtaposition is difficult to decipher given the tight cluster and the overwhelming sameness of the sculptures, creating an overall feeling of hallucination.

As a counterpoint to the petrified sculptures on earth, the next sequence shows moving clouds in the sky represented in a similar method of encrustation as aforementioned. Again, the persistent presence of the moving clouds is symbolic, just like in the split-screen image in the first chapter whereby it is only through the moving fogs that one perceives the passage of time against the immutable mountains, as well as the distinction between the twin images of cloud and mist – both states of air which signify in *Ki or Breathing* the essence of the universe and its motion, as well as the energy and force behind it.

Towards the end of the second chapter, the impressionist tone intensifies in the last full-screen scenes to show slow pans of a gloomy forest in a bluish hue, which then turns into a tableau reminiscent of Georges Seurat's pointillist painting. The contrast between light and shadow is radicalised to the extent of making the natural scene almost non-figurative, like a collage of light spots and other informal stains. The impression of colour and light is intensified in the third chapter whose imagery emphasises the incessant changes and movements of the sea and the perpetual coming-and-going of

its waves. While a ghostly female spirit from the previous chapters performing in the style of the Japanese *ankoku butoh* (a fusion of Japanese tradition with the avant-garde) is seen wading by the shore, the vast horizon behind her undergoes gradual changes in colour: the waves turn dark then red while the cloud banks turn bright and gorgeous orange, yellow and green.

Matsumoto, a pioneering Japanese experimental filmmaker, realised in the visual epic *Ki or Breathing* an array of visual experimentations that corresponds perfectly with constant change in the cosmos, however latent the latter may seem. The visual virtuosity

is intensified and completed by the soundtrack of Japanese composer Toru Takemitsu who was heavily influenced by Claude Debussy and created a series entitled *Waterscape* containing scores under perpetual tonal metamorphosis. As a whole, the vision along with its soundscape in *Ki or Breathing* exemplifies Dominique Noguez's comment on Japanese experimental cinema: "In Japanese films, the visible is a grace which we deserve, which we entrap with perseverance." (*Dans les films japonais, le visuel est une grâce qu'on mérite, qu'on piège avec persévérance.*)

Sylvie Lin

© Coll. Centre Pompidou. Courtesy of the artist.

Hatsu Yume (*First Dream*) is a 56-minute video realised by Bill Viola in 1981 while he was the artist-in-residence at Sony's Atsugi research laboratories in Japan. During Viola's stay, not only did he have the opportunity to broaden his knowledge of Oriental traditions and thought, but his audiovisual experimentations also benefited from the significant technological resources made available to him by Sony.

Viola's video opens with a sunrise, as if embodying the potential of beginnings; there is nothing rigid, nothing defined, no certainty as yet – anything is still possible. Light and water as metaphors for life are omnipresent in *Hatsu Yume*: "I was thinking about light and its relation to water and life, and also its opposite – darkness, or the night and death. I thought about how we have built entire cities of artificial light as refuge from the dark. ... Video treats light like water – it becomes a fluid on the video tube. Water supports the fish like light supports man. Land is the death of the fish – darkness is the death of man."

At the beginning of the video, the power of water is contained in the image of waves rolling onto the shore in extremely slow motion. This image gives way to the equanimity of a lake's still waters, and that of thick fog enveloping the mountains. The video progresses with the rhythms of light: from day, with large open spaces; to night, and obscurity, in the labyrinthine avenues of a large city; from the silence of meditative sequences; to the clamour of an almost chaotic montage. Although these opposing concepts are often shown in the same image, they do not cancel each other out. Hence, at the

end of *Hatsu Yume*, when darkness floods the screen, the city's neon lights, the excessively lit entrance of a hotel, and the cars' lights seem to be attempting to sustain 'life'. Night reigns over the sea, transforming it into an immense black body, but there is always a source of light to remind the viewer of life's energy, whether the light is coming from the lamp posts of the port or the searchlights of a fishing boat moving slowly across the screen.

There is sound but no speech in *Hatsu Yume* whose structure has nothing in common with the narrative. The work is built upon mental associations, evocations, mysteries and uncertainties, and does not resort to anecdotes. The images follow one after another without a causal relationship; they cannot be deciphered using the mechanisms of conscious thought. The gaze is directed to seek meaning in the depths of the psyche. The images and sequences form an ensemble, and they interact amongst themselves through the forms they contain as well as the different emotions they provoke. "From the beginning I have been preoccupied by the same thing: keeping in touch with the part of me I call 'the part before speech', that which is pre-discourse. The speech act comes after the thought – I am very much interested in the emergence of thought."

Like thought, the images of *Hatsu Yume* are often constructed in superimposed layers. To perceive the passers-by, whose presence is insinuated by the soundtrack, the viewer's gaze must venture into the depths of the image, beyond the thick layers of bamboo. In another sequence, Viola uses the background to allude to the enormity of a mass of rock. Initially, the small figures in the foreground of the

© Coll. Centre Pompidou. Courtesy of Electronic Arts Intermix (EAI), New York.

image lead the viewer to presume that the rocky mass occupying the majority of the screen is a hill, only to discover at the end of the sequence that the 'hill' is only a small stack of rocks, certainly no taller than a small child.

Hatsu Yume means 'first dream' in Japanese, and Japanese folk tradition attributes particular importance to the first dream of the new year. According to popular belief, the first dream of the year determines the dreams that occur throughout the remainder of the year, and prophesies the future of the dreamer. *Hatsu Yume* can be seen as Viola's first dream, in which he experiments with the potential of the video image, returning to the origination of this medium, defining a video language.

Yekhan Pinarligil
Translated by Yin Ker

Ko Nakajima

■ *Mount Fuji*, 1984

K o Nakajima is one of the pioneer Japanese artists of video art. After his beginnings in animation video, he made use of new technologies to appropriate and develop different software that allowed him to create visual collages in movement. Each work is the expression of a unified research, progressively unveiled in the process of discovery of a life's oeuvre.

Mount Fuji dates from the year 1984, at a time when Nakajima had already affirmed his style of manipulating images, and had established his universe distinguished by elements of nature and infused with Oriental philosophy. This tape is emblematic of the researches he conducted thanks to the invention of the aniputer, a machine which allows one to distort, superpose and embed images with ease, created in collaboration with JVC's research department. Against the rhythm of repetitive music, different images of Mount Fuji compose geometric structures, forming a Rubik's cube's perspectival frame cut through by photographs which regularly come and drift away before the viewer.

Mount Fuji is a highly mystical site in Japanese culture, a religious and national symbol. It is at the heart of numerous works, placing man in relation to a mountain's ancientness and its fundamental ambiguity – the possibility of a volcanic eruption dwells within the impression of stability and permanence. Playing with static and flat images that cut across the screen, Nakajima brings to mind the tectonic drift of plates which could at any time erase the benign image of Mount Fuji.

If the effects beget an aesthetic that is a little old-world today (though very representative of the period), this video provides an account of artists' capacity to appropriate technological innovations – to bring about them even, thus revolutionising the history of forms. It is an approach we find in the work of Chinese artist Cao Fei, for example, where fantasy intrudes into reality through its recourse to the novel possibilities of digital animation. Nakajima is hence the precursor of an artistic practice that works hand in hand with industrial research.

Mathilde Roman
Translated by Yin Ker

Thierry Kuntzel ■ *Autumn (Mount Analogue)*, 1997

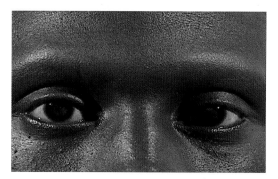

hierry Kuntzel's installation *Autumn (Mount Analogue)* was completed in 1997, four years after the artist's solo show at the Galerie Nationale du Jeu de Paume, where he showcased the installations *Summer (Double View)*, 1989; *Winter (The Death of Robert Walser)*, 1990; and *Spring (Springtime Step)*, 1993, all grouped together under the title *Four Seasons Less One*. In that show, the seasons were assembled in a cross-shaped arrangement, each one of them occupying one of the branches of this cross (the fourth branch being earmarked for autumn), while the central part, *Less One*, set in a dark, acoustic room, forming an obligatory passage for proceeding from one season to the next.

While *Winter (The Death of Robert Walser)* and *Spring (Springtime Step)* consist of triple projections of average and equal dimensions, *Summer (Double View)* is made up of a very large projection opposite a single monitor. This same arrangement applies to *Autumn (Mount Analogue)*, as well as *Autumn (In Praise of Shade)*, a variation on *Mount Analogue*, completed in Kyoto in 1998 for the *Eye & Mind* exhibition held at the Gunma Museum of Modern Art in Japan.

The two videos of *Autumn (Mount Analogue)*, each lasting 5'51", with no sound and in colour, are designed to be shown as a loop, and synchronised. The video made for the monitor consists of a still shot of Ken Moody's eyes, Moody being the model who appears in all of Kuntzel's seasons. There is a close-up shot of his face, his eyes opening and staring hard at the viewer throughout the video, then closing again in the final moments. Around the second minute, a rock is fleetingly and almost imperceptibly reflected in the model's iris, the sole 'event' in the whole installation. This image appears like a kind of forewarning of the video projected opposite Moody's face. This video actually ends on the image of this same rock, after 'traversing a

landscape', whose visual effect is akin to a dream experience: a succession of hills and mountains, then forests and fir trees, files past gradually in a very fluid process of superimposing then erasing of the images, like the effects of persistence, culminating in the image of the rock. The actual substance of the imagery is being presented in this piece: the colours and the brightness of the light vary with the shots, and the pastel shades of the mountains make way for the bright greens of the firs and, last of all, the darker image of the rock; likewise, the movement results just from crossing the landscape and the sequence of images, themselves still, to a very calculated rhythm, alternating cadences. The absence of sound prompts the viewer to be particularly attentive to the passing of time evoked by these images of a moving landscape, forever developing.

The sober quality of the images and effects in *Autumn (Mount Analogue)* is peculiar to all of Kuntzel's installations, while pictorial references often lie at the root of the way his works are conceived, for example that of Henri Matisse in the installation *The White Sideboard* (1980), and Nicolas Poussin in *Summer (Double View)*. So it was Jean-Antoine Watteau whom Kuntzel had in mind when he came up with the installation *Autumn (Mount Analogue)*, about which he wrote: "I remember – or I dreamed about – a hanging at the Louvre in Paris where

© Coll. Centre Pompidou.

Watteau's *Gilles* was placed opposite *L'embarquement pour Cythère*. It was violent and beautiful, that separation. I'm hoping to keep a trace of it in the installation *Autumn*."

Frédérique Baumgartner

Translated by Simon Pleasance

Jun Nguyen-Hatsushiba

Memorial Project Nha Trang, Vietnam: Towards the Complex – For the Courageous, the Curious and the Cowards, 2001

© Coll. Centre Pompidou.

This work is also in the Singapore Art Museum collection.

Jun Nguyen-Hatsushiba was originally a painter, but devotes his time today to focus on video and installation, which he combines with performance. Because of his triple identity – Vietnamese, Japanese, and American, the artist takes a unique look at the history of Vietnam, concerning himself mainly with the post-war period. Through the use of materials and objects conjuring up images of everyday life in Vietnam and its disparate economy (rice, dried fruit peels, mosquito nets, rickshaws, visiting cards, etc.) in his work, the artist investigates the impact of historical events on present-day Vietnam, and the relationship between tradition and modernity, through the perspective of collective memory. Since 1994, his work has been thus organised around a memorial project for the thousands of boat people who tried to flee from Vietnam at the end of the war, fearful of political reprisals.

The installation *Memorial Project Nha Trang, Vietnam: Towards the Complex – For the Courageous, the Curious and the Cowards* is one of the links in this project. It consists of a projection of a 13-minute sound-and-colour video in a dark room, shot entirely underwater at Nha Trang in Vietnam: six characters (fishermen whom the artist met on the spot) try to escape underwater, struggling to pull three rickshaws over the rocky, sandy ocean bed. The weight of the rickshaws, the difficulty of moving underwater, and the divers' need to surface from time to time to breathe, all underscore the tricky and hazardous nature of this slow 'performance', at once chaotic-looking and dreamlike. This procession over, the men abandon their rickshaws and discover, a few yards further on, several mosquito nets affixed to the bed of the azure ocean, lightly tossed by the current. For Nguyen-Hatsushiba, the mosquito net – that simplest of shelters – here acts as a grave for the souls of people who perished in their attempt to flee from Vietnam after the fall of Saigon in the summer of 1975. The procession thus takes on a mnemonic value, a kind of pilgrimage with a poetic aspect, paying tribute to the boat people. The rickshaw, a symbol of Southeast Asian cities, also refers to the consequences of the war – many soldiers became rickshawmen at the end of the war, but from an economic and social viewpoint, the present Vietnamese government is keen to get rid of rickshaws, on the pretext that they are a reflection of an old-fashioned economy.

As the first instalment of a trilogy, *Memorial Project Nha Trang, Vietnam*, is followed by the work *Happy New Year – Memorial Project Vietnam II* (2003), composed of a dragon dance filmed underwater and accompanied by an undersea firework display, commemorating the surprise Tet offensive, on 31 January 1968, the first day of the Vietnamese New Year, by North Vietnamese troops.

Frédérique Baumgartner
Translated by Simon Pleasance

Rachel Reupke's works are aimed at creating short circuits between analogue and digital photographic images, between static images and those in movement. All of her works organise principles for navigating between these ambiguous kinds of images. When they take the form of temporal loops, they oscillate between the extenuation of their form and the expansion of their duration. While she uses the language of film (mastery of the composition of the image, evocative power of the soundtrack, fictional elements, special effects), Reupke sets herself apart from it through the systematic utilisation of static shots, the absence of editing and the disruption of the relationship between the figure and the setting.

With *Infrastructure* (2002), a work in four parts, the artist represents an imaginary transport network all along a valley in the Alps – an airport, a railway, a motorway, a port – which appears in the centre of the scene while an uninterrupted flow of traffic moves through the space. The main action is presented to the viewers like the flow of actions on SimCity (the simulation game), while at the same time, a group of fleeting, random secondary actions in miniature capture their attention and incite them to scan the frame continuously for these secondary motifs.

As Reupke explained in a 2005 interview: "At the time I made *Infrastructure* I was fascinated (and still am) with cinematic special effects. Not just the latest developments in CGI but the whole history of the craft going back to the earliest filmmaking – American Civil War naval battles faked in the studio using water tanks and models, for instance … It was this tension between the visible and invisible that I wanted to explore with *Infrastructure*. Referencing Alfred Hitchcock, in particular *North by Northwest* and *The Birds* (films which today look very painterly), I constructed the images according to the same technical principles used then; a combination of stills photography and live footage assembled using simple mattes. I took what might in conventional cinema be used as an establishing

shot, lasting no longer than three or four seconds (each second a precious chunk of the budget) and leave it on screen for three or four minutes, giving the viewer an opportunity to really scrutinise and question the image."

Here, different scales of and within the image, the different places, realities and timeframes are brought together within the sequences themselves. The static nature of the shots and their length (three or four minutes) transform the viewer's gaze into that of an experienced observer invited to discern the many tricks of the image.

Pascale Cassagnau
Translated by Miriam Rosen

© Rachel Reupke. Coll. Centre Pompidou.

Rachel Reupke

The shaping of landscape is at the heart of English artist Rachel Reupke's oeuvre, in line with traditional photography or pictorial representation. Caspar David Friedrich and Andreas Gursky are essential influences. Reupke's works are made up of static shots and panoramas manipulated and organised using the computer, with which she introduces a narrative rhythm and invented elements.

Did an error slip into the image? *Now Wait for Last Year* successively unreels three static shots of the city of Beijing: a large urban junction, an ensemble of showflats and a conglomerate of buildings with a tunnel cutting through. Each of these views assumes an artificial character, in their acid skies as much as in their occupants with neither aim nor face; three edifying images of a modern city where life seems good. Each view is shown for a long time. The viewer thus readily examines and questions the images. By turns the images uncover effect, dupery, movement and figures; oscillations between the animated foreground and the static middle ground, between the tension of the visible and invisible, between kitsch Maoist aesthetics and science fiction's catastrophist scenario. Like the painter or the photographer, the videographer claims to be fascinated by the constraint imposed by the creation of a work concluded in a single image, as well as by the narration of the totality of an action or a story within one frame.

Shot on a residence in Beijing, while major works for the 2008 Olympic Games were being carried out, the artist was inspired by this city going through a violent architectural boom and its capacity to anticipate its urban history. This video parodies the commercial clichés served up to the Chinese population and the rest of the world. Reupke said that she was interested in the public front of this development: the urbanism exhibitions, the showflats, the billboards, the illustrations of construction projects and the slogans on the standard of living at every street corner. Beijing and Shanghai are cities which embellish their future with promotional banners, as has been the case with other large cities of a Dionysiac urban development such as Dubai or Abu Dhabi, whose museums mark their consecration. Reupke usually takes special care in adding sound to her videos, but this work is silent in order to reinforce the impression of a postcard.

Now Wait for Last Year is also the title of a metaphysical science fiction novel by Philip K. Dick about an alternative time. Reupke, who is particularly intrigued by science fiction, here delights in leading on the viewer in disconcerting back-and-forths between the perceptible and the imperceptible, between mobility and fixity. Beijing represents the ideal protagonist, a city where each junction exhibits and anticipates its future in a poster or a video. Are we visualising a present, a time to come, or a future – or would that be already in the past? Where did this postcard come from? When was it sent?

Florence Parot
Translated by Yin Ker

© Singapore Art Museum collection.

This video features the work of an imaginary graffiti artist who goes by the alias 'Uh'. The viewer sees the aftermath of Uh's illegal act of painting his moniker onto numerous walls of Ho Chi Minh City's urban landscape. As pedestrians and motorcyclists enter the fictive video space and pass through, viewers witness the tragic breakdown of the artist's unrealised imagination as the absurd illusion is unravelled.

"In many of our projects, we try to create disorder, hoping that disorder in such particular instances can become another 'sense of order' to an audience that may be all too afraid of change, or unaccepting of other possible ways of engaging with their current cultural/social structures. We like to play. We align ourselves with different cultural producers. We like to let ourselves get ingested into the bellies of big social beasts such as television or the various manifestations of pop culture. We feel that true criticality comes from the change that can happen from the inside of a system, and not from analytical discourse posited from external positions."

This video is part of a larger body of work that deals with the country's rapidly changing landscape and the youth culture that is trying to navigate these changes, even as young Vietnamese adapt and develop new strategies for individual self-expression.

Through this video, originally titled *Hesitation Proclamations: Uh, A Proposal For A Vietnamese Landscape?*, The Propeller Group interprets the complex and contradictory relationships between Vietnam's youth, the influence of Western culture and the rapid urbanisation taking place in the country. The work references the infiltration of American 'ideals' among the youth (via rock music or hip hop) and contrasts this with the scars and wounds of the Vietnam War.

Patricia Levasseur de la Motte

Brasilia/Chandigarh, 2008

The advertisement models that were previously the protagonists of French artist Louidgi Beltrame's videos have been replaced by buildings. Henceforth, the featured human figures are mere pretexts for the unfurling of the plot and the narration of the set's story.

Beltrame's work is about modernist architecture and its vestiges, both documentary and fictional. *Brasilia/Chandigarh* puts in dialogue two giants of the history of modernism: Oscar Niemeyer and Le Corbusier. Then Brazilian president Juscelino Kubitschek commissioned Niemeyer in 1955 to build Brasilia as a new administrative capital for the country so as to open up the megalopolises of Rio de Janeiro and Sao Paulo, and to draw the population and economic activity inland, and hence better distribute wealth. After the partition of India in 1947, the state of Punjab was divided between Pakistan and India, and Indian Punjab was in need of a new capital to replace Lahore, which had become part of Pakistan. Then Indian prime minister Jawaharlal Nehru decided to entrust the construction of Chandigarh, the "new city, symbol of the freedom of India unfettered by the traditions of the past … an expression of the nation's faith in the future", to Le Corbusier.

Brasilia/Chandigarh is three characters' shared wandering within these megacities: a meditative man for Brasilia, inspired by writer Adolfo Bioy Casares' *La aventura de un fotógrafo en La Plata*, and two women for Chandigarh. Thanks to video, the artist's skilful montage shifts the spectator between the two continents, creating a third space that is both geographic and temporal. The man of Brasilia is no doubt the metaphorical representation of the artist at work, photographer-topographer or researcher-traveller; it is the two women from Punjab who speak and inform us about the man

from the Brazilian state of Mato Grosso. Irish musician Dennis McNulty's metronomic music tinted with nostalgia layers an anterior future, the temporal paradox of the narrative, and plunges the characters into the immensity of these concrete steppes.

What is the present condition of these postcolonial undertakings that were supposed to take these cities of the South into modernity? The visions of a free and triumphant future are now vestiges of utopia. During Brasilia's construction, Niemeyer, a committed communist, was conscious of what it represented for Brazilian life and believed that it would be a happy city. But once the city was completed he observed that, in common with many Brazilian cities, discrimination, overpopulation, injustice and the gap between the rich and the poor remained inevitable. As for Chandigarh, even while the literacy rate hits a new record and the city prospers, the concrete architecture steadily deteriorates with each monsoon and the furniture designed by Pierre Jeanneret (an architect and designer who collaborated with his cousin Le Corbusier) are anarchically despoiled. The city at the foot of the Himalayas continues to grow; previously in harmony with its magnificent natural environment, it is no longer truly in sync with the elements today. Beltrame highlights these two enterprises of political will to illustrate the extent to which they were able to influence the development of the last century and to reflect on the grandiloquence of these utopian vestiges, and what they mean for the future.

Florence Parot
Translated by Yin Ker

Jun Nguyen-Hatsushiba ▪ *Breathing is Free: 12,756.3, 2008–2009*

Breathing is Free: 12,756.3 tracks the artist as he attempts to run the distance of 12,756.3 kilometres, the diameter of the earth. For this video installation, the artist has selected his memorial running video from six Asian cities: Ho Chi Minh City, Tokyo, Taipei, Tai Chung, Luang Prabang and Singapore. Running involves a combination of a breathing pattern, physical capacity and mental control. It becomes more difficult as the runner goes longer and further, eventually relying on his or her mental state to keep on moving.

The recorded data of distance, location and speed are employed to discuss the hardship of 'refugees' and physical struggles. It is conceptual yet physical; a real struggle, not a performance. "Running has been a part of many aspects of human existence. We have to run to hunt, to fight, to compete, to conquer, to condition, to escape, to survive, to move, to migrate. Inevitably, it is a given power of humanity, a force as invisible as potential energy in coal. We possess the vitality to initiate such marks of footsteps." *Breathing is Free: 12,756.3* is the culmination of the artist's memorial projects to date to challenge his own mind and body to discuss layers of ideas through the action of repetitive foot strikes – running. It is also a form of memorial, as so many refugees have had to and still continue to run away from their homes for a better life and, sometimes, just to survive. The artist's running, his experience and struggle sets the backdrop for this long-term project.

In the installation, the six videos are transformed into a frame-by-frame sequence to allow the viewers to experience the notion of movement and time as the artist struggles through his run. The abstraction of shapes, lines and texture vibrate in and out of the scenes as the video plays 'reality'. The sequence blurs and sharpens, giving multiple dimensions to life, simultaneously flattening the artist, making him the subject of the place as well as the image. The artist is portrayed as mutating and migrating between the place and his physical self, leaving his trace as offerings. In slowing down the speed of the video, the combination of the movements of the artist running, the camera used for the recording and the surrounding environment – people walking, cars passing, buildings – gives one the impression that, in some of the sequences, the artist runs against a fixed photographic background. In this installation, the video explores and brings out this photographic component. The still images capture the most meaningful sequences of the video. The combination of stills and slow motion allows the viewers to easily appreciate the full sense of the 'photographic memory' of the videos.

Patricia Levasseur de la Motte

Keith Deverell, Sue McCauley, Meas Sokhorn and Srey Bandol

■ *The Hawker's Song*, 2010

One of the first major video artworks to be made in and about Cambodia, *The Hawker's Song* was created through an international collaboration between Australian artists Keith Deverell and Sue McCauley, and Cambodian artists Meas Sokhorn and Srey Bandol, with soundtracks composed and performed by Corey Sands and Deverell. The components of this work were first displayed in Phnom Penh and Melbourne in September–October 2010.

The Hawker's Song focuses on the lives of Cambodian street hawkers, their songs, their daily hardships and the effect of urban development and modernisation on their lives. Framed in both HD video and Standard 8 Film, the work draws on notions of the past and present, of the traditional and the modern. It investigates through poetic sound, performances and image compositions, the clash between rapid urbanisation (represented by new shopping malls and multi-storey office blocks) and traditional modes of commerce and communication, symbolised by the oral traditions of street hawkers selling their wares in the streets of Phnom Penh.

Hawkers, found throughout Asia, are street vendors who utilise mobile carts, bicycles, and various tools and containers to transport their goods and services to parks, main streets and alleyways. In Cambodia they often use songs and instruments to attract customers and form part of the urban landscape and soundtrack. As an emerging economy, urban centres in Cambodia, particularly Phnom Penh, are changing constantly with new injections of foreign investments and social influences from other countries. These investments have brought in rapid growth, with little consideration for the residents. Skyscrapers are inappropriately sited and superficial pre-fabricated 'new towns' mushroom around the city centre. In this new environment the hawker's way of life is being marginalised and they face an unknown future in the development race.

The themes in *The Hawker's Song* are universal. The local issues in Phnom Penh are of similar concern in Melbourne and elsewhere, especially in Asia. The competing interests of modernisation and the preservation of unique cultures are grave concerns for people in cities all over the world.

Patricia Levasseur de la Motte

V.

Memory:
Between Myth and Reality

In the post-Marxist era, especially in countries with emerging contemporary cultures, artists prefer to use digital media like photography and video to express themselves.

The evolution of the new geopolitical map of creation has picked up pace over the past few years, affecting most parts of the world, including the Balkans, the Middle East and Southeast Asia. It should be remembered that from the 1960s to 1980s, video artists came largely from North and South America, Japan, and Europe.

Artists focus on questions linked to the reality of their world, of our world – political reality (Liu Wei), ethnological reality (Sima Salehi Rahni), cultural reality (Araya Rasdjarmrearnsook), religious reality (Than Sok), and sociological reality (Arahmaiani) – and transform them into artistic works that are generally poetic. *Dial H-I-S-T-O-R-Y* is the symptomatic title of Johan Grimonprez's work that revisits historical events in a poetic, and certainly subjective, way.

By adopting the documentary style, artists stay close to historical reality. They sometimes replay, interpret, and comment upon isolated fragments of reality (Richard Streitmatter-Tran) through technical interventions like cuts, shots, sound, language, and special effects (Dinh Q. Lê). The format of documentary rests upon the tradition founded on experimental cinema and the works of filmmakers like Chris Marker.

Today, a new generation of artists offer a distinct perspective on their community that has become global, most notably through new media such as the Internet. Video thus acts like a memory exercise of societies, transposing events often situated on the boundary between myth/fiction on one hand and reality/history on the other.

Nam June Paik

■ *Guadalcanal Requiem*, 1979

In the 1970s, Nam June Paik directed several 30-minute programmes for the American production company WNET-TV that were broadcast on Channel 13. *Guadalcanal Requiem*, which was created in 1977 and re-edited in a shorter version in 1979, was among those produced for television, like *Allan 'n' Allen's Complaint* (1982), *Living with the Living Theatre* (1989), and *Global Groove* (1973). These videos are, first and foremost, discourses on history and the importance of the interpretation and understanding of the past. They also demonstrate video techniques and the use of the video medium by television. Paik does not intend for these works to assert any particular message, but rather aims to liberate the viewer from the monopoly of conventional televisual productions. Conversely, the television becomes the means of taking art out of its formal framework, enabling it to reach a larger audience.

Guadalcanal Requiem is one of Paik's most politically engaged works. It unfolds in Guadalcanal in the Solomon Islands where a World War II battle between the Americans and the Japanese took place between 1942 and 1943. Paik visited the island in the late 1970s to film the combat sites in collaboration with cellist Charlotte Moorman.

Guadalcanal Requiem shuffles different temporalities. By combining in situ images with black and white archive images and interviews, Paik composes a testimony of the past. Short sequences of war records, and images of Paik's performances from the 1970s are juxtaposed with accounts from the island's inhabitants, American veterans, and Japanese soldiers. Images of Moorman playing the cello at the island's war memorial are similarly juxtaposed with the performance of *TV Bra* (1969), which took place in a studio in New York and was presented again to the public on the island.

The video documents the Battle of Guadalcanal by presenting its historical and geographical context, while also setting up a process of recollection and of commemorative rituals created by Paik and Moorman on the island, the landscape of which is ravaged by war. In working with memory and contemplation, they accomplish a series of rituals. Moorman first plays her instrument on various parts of the island before wrapping her cello in a felt cover, evoking Joseph Beuys' *Homogeneous Infiltration for Piano* (1966). As Moorman, swathed in canvas, crawls along the beach with her cello strapped to her back like a rucksack, Paik drags a broken violin behind him, bringing to mind his *Violin with String*, realised in 1961.

Using montage and Paik's characteristic post-production techniques, these images from varied sources are juxtaposed, linked, and reworked. Paik employs the video synthesiser, the Abe-Paik in particular which he conceived in 1969 with engineer Shuya Abe. This equipment allows the generation of forms and modulations, the synthesising of colour, and the creation of distortions on the video image.

The fragments of memory and episodes from the past, which are revisited through Moorman's performances and Paik's images, attest to the importance of the imagination in representing and understanding the trauma of war.

Priscilia Marques
Translated by Yin Ker

Sans Soleil (Sunless) is a meditation on the analogous destiny of two countries as different as Japan and Guinea-Bissau in four acts. Chris Marker traces a journey in time and space. Not only does this comparison affirm a temporal dissymmetry, it also expresses a difficulty in extracting oneself from the frame of time. Marker is not simply challenging the opposition between the wealthy and poor countries, but the attitude towards the conservation of self and things – the relation with change and death in other words.

"I would have spent my life trying to understand the function of remembering, which is not the opposite of forgetting, but rather its lining", reads the toneless voice of *Sunless*. *Sunless* is at once an essay with several voices, images composed as in a collage, a musical and sonorous arrangement and a travel journal. But *Sunless* is above all an 'archival storage' which reproduces aesthetically the process of memory. How can that which disintegrates with time be held back, that which is destined to the residual and to oblivion? How can memory be ordered?

According to Barbara Lemaître, Marker uses the 'memory-joint' (*raccord-souvenir*) device which she defines as what allows one to "cross the gap between two motifs, two images, two temps, etc. which are far-flung in principle or radically disconnected". The shots are brought together following a rationale which is classificatory instead of chronological.

Sunless is a work which progresses bit by bit in stubs, with flashbacks, reminders and speculative hypotheses (absolute memory). It is in this "back and forth" movement that he weaves his gossamer and sets up a temporal and spatial tree chart of memory. Memory full of holes is thus recapitulated by the cinematographic device. The question of 'retrieval' and the aesthetics of recovery are elements which forge Marker's work and can be found in *Sunless*.

The traveller-filmmaker-writer returns to these images and questions their functions, what they connote and what remains in them of these lived realities. The camera's viewfinder acts as the eye, only amplified. It heightens the acuity of the gaze's perception, while strengthening the power of the person behind it. As such, he lives his relationship with others and the world more intensely, for he is not indifferent. It is the fulguration of the moment which is called upon as the moment of truth, which unveils itself and which the eye alone is incapable of apprehending. The ephemeral becomes the object of awareness. The gaze which shapes the process of memory orders the residual, apprehends better the fulgurant in the moment and what would have remained unspeakable without the collaboration of the camera which designates and the photographic film which registers. What is doomed to fade away (the impermanence of things) is kept in an inter-mediary station between being and oblivion.

But the video also makes history "a retrieval, an inclusive story: the viewer's mind scouts it; between here and there, today and yesterday, a candid game of cross-references and reciprocal inclusions hatches".

Sunless is a reflection on the status of the image and its ultimate destiny. The video begins with an image shot in Iceland. Three children clinging to each other slowly recede from the camera. This image of happiness is simultaneously the problematic crux of the matter and the point of departure, the "first stone", according to Marker, of an imaginary film. It is problematic in its content which is "the fragile image of a moment heralding its imminent end", and in the relation it maintains with the other images (Marker tells us the impossibility of linking it). Filmed by Haroun Tazieff five years later, images of the same location buried under the flow of lava from a volcanic eruption answer to this same image, giving

© Argos Films.
Photo Brigitte Rodoreda.

it a future and en end. An etiolated space displaces the first image of happiness. It is the impermanence of happiness in particular and of things in general. Marker's work consists of making permanent the image of a reality destined to fade: "The image is hence exactly like the ceremonial objects of *dondo yaki*, 'debris with the right to immortality.'"

Lou Svahn

Translated by Yin Ker

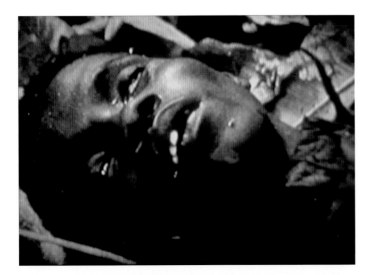

Shuntaro Tanikawa and Shuji Terayama

■ *Video Letters*, 1982–1983

Video Letters is a video correspondence between Shuji Terayama and Shuntaro Tanikawa. As with a book, the chapters of a shared story emerge piecemeal and form an authentic video exchange. At the heart of the exchange is the power of anticipation (the motif of the red thread which traverses and intrudes on the frame is one recurrent expression), and its combination with the poetic strength of a denuded world (the rustling of leaves, or still, the characters 'dissolving' in space).

With *Video Letters*, poets Terayama and Tanikawa become what we could call 'collectors of the fragmentary'. Gleaning hither and thither, the savouring of words, then their meanings, the images are conditional upon their context, and may echo the '*fuites d'interlocution*' borrowed from Roland Barthes.

In *Video Letters*, there is a dramatic composition, the foremost elements of which are the dynamic and the static, as well as the sense of space and fluidity of each element. Details merge in an evanescent atmosphere, permeating beings and objects. In the process, man unveils himself by what he throws on the ground (personal curios, book, clothes, medicine, food, etc.), or what he 're-edifies' (scattered scraps of torn photographs flattened out side by side). The camera allows an actual visual correspondence, like clearly addressed postcards – 'From Terayama to Tanikawa' or 'From Tanikawa to Terayama' – which initiates a new modality of fiction.

But it is also their self-portraits the two letter writers confront the viewer with. Between figurative presence and the reminder of absence, the faces that appear in the images transform into visions through the fascination of the viewer's gaze. Photography and videotapes provide, by the fact of 'having been present', the proof that the real actually happened, that it is discernible. But which or whose real is it? We are, writes Jean Borreil, like "impossible subjects that never resemble our photographs, we do not know which are our features". "Is this me? No, it is just a photograph. And this voice that speaks, is it me? No, I do not even exist anymore."

The motifs of faltering identity (identity papers strewn on the ground), and disfiguration (Tanikawa's 'face-landscape' making all sorts of grimaces and deformations while facing the camera) refer to the idea of an almost-spectral portrait, and that which cannot be figured par excellence. Thereafter, video becomes like a mask, or like the double of death, which is forever relegated into the world of the living. In *Video Letters*, there is something of the nature of the persistence of the portrait.

In their way, these letters are as much testimonies to the individual's situation, and to his or her fragility, as they are to the strength he or she musters at the moment of decline: Terayama passed away on 4 May 1983.

Lou Svahn
Translated by Yin Ker

Lee Wen

■ *Journey of A Yellow Man No. 3: Desire (Lee Wen: Documentation of Performances on Video)*, 1993

Documented on video, *Journey of A Yellow Man No. 3: Desire* is a 4'23" précis of Lee Wen's third performance in his full-body mask of the Yellow Man – the persona that placed him on the international map of contemporary art. For five days from 11am to 7pm, in July 1993, Lee improvised with 15 kilograms of rice, eight chains painted red, and six metaphorically charged 'objects of desire' – a bandaged guitar, a bird cage filled with books, a glass jar with a plastic flower on a bed of coins, etc. – amidst an installation of graphic works at the Substation, an experimental art space of historical significance in Singapore. Through shifting forms and texts created with rice and chains on the ground, Lee explored the relationship between desire and society: the nuances of bondage and security, and luxury and necessity, in an increasingly consumerist Singaporean society.

Lee embarked on the journey of the Yellow Man the year before in 1992, when he was studying art in England. Garbed in yellow briefs and covered from head to toe in yellow paint to exacerbate his 'Chinese' skin to the point of farce, the persona was born to counter racial prejudgement. But it quickly developed beyond the domain of ethnicity to challenge other preconceptions, always with the humour and irony that is Lee's brand. Over the past three decades, his avatar has performed in spaces as varied as a gallery, a downtown street, and a wheat field, each time attuned to the location's social and political parameters through the use of specific cultural signifiers, chosen to reiterate the principle of cultural and historical relativity and specificity – in this case, the dollar sign and rice. Today, the Yellow Man is an ongoing pilgrimage dedicated to the deconstruction of stereotyped identity, and to the greater end of emancipation and self-realisation, a tour de force that has resisted the troubled fate of performance art in Singapore, the development of which was arrested by the suspension of funding between 1994 and 2003.

Journey of A Yellow Man No. 3: Desire in video is indicative of this odyssey that is Lee's real oeuvre. From the angle of art history, we are reminded of the genesis of performance art as the fruit of cross-fertilisation between theatre, video and visual art, as well as the purely functional aspect of video (when it is not exploited as an artistic medium in its own right) to document ephemeral installations and performances since the 1960s. Its background and message alike drive home the urgency of a multiple historicity: one that encompasses empathy for the Other's experience, especially in the context of this exhibition, which presents historical works marking the beginnings of the medium in West Europe and North America, at least three decades before its advent in Southeast Asia. As Lee says, "It remains difficult to keep a constant vigil on our perceptions so that we do not fall prey to false consciousness and prejudices, nor become victims of propaganda from the market and the media, and other distortions." Admittedly ignorance is natural, but if humanity is still of concern, then resignation is not an option in the face of the increasingly globalised world that is ours.

Yin Ker

205

Johan Grimonprez ■ *Dial H-I-S-T-O-R-Y, 1997*

What do we usually do when we are confronted with impressions so strong, so new, and so fearsome that they exceed our capacities? We push them aside, by likening them to make-believe and fables, or else by incoporating them in the daily milieu: *dial a story*. This, of course, is just an escape reflex. Needless to say, this attraction to horror recurs here, there and everywhere in cultural history, but then eyewitnesses are invariably punished by death: the horrifying Medusa turns all those who look at her into stone, and Lot's wife is turned into a statue of salt when she turns round to look at the terrifyingly beautiful fall of Sodom and Gomorrah. The moral of these stories might well be the following: he who looks at horror becomes guilty.

In this day and age of live television programmes, it would seem that this moral judgement has become obsolete. And yet a remnant of shame hovers over the tense face of the old Japanese man staring at the sight of an aeroplane being hijacked through the window of an airport in Johan Grimonprez's film compilation, *Dial H-I-S-T-O-R-Y*. It is seemingly an instinctive moral reaction to the shamelessness that we have shown by unintentionally witnessing the private fate of people we do not know. In any event, this expression lends the eyewitness a dignity only rarely glimpsed among the film's other protagonists.

Victims, guilty parties, the public and media are in fact being increasingly caught up in the whirlwind of collective fascination, and Grimonprez thus endows his brief take of a hijacking with a structure that proceeds towards the presentation of a "Hijacking Party". To begin with, there are the first dispatches, still uncertain, then we see the freed hostages excitedly recounting their ordeal in front of whirring cameras. Off to one side, charismatic hostage-takers looking like Greek gods stating their demands in a rather formal but still charming manner. And whereas those first skyjackers were offered not so much as a lousy sandwich, their successors are entitled to champagne and petits fours.

© Coll. Centre Pompidou.
LEFT: Photo Johan Grimonprez and Rony Vissers.
RIGHT: Photo Philippe Migeat.

Over the years, hijacking scenarios have become more and more dramatic, and the only responses that governments have come up with to combat the fear of flying are simple psychological profiles of terrorists, state-of-the-art security and safety techniques, and wisecracks to mask embarrassment. Everything assumes a scale that finally turns into a dangerous game of speed: "Each plot moves deathwards", as it is said in one of the Don DeLillo extracts discreetly distilled in the film, which Grimonprez uses as an aesthetic subtitle beneath the flow of images, just as he does with the original and shrewdly composed soundtrack.

The laconic caption beneath one image reads: "1970, Tokyo streets deserted: millions watch first televised hijack". And ever since, cameras chase the blood-bespattered injured right to the ambulance, and haul freed little girls and half-dead terrorists in front of their microphones. They show bullet holes in the aircraft's fuselage, dead kidnappers and pints of blood being wiped up before our eyes. But what

do all these details mean? In the endless loop of images of horror, they do not mean a whole lot, because we gradually shed our ability to grasp horror.

But after the umpteenth repetition of shocking, in-your-face imagery, chance playing its part, emotion is no longer very far removed from the banality that we can "choose" on the screen. This is precisely what Grimonprez shows with what he calls his "poetics of zapping": sausages being barbecued right beside absolute horror. Then mice and frogs staggering about, and this totally superfluous tidbit of information telling us that people who like dogs live longer than people who like cats. And thus it is from the artist's subjective way of looking at television images, and even by means of television, that a critique of the media originates. Without any pedagogic pathos, but like a fragmentary narrative commentating on itself: *Dial H-I-S-T-O-R-Y*, as a matter of fact.

Gaby Hartel
Translated by Simon Pleasance

© Coll. Centre Pompidou. Photo Philippe Megeat.
Courtesy of RMN.

© Centre Pompidou. Courtesy of the artist.

At the time of the student demonstrations on Tiananmen Square in Beijing in 1989, Liu Wei was a student at the Beijing University. Before the repression by the Chinese government on 4 June, Liu was able to take photographs that have become evidence of what has remained silenced under the Chinese regime. *Floating Memory* contains these photographs, along with other image sequences pertaining to Chinese propaganda, the past, the present, and other symbolic scenes. Arranged using bifurcations and superimpositions, the video imitates the way memory works.

The beginning of the video shows boy scouts blowing trumpets, political slogans printed on banners, etc. One of the following scenes shows children tracing a line on a wall, a sequence from *City of Memory* (2000), another video by Liu on the theme of violence in China's education and its affect on the growth of children under the extreme leftist ideology of the Cultural Revolution. The allusion to children – who are allegorical of naivety – forecasts the long years of repressed individual growth due to the violence inherent in China's education system, and political and societal structure. This violence finds its perfect incarnation in the Tiananmen Square protests of 1989. The following shots shift to today's Tiananmen Square, pictured in all its prosperity, accompanied by a soundtrack whose lyrics present a cynical take on the capitalist society. The camera focuses on the portrait of Mao smiling down on the Square, wearing, as Dou Wei describes it on the soundtrack, "a pretentious smile".

The prosperous atmosphere gradually fades as the images shift into monotones of grey, and the boisterous music fades. We see a young man with a camera in his hand looking back at the Square. He takes photographs and sees a wall turn fleetingly red at the end of the scene. The rest of the video alternates images of hands sorting through photographs and negatives depicting the events of 1989, with close-ups of certain photographs showing protesting students and their frailty. Interspersed with these are images of the young man looking at the memorial on the Square, lit up in the evening, recalling the eve of the violent repression.

Images of the protests, the protagonist, and the Square (where the passers-by are shown walking backwards, as if retracing time), fade in and out, superimposed with images of hands sorting through old photographs and close-ups of a wall (the latter implying dictatorship). Other monotone scenes show a crowd climbing stairs, and a blind man walking with a stick: an anonymous and collective procession in a historical dimension. While the last scenes of fog and falling rain hint at the hazy and dreamy tone of one's memory, as well as the irretrievable past and lost lives, the bold characters on the banner above the students' heads reappear: "We must not die today".

Sylvie Lin

Trinh T. Minh-ha ■ *The Fourth Dimension*, 2001

The Fourth Dimension is a journey to the heart of Japan at the dawn of the 21st century: a literal, allegorical, spiritual, musical, cultural, and political voyage. "The image of Japan," says Trinh Minh-ha, "as mediated by the experience of 'dilating and sculpting time' with a digital machine vision." As she traverses Japan by train, manipulating, for the first time, a digital camera and the liberties it offers in terms of both its handling and the resultant visual, Trinh never reveals her exact location to the viewer, thus intimately integrating the viewer into her travel, making them the ears that listen, and the eyes that watch as the country emerges in all its contrasts.

Since World War II, Japan has oscillated between a philosophical sustenance of tradition and an unprecedented economic and technological development. Refusing to relegate her sacred rituals and folk beliefs to the past, the country keeps these memories alive while appropriating the Western model (American in particular), and adapting it to a vernacular modernity. Using shots and montage of captivating poetry, Trinh transports us to a contemporary reality on which she comments in voice-over, associating quotes from Japanese sages, reminders of historical facts, and observations on day-to-day rituals to her phrases and thoughts. The images unfurl in a horizontal movement following the course of the railway, while seeking to inject this fourth

© Coll. Centre Pompidou. Courtesy of the artist and Moongift Films.

© Coll. Centre Pompidou. Courtesy of the artist and Moongift Films.

dimension upon which we get a voluntarily elliptic definition almost at the end of the film – "the fourth dimension: to be attentive to the infra-ordinary". The ordinary and the extraordinary accompany this infra-ordinary, modifying our visual and aural perception. Trinh deliberately plays on the former by manipulating her camera's technological features. The frames are in movement and the colour travelling mattes reveal or camouflage the landscapes: urban and rural views, details of interiors, and musicians' and dancers' gestures. The artist, in the same unique way she had been able to look at Senegal and Vietnam, proposes a dilation of rhythmic encounters in this diminutive space that ensues from the infra-ordinary. The arms of the women, men and children wielding batons while beating

the drums resonate to the sound of these rhythmic encounters; the percussion gives tempo to the entire film. While music and Trinh's whispering voice are omnipresent, it is nonetheless a feeling of meditative silence that prevails. It seems that this journey and the vibration of the body seated in a train are suspended the moment images depicting the elements of nature appear, for Trinh films water, the sky and trees in a hypnotic manner, and the photogenic side of Japan is at its most beautiful when captured by her lens.

Trinh devotes an important part of her publication entitled *The Digital Film Event* (2005) to a study of *The Fourth Dimension*. The artist's remarkable analysis accompanying her visual work makes it possible to comprehend the poetic, philosophical,

literary, and social and political confrontations that she establishes in reference to the techniques she employs. In Trinh's work, all representations beget a reference. The shots showing traditional Japanese gardens come with detailed information on their origin: a Korean refugee created them in the year 612, becoming the 'pathmaker'. In the same way, the woman, a leitmotiv since Trinh's first works, is featured in close-up allowing the extremely sensitive perception of the vibration of the skin and lips, and the fluttering of eyelids. We read "Women's Time, Japan's Time" in one of the captions, fragments slipping into the images throughout *The Fourth Dimension*. Trinh worked with the gender department at the University of Tokyo while preparing her video, and the most contemplative sequences echo shots of headlines highlighting the country's political reality of the 1960s. She cites the bloody suppression of the student uprisings in June 1960, as well as Kamba Michiko, activist and figurehead of the feminist cause.

While the haikus of Basho, the great classical poet of the 17th century, mark the beginning and end of the film which closes with the image of an immaculate lotus floating on water, Trinh never forgets that temporality, absence, memory, frontiers and history – even fragmented – are notions underpinning her artistic and theoretical research. The storyline of *The Fourth Dimension* published in her book reads like verse. Poetry and critical thought satisfy each other within a postcolonial reflexion articulated beyond cultural limits. Trinh also reminds the viewer that "time is liquid".

Elvan Zabunyan

Translated by Yin Ker

Richard Streitmatter-Tran　■ *Missed Connections*, 2004

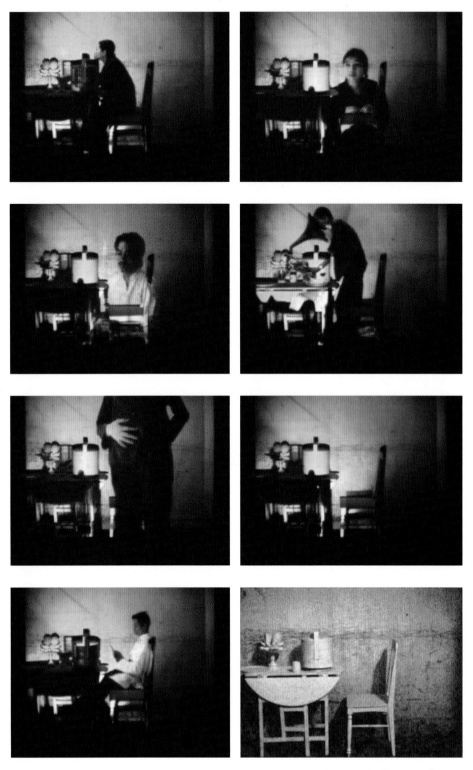

Filled with nostalgia, at first sight *Missed Connections* seems to explore a time of endless solitude. The video takes the viewer through a series of scenes in which four individuals separately enter and exit an intimate home space. Only one character at a time occupies the space demarcated by the screen and the presence of a table unifies their seemingly disparate narratives. The table is set with various objects from everyday life and it remains the central motif around which the characters' activities revolve.

At the beginning of the film, a connection between all the individuals is implied as they mirror each other's actions. However, as the film progresses, this connection is lost as each character pursues his or her own simple activity: eating, resting, playing, sewing, reading, etc.

Throughout the video the viewer is given the sense that the individuals are waiting, perhaps for another person. This suggestion is echoed visually by the abrupt severance of the far end of the table by a shadow, thus suggesting a place set for another person, at once included yet absent from the scene. The atmospheric soundtrack lends *Missed Connections* much of its poignancy, and the overall mood of isolation and missed opportunities for connection can be perceived as a statement of our modern condition.

The themes of memory and nostalgia permeate this film. The presence of a pregnant woman may refer to the time in the artist's childhood when he grew up in the United States, making him miss an inherent connection with his native country. After completing his studies, Streitmatter-Tran returned to Vietnam and had to learn the language. The fact that the video is speechless testifies in some way to the artist's difficulty in reconnecting with his Vietnamese roots. As an attempt to integrate his imaginary past in Vietnam, the artist features himself in a few scenes. Constant references to a re-created past and a real present can be occasionally seen through the simultaneous use of both black and white, and colour images.

Patricia Levasseur de la Motte

215

Up close, a shrivelled leaf artfully crafted to suggest a female profile pivots and flutters under the flickering light of a candle flame, as does its shadow. A caption announces that we are looking at the fire ordeal of Sita, Rama's wife from the *Ramayana* – the Sanskrit epic whose import in Southeast Asia is not to be underestimated. Non-speaking with only Arahmaiani's improvised vocals and synthesised sounds throughout the video, subtitles in Jawi and English by the artist make known the protagonist's tragedy:

"Is it possible that I could make a bargain with fate and not become part of your legend?
Will it make my path easier and
free of suffering?
I've never regretted the path I've had to take even if it were strewn with every kind of thorn.
Is there another possibility for me so that I don't need to bear the entire burden of a person who must be under suspicion, their purity doubted;
a creature pushed aside who can't be trusted?
I am a dry leaf tossed aloft by the wind.
Falling into the pyre and becoming
part of the fire."

Contrary to the legend in which Sita, the epitome of feminine virtue, survives the sacrificial fire unscathed, proving her chastity despite the long captivity by Ravana – but is nonetheless later banished by Rama who succumbs to popular opinion against her, Arahmaiani has the body of Sita presented as a fallen leaf sublimated by fire, uniting with the element which both consumes and creates. Despite Sita's unwavering dedication to the heroic code, matching that of any of the male literary he-

roes known, she has been alienated and victimised by demon and god alike. In relinquishing herself to the flames, she sheds the body confining her to the patriarchal framework, negating the narrative of the male heroic to embrace an ethos that celebrates the female principle of regeneration. This is the form her redress must take, for this alone can liberate her from the male *logos*, allowing her to even rise above it. Through Sita's transfiguration, Arahmaiani hence turns the tables entirely.

One of Indonesia's most prominent female performance artists, Arahmaiani avows a woman's right to play by her own rules with *I Don't Want to be a Part of Your Legend* – this time without adopting a confrontational stance or involving her own body as is typical of her practice in general. Again, she juxtaposes symbols and references Hindu, folk and Islamic – the ancient epic of Hindu origin, *wayang rumput* (grass puppets) and Jawi script whose history is inextricable from Islam in Indonesia – to reflect the archipelago's rich history and culture. As much as the vacillation of Sita's representation between a withered leaf and a female silhouette (not unlike the rabbit-duck optical illusion in principle) demonstrates the relativity of perspective whereby perception is as much a product of mental activity as it is of the stimulus, the syncretism in this autobiographic work proposes that constructs of sexuality and culture are neither univocal nor monolithic.

Yin Ker

In *A Day to Remember*, Liu Wei questions 16 students outside the Beijing University on 4 June 2005, the 16th anniversary of the Tiananmen Square protests in 1989. He asks each of them the same question: "Do you know what day it is today?" Some of them look the other way and keep going without replying. Others give incorrect answers such as Environment Day or Father's Day. Most of them are silent at first and then say they have no idea. However, a few do attempt to answer the question. Thus, the third young man questioned says, "It's the anniversary of 4 June. I can't say very much about it, very few people talk about it. I don't know much about it. Bye." Another replies, "I'm sorry but I can't give you an answer. I know what you're talking about. I can't answer." Many of them slip away because of the camera: "I don't want to be filmed, don't film me."

Liu Wei next shows the viewer a man soundly asleep on a bus, like the students who were at the heart of the protest movement 16 years earlier but are now unable to speak about it or even recall it. He has come up against a wall: a wall of forgetting, because many students really did not know what 4 June corresponded to, and a wall of fear, since most of them refused to answer while they were being filmed.

Finally, Liui shows us Tiananmen Square, with its surveillance cameras, its streams of police, tourists getting out of a bus and taking photographs, red flags floating against the greyish sky. He poses the same question to the passers-by contemplating the square around him. He receives the same evasive or incorrect answers until he arrives at the 20th person, a woman:

"It's the anniversary of the student revolt."
"Do you want to say something about it?"
"No."

Young people are sitting on the sides of the square, smiling, talking with one another.

It is a day for remembering, but a day that appears to have been erased from peoples' minds, or repressed into the depths of their beings. A day like any other, which has lost all its meaning and symbolic impact. A day to be hidden, repressed, forgotten.

Elodie Vouille
Translated by Miriam Rosen

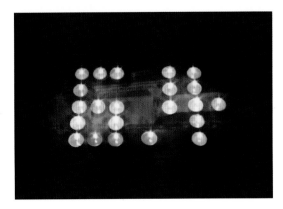

A powerful video installation, *The Farmers and the Helicopters* however opens quietly with dragonflies filling the entire screen. Symbols of courage and peace, dragonflies also have traditional medicinal uses in Asia. Called *chuon chuon* in Vietnamese, a poem says that when dragonflies are happy, they will stand on a branch of a tree; when they are sad, they will fly around randomly, a warning sign that rain is about to come. The sibilant buzz that the dragonflies typically make eventually gives way to the drone of the helicopters, and the latter becomes the dragonflies' poetic counterpart.

The Farmers and the Helicopters' three-channel video installation consists of interview footage of Vietnamese farmers intermixed with clips from Hollywood Vietnam-American War movies (like *Apocalypse Now*) and short documentaries of helicopters during the war. To fully understand the power of the work, the viewer has to remember that the Vietnam-American War was the first war in the world where helicopters were extensively used (over 12,000 American helicopters). The impact on the population in Vietnam was profound and is still present in Vietnamese minds today.

In Dinh Q. Lê's video, the spectrum of memories evoked by the sight and sound of a helicopter is given free rein. Among the people interviewed in the video, some recall the fear, terror and the indecision they experienced. Some even cast judgement on the war machines.

> When I was very young,
> my parents taught me, that if
> I saw a helicopter flying, not to run.
> I was told to walk
> slowly as usual, and not to
> try to hide anywhere.
> I was very scared. They said that,

> if you run or hide in the bushes,
> the helicopter would shoot you dead.
>
> Le Van Danh

> In my opinion, what we have
> lived through and witnessed,
> definitely, we will never forget.
> But our children and
> grandchildren did not live
> through this historical period.
> They don't know. When we tell
> them about it, they listen
> to the stories as if they are listening
> to folk tales. They don't know,
> and can't imagine it.
>
> Pham Thi Hong

Ironically the helicopters in this installation serve both as a symbol of the end of the helicopter as a war machine and the beginning of the helicopter as a machine of peace in Vietnam.

> Now I see the helicopter
> more as a companion. Why?
> Because it has peaceful purposes,
> such as rescue operations and
> emergency medical evacuations.
> It's our means of transport.
> There's nothing to fear from it.
>
> Vuong Van Bang

This new vision is echoed by Tran Quoc Hai. Over a six-year period, the self-taught mechanic built his own flying machine and created an affordable helicopter that could help evacuate people in emergency situations and assist in farming. Fear gives way to fascination in the way helicopters are viewed.

I didn't know much about helicopters then,
but I believe it was called "chinook".

© Singapore Art Museum collection.

I don't remember when
I became infatuated with
helicopters but I can sit for
hours watching helicopters
without ever getting tired of them.

Tran Quoc Hai

This powerful machine once had the power of life
and death in Vietnam. Today people prefer to look at
the benefits of the helicopter, its ability to assist and
save. But memories always remain, as witnessed by
the interviews and footage in this work. The stark
reminder is that one must never forget.

Patricia Levasseur de la Motte

In grade school, I saw helicopters
land, take off, drop off supplies,

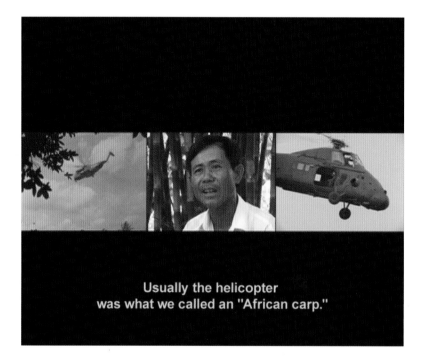

Usually the helicopter
was what we called an "African carp."

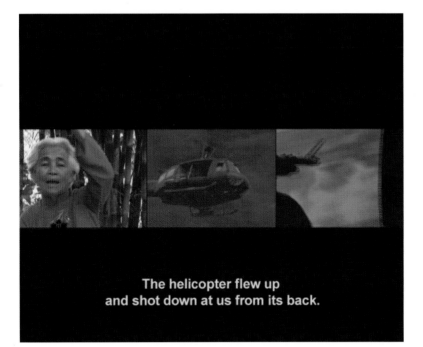

The helicopter flew up
and shot down at us from its back.

We should see it as a companion.
There's nothing to fear from it now.

Araya Rasdjarmrearnsook ■ *Two Planets*, 2008

Since her beginnings in intaglio printing, loss as well as its reconciliation has been at the heart of Araya Rasdjarmrearnsook's oeuvre. Her earlier video works include the morgue series in which the artist attempts at communion with cadavers (such as *Reading for Female Corpse* and *I'm Living*). In this video installation, *Two Planets*, the leitmotiv of loss takes on a twist: gone are the enclosed spaces, the stillness laced with pathos and the artist's monologues to the dead who do not respond. Here, Rasdjarmrearnsook takes us out to the open fields of the Thai countryside where she gives local farmers free play to air their views on four masterpieces of French impressionism: Millet's *The Gleaners* (1857); Manet's *The Luncheon on the Grass* (1863); Renoir's *Ball at Le Moulin de la Galette* (1876); and Van Gogh's *The Siesta* (1889–90).

In *Two Planets*, the object of loss is the significance of these four iconic paintings in their transfer to an *other* context: on the other side of the globe after an interval of more than a century. What would have been irrefutable for students of art and a litmus test for the purportedly genteel urbanite becomes as irrelevant to the farmer as a sickle is to the banker. Seated on the ground with their backs to the camera, about a dozen men and women known to each other share candid comments on a framed reproduction placed before them: "If you look at the painting closely, you'll see they take care of their feet better than their faces."; "Her face is so fresh like white chicken drop-

pings (so white and soft)."; and "See the shoes look like numbers 0 0 and the sickles look like 5 0. The lottery number zero means you won't get anything." etc.

The Thai farmers recognise these paintings in their primary signification as an image – not unlike a picture made by a neighbour's child – without the preconceptions of 'art', making free associations from their own perspective. Their responses are thus spontaneous and ingenuous. Having lectured on Western art history at university level in Thailand for many years, Rasdjarmrearnsook is painfully aware of the abyss between experience and regurgitated knowledge, which non-Western art students grapple with vis-à-vis Western artworks borne of an entirely different historical and cultural process too

often assumed to be universal. It is the local farmers' absence of pretence that lays bare this chasm.

Where does this leave the museum visitor who does not necessarily know more about the paintings – apart from the obvious facts provided in the caption – but who does not possess the farmers' candour? Who is doing the signifying and who is merely present? The audience is caught between the farmers and the paintings, the passive observer of action on a planet split into contrasting pairs: the dead and the living, the city and the countryside, the haves and the have-nots, the East and the West. Communication remains thwarted as with the corpses but Rasdjarmrearnsook no longer mourns.

Yin Ker

© Singapore Art Museum collection.

Than Sok

■ *Negligence Leads to Loss; Attention Preserves*, 2009

Than Sok's current artistic practice considers the spiritual practices of his people. In his installation *Negligence Leads to Loss; Attention Preserves*, traditional communal mats and meditation pillows invite the viewer to sit in the gallery between two different spirit houses – an ornate structure serving as the projection site for a video showing a humble shrine. In Cambodia, wealthier urban families have the means to buy ornate, gold-painted cast cement spirit houses, known as *ktome*, while poorer rural families usually build their own *ktome*, using wood to construct a simple structure.

Found in the majority of rural Cambodian homes and in the northeast corners of Buddhist temple grounds, the shrines serve as the place of communication with Neak Ta. Khmer cultural scholar and professor Ang Choulean defines Neak Ta as the most omnipresent figure of the divinities that inhabit the supernatural world of the Cambodian countryside. Incense and prayers are offered to Neak Ta daily and especially in times of need.

In Than's installation, the wooden shrine is replaced by a handcrafted house built from the material normally used as an intermediary for prayer – incense sticks. The video documents in real time the fictive ceremonial: anonymous hands setting the *ktome* ablaze followed by a performance of dancing flames, and the gradual and violent dismantling of the structure. Before the *ktome* is totally destroyed, the viewer can witness a brief prayer ceremony before it disintegrates into a pile of ash pulsing with heat.

The contradictory actions of arson and prayer provoke the eponymous title from a Cambodian proverb: *Negligence Leads to Loss; Attention Preserves*. The artist notes both a survivalist instinct and reliance on karmic philosophy in such proverbs whose meanings, imbued from times of war, remain in use today, "We cannot know the other actions of the person who prays. Yet we are told from our religion that everything happens for a reason."

Than offers insight into Neak Ta – one aspect of the unique historical fusion of animist, Hindu, and Buddhist practices in Cambodia. The contemplative quality of the video invites the viewer to simply sit and meditate.

Erin Gleeson and
Patricia Levasseur de la Motte

Sima Salehi Rahni

■ *Circle*, 2009

O f the same title as Jafar Panahi's film, *Dayareh (Circle)* (2000), and similarly inspired by the feminine condition in contemporary Iran, is Sima Salehi Rahni's three-channel video installation made for her MFA project at the LASALLE College of the Arts, Singapore. However, unlike the film to which Salehi Rahni makes no intentional reference, *Circle*'s protagonists are metaphors. The chador, the well, water, and pestles and mortars enact the cyclical rituals that are the social, economic, and political structures confining 'the second sex'.

Shot on the Indonesian island of Batam, 17 local women, draped in chador, solemnly engage in vapid activities: they stride across plains of scorched grass under the sweltering sun; they stand facing the sea like megaliths; they peer into a cement well; they sit in a circle to gurgle; they pound water; they yodel. Without speech, there are only the sounds of wind, gurgling, pestles striking mortars, and bodies brushing against grass. Silence, in the stead of dialogue, becomes their voice. The vacuity of the rituals that are repeated, literally on a loop, culminates in the pounding of water contained in mortars.

But the destiny of *Circle*'s 'actors' is not set in stone: the purificatory qualities of water are ultimately lauded when the artist, who inserts herself in the coterie, douses herself; the chador which represents either subjugation or liberation depending on perspective – though never independence – is taken by the wind. The monotony of the circle breaks. Indeed, the significance of *Circle*'s metaphors is multiple if not ambiguous – thus deliberately inviting rumination. Beneath the ambivalence of references lies a subversion that is surreptitious but constant. In the same way that the fragmented and shuffled sequences, locked in a three-channel display, oblige the audience to confront the same scene from different points of view, they confound and

appeal to an alternative approach that calls upon the imagination. The appreciation of *Circle*, like the interpretation of Iran's feminine condition, must adopt shifting paradigms.

As Singapore-based Salehi Rahni, discovered, from the plateau of Tehran to the island of Batam, there are commonalities shared by societies governed by men. And there is always new potential for poetry. The result is this maiden work written in moving images. As much as *Circle* might embody one of the quintessential attributes of Iranian art in the restraint and lyricism with which it conveys irony, this quality does not confine the reading of the work to a narrow vision of what 'Iranian' means. Like Shirin Neshat, whose oeuvre never renounced Iran while embracing new experiences, Salehi Rahni's relationship with her native land is engaged in constant dialogue with fresh encounters on new soil, as the setting of *Circle* demonstrates. Indeed, she would probably disagree with Rudyard Kipling's vision of an antagonistic world whereby "East is East and West is West, and never the twain shall meet".

Yin Ker

© Singapore Art Museum collection.

VI.

Deconstruction and Reconstruction of Narratives

The sixth section of the exhibition explores the crisis of narratives and the end of representations with works from the 1980s to 2009: six artists deconstruct images and sounds from their cinematographic culture (Jean-Luc Godard, Pierre Huyghe, Yang Fudong, Isaac Julien, Tun Win Aung and Wah Nu). Video art has much evolved since Guy Debord's *The Society of the Spectacle* towards spectacular installations involving video projections, large screens and multidirectional sound in specially devised dark spaces that resemble auditoriums for some (Julien) and staged exhibitions for others (Huyghe).

Video artists now look to the professionals of documentary, narrative film and television series for resources. Shooting with professional teams, and editing and sound mixing in studios are common practices in art. Sound itself has become an incontrovertible element of video installation and is handled with great care.

Some artists shoot their own images and record their own sound (Julien, Yang), while others appropriate images and sounds from existing films, borrowing and mixing filmed images and recorded sounds (Huyghe). The purpose of these manipulations of images and sounds is to recreate newly structured narratives that are closer to contemporary concerns.

Installation here gives way to various modalities. By including the visitor in the work's space, the visitor actively becomes one of the work's constituent and necessary parameters.

Jean-Luc Godard

Jean-Luc Godard has always linked his cinematographic oeuvre to the process of thought behind its creation. In *Scénario du Film Passion*, video is the medium he chose to present this reflection, to make himself heard, to list, to designate, and to show what happens when one embarks on a quest for images. It becomes the metalanguage of cinema, the space-time of his reflexivity.

As the title indicates, *Scénario du Film Passion* offers a journey of the narrative frame of the film *Passion* (1981). However, instead of being written before the production, the screenplay comes after, and it primarily seeks to question the way a film is created; the way a story is written and shared with the team involved in the filmmaking process. *Passion* already shows a director in crisis trying to make a movie; the set, the stage, the actors, the extras, the producer, all the ingredients are there and yet it is not coming together. With *Scénario du Film Passion*, Godard thus makes a video about a movie whose subject is already the cinema as work. Behind his cutting table, facing the screen with only the luminosity from his projector as lighting, Godard speaks to the image, listing what he has tried to do and identifying all the entangled layers. In this head-on situation, he asserts the necessity of seeing before writing, for the image is primal to him.

Scénario du Film Passion rejects the authority of the screenplay in cinematographic production and the pressure put upon the director to present his project as a screenplay in order to obtain funding. The viewer sees "the possibility of a world" in construction, the progressive building of an image where there used to be only a blank screen. Words relate what must happen in order for the image to be constructed: the work of the invisible, the confidence in the images that emerge and gradually find their place on the screen. The trajectory recounted by Godard is resistant to cinema's normative economic condition, an attempt to see differently. Godard's process is first of all addressed to his team and the actors, to spur them on a quest for the image to be created, by invoking paintings by Francisco Goya and Diego Velasquez that shine in their obscurity. To film while seeking to find the grand compositions, from the history of painting, in the realness of bodies, their positions, and their movements, to reproduce the grand themes of humanity from a banal story made up of love, betrayal, work and workers' struggles. Above all, it is about leaving the work open to possibility, waiting for the connections to be made, and for chance to guide the work's progress, just as Mozart's musical piece – which Godard purchased at an airport – sets the tone and opens up sudden possibilities.

Through this reflection on screenplay, Godard rejects the economic model of cinema that would have demanded Paul Cézanne "make a few sketches of an apple before asking his dealer for money". He perseveres on the path of a cinematographic creation that is strongly associated with the way artists worked with video, allowing himself to seek the image freely before designating it. The technical ease of this medium and its low cost surely gave him the liberty to film in an intuitive manner, to immerse himself in the image without mastering it, and to campaign for a videographic composition broken loose from the codes of cinema. Godard, who began his career writing press releases for Fox Studios, is very familiar with the political machine of writing that goes along with cinematographic production, and has already expressed interest in this in *Scénario de Sauve qui peut (la vie): Quelques remarques sur la réalisation et la production du film* (1979), a video to receive an *avance sur recettes* and is unfinished in terms of the image. *Scénario du Film Passion*, which

was made three years later, extends the analysis of the context of production which interests him as much as the films themselves, because they involve cinema as work. As the narrative develops, extracts from *Passion* appear and impose themselves as evidence for Godard's mind and the journey he has undertaken. Cinema becomes this extraordinary art whereby the narration of stories is a perpetual game between reality and fiction, between words and the image, and between the thought and the unthought.

Mathilde Roman

Translated by Yin Ker

Chris Marker

How does Chris Marker arrive at *Immemory*? What is *Immemory*? The three French adjectives condensed into this English word suggest something so familiar and so ancient that its memory is lost. Does it not describe the impossible character of a personal memory which is Memory itself? A Memory by which, as in God or the Machine, the whole memory of the world is brought full circle. This is the memory of the future, of the year 4001, with regard to which Marker has teased out the paradox by conjuring up the viewpoint of the "imaginary film" which he is both making and not making, in making *Sans Soleil (Sunless)* (1982) (p. 198).

For a long time, the all-purpose 'I' where Marker excelled was the 'I' of chronicle and journey, feeling and persuasion, and the sharing of ideas and sensations. It is involved in an active, political and cultural memory, with which it has a playful relationship of co-habitation: the memory of the world whose voice and witness it becomes. But it has not yet involved itself within its own memory, to the point where the attempt and a fictionalisation of life combine to merge within a single matter, at the whim of the methods of their formal manifestation: writing, photography, film, video, etc.

The result is that it is hard to say since when Marker has devoted his efforts to *Immemory*. He has clearly been working at it since he defined a production framework for it with the Musée national d'art moderne in 1993. But also since then, he has been trying out a kind of personal language creatively on his computer, and entrusting more and more of his memory to the machine. He possibly started work on *Immemory* as soon as he chose to write and make films; as soon as memory, with the war and the camps over, became his problem – almost his sole subject. He enters *Immemory* as soon as he remembers, remembers that he remem-bers, and starts to accumulate, in the ever more disproportionate treasure of his archives where he has kept "everything", the traces of his life refracted in the lives of so many others: private lives, public lives, the tiniest vestige of which henceforth, like the Land of Israel at the beginning of *Description of a Battle*, "first of all sends you signs". So as soon as you digal-most haphazardly in the treasure of *Immemory*, you will find the telegram sent to Marker to tell him of the death of the musician Bola de Nieve, in October 1971, which we stumble upon in the Photo zone, Cuba section, chapter January 1961. Thephotos in Uncle Anton's Album, one of the perceptible centres of the CD-ROM which we penetrate, for example, by following a branch line of the Hitchcock section inside the Memory zone, or Castro's speech opening the literacy campaign, in which we hear the famous words *Patria o muerte, venceremos* which open the same chapter January 1961. Or, in the *Vertigo* section of the Cinema and Memory zones, the photo of the section of sequoia of *La Jetée*, inserted in a photogram of the sequoia section of *Vertigo*,before which Scottie and Madeleine stood stock-still paralysed by the ordeal of love and time.

We swiftly realise that *Immemory* cannot be just one among many works in Marker's oeuvre. Whatever he may or may not do after his CD-ROM, we can clearly see how this already appears to be a magnum opus and a masterpiece, in accordance with its artisanal reality and its programme value. Its interactive nature involves a virtual dimension (Umberto Eco had already made a distinction between the simple "open work" aimed at giving rise to a plurality of interpretations, and the "work in motion", planned to vary in accordance with its performers). But the virtuality of *Immemory* has to do above all with the relationship between the boundaries which the work provides for itself and the limitlessness that it opens up.

Immemory is no longer an essay, haunted, like *Sans Soleil (Sunless)*, by the fiction of a self-portrait traced in it between the lines; it is a self-portrait informed by novel forces, which are still partly unaware of one another, and the self-portrait knows it. The unusual thing about *Immemory* is that it is the repository of a body of work and a life which have taken as their subject this century as a place of memory of all the memories of the world.

"I claim, for the image, the humility and the powers of a Madeleine." So this involves experimenting, by rendering them virtually possible for a reader, with all the ways and links making it possible to proceed from one image to another, through the zones which cover the story here, or rather the experience of a life, under the auspices of its geography. Help is provided by an index, offering direct access to all the points listed in the eight zones which *Immemory* is made up of. But above all, within a zone, as from one zone to the next, thanks to the possible bifurcations, the shift from one image to another helps us feel that with neither secret nor centre, it is through conveying one's heartbeat from one memory to the next, that memory is ceaselessly and endlessly constructed, like a network.

Raymond Bellour

Translated by Simon Pleasance

© Chris Marker. Coll. Centre Pompidou.

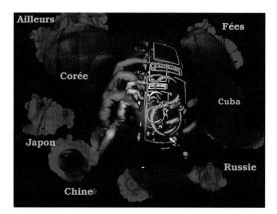

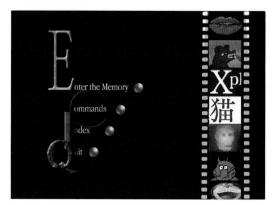

The Third Memory is presented in the form of a display of heterogeneous documentary and fictional elements in order to highlight the different gaps that have been formed between the reality of a news item as experienced by its author and the cinematographic spectacle derived from it by the Hollywood film industry. Like a police re-creation (say, of a crime), a situation and an event are re-enacted, re-performed, using a method involving the reappropriation of representations (of film and the media in this instance), which Pierre Huyghe has been exploring in his work for several years. What is involved here, and what is the chronology of the facts?

On 22 August 1972, in Brooklyn, New York, at 2pm, there was a bank hold-up, during which hostages were taken by the two men involved, John Wojtowicz and Sal Naturile. When it was all over, Naturile was dead and Wojtowicz had been arrested. The entire event was given wide coverage in the media. The motive for this crime, as revealed by the media, was to finance the sex change operation wanted by the man with whom Wotjowicz was in love, Ernest Aron. An article published in *LIFE* magazine would subsequently inspire Sidney Lumet to write a script for the film, which would end up as *Dog Day Afternoon*, which was released in 1975, with Al Pacino starring in the lead role.

Twenty-seven years after those events, Huyghe asked Wotjowicz to reconstruct the heist and thus make rectifications to Lumet's fictional rendering, in which Wojtowicz failed to even recognise himself. A new film was shot in a studio, with the author of the hold-up re-enacting the situation and commenting on it, based on the way he recalled it. Huyghe thus gave Wojtowicz a chance to reconstruct a truthful version of his story and image of himself, which had been confiscated from him by the imagination and production of somebody else, and permitted him to "have

his say and become the actor of his own memory". In the first room, the installation consists of a double projection on a screen wall, the editing of which deals with an excerpt from Lumet's film, documents from that period, the 1970s, and the reconstruction of the events in a studio by Wojtowicz, filmed from different angles and directions, and at times talking straight at the camera. In the second room posters are affixed to the walls, along with press clippings and a video showing a segment from the *Jeanne Parr Show* dated 25 January 1978, with Wojtowicz in a link-up from his prison cell, and Aron who has turned into Liz Debbie on the set.

This whole complex and precise construction, split into two areas of reconstruction and documentation around one and the same event, constitutes an exhibition in its own right. Huyghe steps up the number of exhibits and pieces of evidence and mixes the true with the false, by putting the prime witness's account at the very centre of the reconstruction. Memory itself becomes subject to interpretation by the very fact of it being updated. At the heart of this anamnestic device lie truth, history, identity and representation. By repeating the event, Huyghe gives what has already taken place a second chance: he reconstructs "the possibility of what was", and borrows the words of Giorgio Agamben, "Memory gives the past back its possibility", if not its truth. Huyghe often uses film to question memory, in the form of remakes and interpretation. Memory is carried by the body, for it is the body of memory: in pieces like *Remake*, *The Ellipse*, *Snow White Lucie* and *Dubbing*, it is the bodies of the film actors which gives the past its possibility. What affects us in *The Ellipse* is not so much that Bruno Ganz reconstructed a time-frame that the cinematographic code had spirited away, and stolen as much from the actor as from the viewer, but that 27 years after *The American Friend*,

he says to us: "I'm still here, here and now, with my story which is also your story, made up of make-believe and reality mixed together." This third memory which Huyghe talks about adds to the memory of facts and their interpretation by way of fiction, the memory of the present body which talks and reports, which expresses its truth, and lays claim to being the author thereof.

What is the author of the crime? What is the body of the crime? The motive for the crime is the identity switch (sex changes costs a great deal of money – it is life-changing after all): the author of the crime is the body of the crime – it is the person who risks his life. When you put your life at risk, you must not make things up, because this life and its story belong to us at the most private and deepest levels. This is what Huyghe expresses by doing away with himself as the author in *The Third Memory*, as reconstructing the story is like reconstructing the body in the sur-

gical sense of the term – it is re-establishing it in its original form, and repairing the damage that chance (illness, accident) or nature (being born a man and being a woman) has made the person undergo. It is a contestation of its representations and its amusing happenings. Film doctors and adulterates bodies as shown by *Dubbing* (1996), where we see (at last) the bodies behind the voices of the French version of an American film – one body talks for the other. This also comes through in *Snow White Lucie* where a body is dispossessed of its voice by the entertainment industry. Restoring the word to the body, reappropriating its story, relativising the event, these are the challenges which Huyghe has assigned to his art. Perhaps freeing oneself from exploitation and returning to production is his true political agenda.

Françoise Parfait
Translated by Simon Pleasance

© Coll. Centre Pompidou. Photo Georges Meguerditchian.

Yang Fudong belongs to the Chinese generation that grew up under the communist regime, but as adults face the drastic political and societal transformation that is a result of China's rapidly developing capitalist economy. Yang tackles the theme of social reality in contemporary China with an emphasis on the psychology of the individual confronting the status quo. In his photography and video works, Yang creates alien decors and situations that evoke both bygone eras and the present. On one hand, with his background in traditional Chinese painting, Yang depicts in his contemporary pieces pastoral landscapes that are reminiscent of the peaceful ideal world represented in traditional Chinese paintings. On the other hand, he distorts these picturesque scenes by introducing incongruous elements that relate to specific moments in the modern era, resulting in an anachronistic setting in which the characters' absurd and nihilistic existence is staged.

These themes and approaches can be found in Yang's video, *Backyard - Hey! Sun is Rising*. The short black and white film can be regarded as a parody, composed of remnants from the Cultural Revolution and ancient China, with a visual stylisation vaguely recalling Chinese cinema of the 1930s and the 1940s, a genre that exerts a strong influence over the artist. While the title indicates the morning, the most precious moment of the day according to traditional Chinese wisdom, the characters appear to be aimless and ineffectual despite their ongoing actions and trajectories throughout the city. Accompanied by a soundtrack of gongs and drums similar to those heard in Chinese warfare films, the video begins with several young men dressed in Cultural Revolution uniforms, who yawn widely before doing their exercises. The scene abruptly shifts to show them climbing hills and pushing

the pillar support of an old house. However their efforts are in vain, as demonstrated by the image of a group of elderly people talking on the other side of the pillar, unaffected by the exertions of the young men. It is an anti-heroic scene that runs counter to Chinese propaganda imagery.

The cluster of young men, sometimes in their white shirts – indicative of their social status as white-collar workers – continue to perform different actions in often incongruous settings: playing swords on bustling urban streets, drinking tea in a modern apartment in the fashion of the refined intellectuals from ancient times, and gazing into the distance in an idyllic garden. The camera fleetingly captures old alleys which have been largely eliminated by the massive urbanisation of mainland China. The collapse of the old political regime and value system handed down by previous generations for thousands of years has consequences for the present generation; the confusion they suffer is expressed through the disparity of the actions and settings in the video, as well as the abrupt jumps of short sequences which are inadequate in constituting any continuity or narrative coherence. The absurd nature of these sequences also results in a kind of inertia that dominates the characters who intermittently curl up on the bed or the ground while holding a sword to their chests, or remain motionless and expressionless while being attacked by their comrades.

Consistent with the preoccupations and approaches in Yang's other videos, *Backyard - Hey! Sun is Rising* represents a pastiche of hybrid elements, like a mental mosaic reflecting the inner conflicts and battles that the individual confronts in the face of mutations. Such works recall similar existentialist questionings already proposed in literary works such as Jean-Paul Sartre's *Nausea*.

© Coll. Centre Pompidou.
Courtesy of the artist and ShanghART Gallery.

The viewers of *Backyard - Hey! Sun is Rising* are confronted with the same feelings of powerlessness and alienation as they watch the characters running in endless circles, silently shouting as the soundtrack overwhelms their voices, and confining themselves in modern high-rise buildings set over a vertiginous cityscape. *Backyard - Hey! Sun is Rising* represents a contemporary vision of a Sisyphean task set in contemporary China in which the characters must navigate the intersection of the country's long history and recent past, as well as the conflict arising from deeply embedded traditional values and the driving force of modernisation.

Sylvie Lin

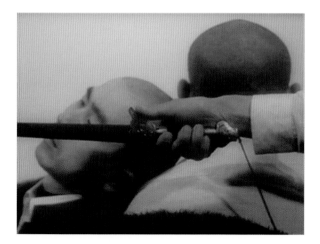

With *Baltimore*, Isaac Julien presents a monumental installation made up of three videos shot on 16mm film, edited, and projected on three quite different screens. The triptych form extends the length of the projection over three timeframes which, through narrative breaks and repetitions, make it possible to construct a narrative which relates, by way of many different references, to a past, present and future history of black culture in the United States. On the last point, Julien did once explain that he was keen to create a "third dimension" using cultural themes borrowed from black science fiction and Afro-futurism, while being simultaneously inspired by the film trend known as blaxploitation from the 1970s.

As an introduction to each video, the shot of a drawing of two black silhouettes opening a large book with white pages announces the start of a story which is set in the city of Baltimore, as seen through its streets and three of its buildings – first the National Great Blacks in Wax Museum, a popular museum displaying wax figures of historic black personalities (politicians, musicians, singers, and writers, as well as former slaves and Egyptian queens); the Walters Art Museum which houses a major collection of works dating from antiquity to the present day as well as some very fine Renaissance canvases; and lastly the Peabody Library which is part of the famous Johns Hopkins University, the oldest research and educational institution in the United States. Over and above a choice of film sets, Julien, who has a deep interest in the issue of archives, proposes nothing less than a comparison – both imaginary and real – between these places that each contain an ancestral memory, and hence giving rise to an extremely contemporary reading of the history of art and culture.

The two characters who recur in all three videos are Melvin Van Peebles, the famous director and actor of the cult film *Sweet Sweetback's Baadasssss Song*, the first independent black film which marked the year 1971 with its huge public and critical success, and Vanessa Myrie, who embodies an Afro-Cyborg, with the features of a woman who calls to mind both political icon Angela Davis, and icon of blaxploitation Pam Grier. As the bionic eye, she appears throughout the video, in high heels, as if trying to escape from Van Peebles. In just a few minutes, using quick cuts following the soundtrack and film extracts including *Sweet Sweetback* alternated with views of working class neighbourhoods in *Baltimore*, Julien creates all the suspense of a detective film. The special effects, the light with its bluish hues, the expertise of the camera movements, and the shots which follow one another at the pace the museum rooms are crossed, all reinforce this impression but, at the same time, the elements presented contradict the sensation of lightness which might be felt in an action movie. This is due to the fact that these wax figures which enact the movements of Van Peebles and the Afro-Cyborg are often painful reminders of an Afro-American history hallmarked by slavery, violence and racial discrimination. Accordingly, the wax slave figures are shown on the screen of the first video just when we hear a shot fired, and when the actress takes off her wig and reveals her shaven head. While the voice of a black leader rings out, and Van Peebles contemplates a metaphysical 'Ideal City' painted by an anonymous 15th-century Italian artist, the camera follows one of the ruined amphitheatres in the painting. The next shot dwells for a long time on Martin Luther King, and then shows the sad face of Billie Holiday. In the second and third videos, the scenes seem to be repeated, but we find new historical figures such as Malcolm X, W.E.B. Dubois, leaders of the Nation of

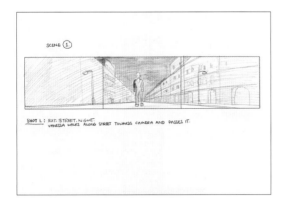

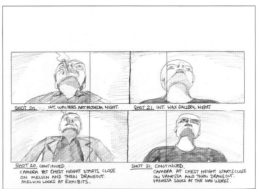

Islam, and demonstrators in the Civil Rights Movement bearing 'Freedom' placards. Shifted into the picture gallery, they become at once actors in their own history and spectators of another history in which they did not really play any part. Julien films them as witnesses of a genealogical experience. He also creates the encounter between Van Peebles and his double by making a chronological short cut which does away with any nostalgia.

While in most instances the wax figures are frozen in their timeless quality as popular icons, by creating a wax Van Peebles for his video, Julien wittily suggests an active memory between the famous director and his character, and through this contrast keeps the story in the present. The meeting occurs in a museum, and the flesh-and-blood Van Peebles looks at his wax alter ego as if he were seeing himself in a mirror. The new spatial dimension created between model and effigy henceforth offers a read-

ing which projects all the historical figures of African-American culture into a political reality which is still valid today. Having become visitors at the Walters Art Museum, which lays claim to 55 centuries of European and Asian civilisation stretching from the ancient world to the 20th century, Julien gives them the part of ferrymen between two parallel histories, between a popular culture and an erudite culture, and creates a novel comparison which overturns the linearity of Western history. When the video *Baltimore* is near its end, we see Van Peebles from behind, walking in the street amidst the sound of sirens and, with a final shot of skyscrapers, we hear a voice which winds up the film: "The party is over, baby, it's reality!"

Elvan Zabunyan
Translated by Simon Pleasance

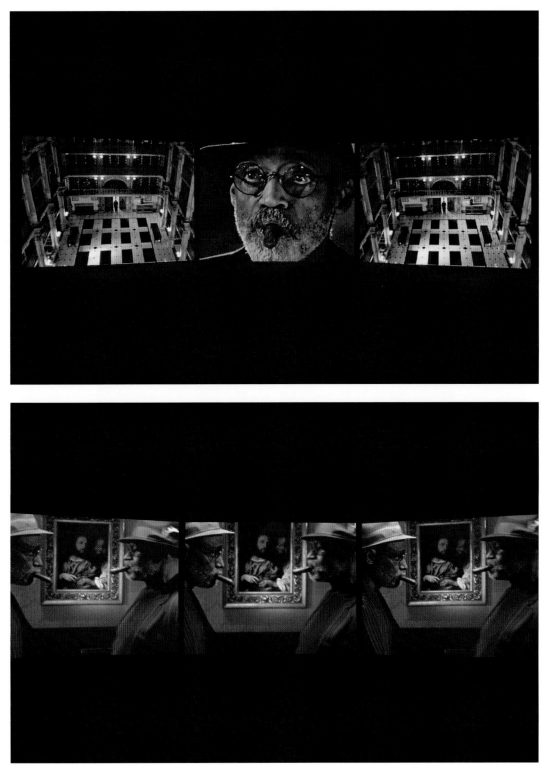

© Singapore Art Museum collection.

A colour monitor shows an old lady seated in an interior, chanting faintly intelligible phrases. On the wall facing her is a projection of edited sequences taken from three black-and-white films from the 1970s. The audience stands between two worlds that cannot be engaged simultaneously: one either hears the old movie soundtrack broadcasted on the speakers or the old lady's soliloquy on the headphones.

Kekeke! Kebalaba! translates as 'It's all right! Please come!' in the Myanma language and is taken from the old lady's chant. The video installation is as much a meditation on sickness, old age, and death – personified by the figure of a fragile old woman on the brink of senile dementia – as it is about the persistence of desire, albeit weak but undiminished by deteriorating physical conditions. Despite losing control of her faculties, the old lady continues to yearn for her loved ones, and for pleasurable sensations.

These unfulfilled longings are made visible in the projection conjuring images of freedom, youth, hope and joy recalling promenades, boat trips and other scenes of merrymaking from better days. Excerpted from the old movies of Maung Wunna (1947–2011), the scenes dilate to engulf the viewer, as if suggesting that imagination is indeed more powerful than the reality, here contained in a relatively small monitor screen. But the film excerpts are not what they seem; they are irreversibly disfigured by the passage of time: blanched images played backward.

The dialectics of *Kekeke! Kebalaba!* are sustained by the confrontation between the two worlds of enactment and documentary. The audience is caught between reality and memory, physically and metaphorically inserted at the midpoint of the work, and left to hesitate between the two time-spaces. It is a distilled time zone created by the artists, the point where reality and memory narrowly brush past each other, never to meet, each compelled by the momentum of its own destiny, like two trains on parallel but separate tracks. Where is the present? Which is the real?

Decrepitude, exemplifying two of the three central tenets of Buddhism in particular, which are impermanence and suffering, is at the heart of this work. These two premises extend beyond the flesh to affect time as well as space. Here, Tun Win Aung and Wah Nu take Myanma cinema into a new time and space in the form of the video installation. Incidentally, preparations for the exhibition of this work corresponded to the passing of Maung Wunna, Wah Nu's father and one of the country's leading filmmakers. Perhaps by evoking the old lady's happier times, it is not without projecting their own childhood memories of a different Myanmar, when the local film industry and intelligentsia still strived within limits.

Greater than nostalgia is a poignancy that gnaws: the irretrievability of time and the irreconcilability of dreams with life. The old lady's calls fall on deaf ears. With its layers of interwoven significance, *Kekeke! Kebalaba!* embodies an endearing characteristic of Myanma art and literature: an art of the double movement of opening and concealing, developed to perfection against a backdrop of ubiquitous censorship.

Yin Ker

251

List of Works

Vito ACCONCI
Turn On, 1974
1 videotape, NTSC, colour, sound, 22'
Musée national d'art moderne Collection, Centre
    Pompidou, Paris, France
AM 1995 - 42

Sonia ANDRADE
Rio de Janeiro, Sans Titre 2, 1975
1 videotape, PAL, black and white, sound, 9'
Musée national d'art moderne Collection, Centre
    Pompidou, Paris, France
AM 2008 - 56

ARAHMAIANI
I Don't Want to be a Part of Your Legend, 2003
1 digital file, PAL, colour, sound, 11'36"
Singapore Art Museum collection

Samuel BECKETT
Arena Quad I + II, 1981
1 videotape, PAL, colour, sound, 15'
Musée national d'art moderne Collection, Centre
    Pompidou, Paris, France
AM 2001 - 56

Louidgi BELTRAME
Brasilia/Chandigarh, 2008
Video installation
Edition 1/5 + 2 a.p.
1 video projector, 2 loudspeakers
1 digital file, 16/9, anamorphic, colour, sound, original
    version in English, 26'
Musée national d'art moderne Collection, Centre
    Pompidou, Paris, France
AM 2010 - 295

Peter CAMPUS
Interface, 1972
Closed-circuit video installation
Edition 1/1
1 black and white camera, 1 light projector, 1 video
    projector, 1 pane of glass
Musée national d'art moderne Collection, Centre
    Pompidou, Paris, France
AM 1990 - 59

**Keith DEVERELL, Sue McCAULEY, MEAS Sokhorn
    and SREY Bandol**
The Hawker's Song, 2010
Audiovisual installation
Edition 1/5 + 6 a.p.
Debris, 6 flat screen television sets, 7 digital files, PAL,
    colour, black and white, sound, 4'30", 3'30", 7', 7', 4'30",

12', non-durational
Singapore Art Museum collection

Valie EXPORT
Facing a Family, 1971
1 videotape, PAL, black and white, sound, 4'44"
Musée national d'art moderne Collection, Centre
    Pompidou, Paris, France
AM 2004 - 416
Space Seeing/Space Hearing, 1973–1974
1 videotape, PAL, black and white, sound, 6'19"
Musée national d'art moderne Collection, Centre
    Pompidou, Paris, France
AM 2004 - 420

Jean-Luc GODARD
Scénario du Film Passion, 1982
Video projection
1 video projector, 2 loudspeakers,
1 videotape, PAL, colour, sound, original version in
    French (English subtitles), 53'24"
Musée national d'art moderne Collection, Centre
    Pompidou, Paris, France
AM 1992 - 123

Dan GRAHAM
Present Continuous Past(s), 1974
    Closed-circuit video installation
Edition 1/1
1 black-and-white camera, 1 black-and-white monitor,
    2 mirrors, 1 microprocessor, 5" delay
Musée national d'art moderne Collection, Centre
    Pompidou, Paris, France
AM 1976 - 1335

Johan GRIMONPREZ
Dial H-I-S-T-O-R-Y, 1997
Video projection
Edition 1/3
1 video projector, 4 loudspeakers
1 videotape, PAL, colour, stereo sound, 68' (English
    subtitles)
Co-produced by New Media department, CGP, Paris and
    Kunstcentrum STUC, Université de Louvain (Belgium)
Musée national d'art moderne Collection, Centre
    Pompidou, Paris, France
AM 1997 - 254

Pierre HUYGHE
The Third Memory, 1999
Mixed media installation
Edition 1/4 + 1 a.p.
2 video projectors, 1 synchroniser, 1 monitor
1 poster 170 x 120, 11 digital images 60 x 80, 2

videotapes, 16/9, PAL, colour, stereo sound, original version in English, 9'46"
Co-produced by New Media department, CGP, Paris, The Renaissance Society at the University of Chicago, and The Bohen Foundation, New York (USA)
Musée national d'art moderne Collection, Centre Pompidou, Paris, France
AM 1999 - 154

Mako IDEMITSU
Yoji, What's Wrong With You?, 1987
1 videotape, NTSC, colour, sound, 17'50"
Musée national d'art moderne Collection, Centre Pompidou, Paris, France
AM 1990 - 152

Isaac JULIEN
Baltimore, 2003
Audiovisual installation
Edition 3/6 + 1 a.p.
3 video projectors, 1 synchroniser, 5 loudspeakers, 1 sub bass
3 videotapes, PAL, colour, stereo sound, 11'36"
Musée national d'art moderne Collection, Centre Pompidou, Paris, France
AM 2004 - 78

Sonia KHURANA
Bird, 2000
1 videotape, PAL, black and white, silent, 3'06"
Musée national d'art moderne Collection, Centre Pompidou, Paris, France
AM 2006 - 145

Thierry KUNTZEL
Autumn (Mount Analogue), 2000
Video installation
Limited edition 1/3 + 1 a.p.
1 video projector, 1 monitor, 1 synchroniser
2 videotapes, PAL, colour, silent, 5'51"
Musée national d'art moderne Collection, Centre Pompidou, Paris, France
AM 2004 - 190

Dinh Q. LÊ
The Farmers and the Helicopters, 2006
Audiovisual installation
Edition 3/5
3 video projectors, 4 loudspeakers, 3 media players/PC systems, 3 synchronisers, 1 amplifier, 3 digital files, PAL, colour, stereo sound, 14'59"
Singapore Art Museum collection

LEE Wen
Journey of A Yellow Man No. 3: Desire (Lee Wen: Documentation of Performances on Video), 1993
1 videotape, NTSC, colour, sound, 4'29"
Singapore Art Museum collection
World Class Society, 1999
Video installation
Edition 1/1 + 1 a.p.

Survey forms, badges, 1 jar, 1 stuffed white globe with wings, 1 stuffed white star, 1 white cloth tube, 1 white plinth,1 showcase, 1 monitor, 1 videotape, NTSC, colour, sound, 4'
Singapore Art Museum collection

LIU Wei
Floating Memory, 2001
1 videotape, PAL, colour, sound, 10'
Musée national d'art moderne Collection, Centre Pompidou, Paris, France
AM 2088 - 89
A Day to Remember, 2005
1 videotape, PAL, colour, sound, 13'
Musée national d'art moderne Collection, Centre Pompidou, Paris, France
AM 2088 - 88

Christelle LHEUREUX
See **Apichatpong WEERASETHAKUL**

Joan LOGUE
30 Second Spots New York, 1980–1982
30 Second Spots Paris, 1983
Ushio Amagatsu 33"22, Lucinda Childs 31"01, Yoshi Wada 30"4, Laurie Anderson 1'1", Nam June Paik 1'30"3, Tony Ramos 1'31"05, John Cage 1'29"09
1 videotape, PAL, colour, sound, 7'50"
Musée national d'art moderne Collection, Centre Pompidou, Paris, France
AM 1985 - 442 and AM 1983 - 512

Sue McCAULEY
See **Keith DEVERELL**

Chris MARKER
Immemory, 1996
Interactive multimedia installation
Limited edition 1/1
1 hard drive 34 MB, 3 Apple computers
1 mural painting, 1 CD-ROM, colour, sound (French and English)
Musée national d'art moderne Collection, Centre Pompidou, Paris, France
AM 1997 - 253
Sans Soleil (Sunless), 1982
1 video projection
1 videotape, PAL, colour, sound, 110' (English subtitles)
Argos Films

Toshio MATSUMOTO
Ki or Breathing, 1980
1 videotape, NTSC, colour, sound, 10'
Musée national d'art moderne Collection, Centre Pompidou, Paris, France
AM 1987 - 1187
Formation, 1983
1 videotape, NTSC, colour, sound, 9'
Musée national d'art moderne Collection, Centre Pompidou, Paris, France
AM 1987 - 1188

Ko NAKAJIMA
Mount Fuji, 1984
1 videotape, NTSC, colour, sound, 7′
Musée national d'art moderne Collection, Centre
    Pompidou, Paris, France
AM 1992 - 32

Bruce NAUMAN
Stamping in the Studio, 1968
1 videotape, NTSC, black and white, sound, 60′
Musée national d'art moderne Collection, Centre
    Pompidou, Paris, France
AM 1985 - 451
Going Around the Corner Piece, 1970
Closed-circuit video installation
Edition 1/1
4 black-and-white cameras, 4 black-and-white monitors,
    1 white cube
Musée national d'art moderne Collection, Centre
    Pompidou, Paris, France
AM 1988 - 954(1)

Jun NGUYEN-HATSUSHIBA
Memorial Project: Nha Trang, Vietnam: Towards the
    Complex – For the Courageous, the Curious, and the
    Cowards, 2001
Audiovisual installation
Edition 10/10 + 6 a.p.
1 video projector, 2 loudspeakers
1 videotape, PAL, colour, sound, 13′
Gift of Lotus and Yves Mahé, Luxembourg
Musée national d'art moderne Collection, Centre
    Pompidou, Paris, France
AM 2004 - 91
Breathing is Free: 12,756.3, 2008–2009
Audiovisual installation
Edition 1/3
6 flat-screen television sets, 6 digital files, NTSC, colour,
    sound, 13′30″, 17′30″, 25′, 9′30″, 15′, 19′30″
Singapore Art Museum collection

MEAS Sokhorn
See **Keith DEVERELL**

Tony OURSLER
SWITCH, 1996
Mixed media installation
Edition 1/1
2 surveillance cameras, 1 surveillance monitor, 1
    microphone, 1 remote control, 5 dummies, 5
    video projectors, 1 fibreglass sphere, 2 sound
    organs, 2 bulbs, 6 loudspeakers, 3 amplifiers, 4
    videotapes, NTSC, 2 CDs, colour, sound (French and
    English) 4′29″ to 35′
Commissioned by New Media department, Musée
    national d'art moderne Collection, Centre Pompidou,
    Paris, France
    AM 1996 - 389

Nam June PAIK
Moon is the Oldest T.V., 1965–1992
Video installation (exhibition copy)
Edition 1/1

11 black-and-white monitors
11 videotapes black-and-white, silent
Musée national d'art moderne Collection, Centre
    Pompidou, Paris, France
AM 1985 - 142
Guadalcanal Requiem, 1979
1 videotape, NTSC, colour, sound, 29′
Musée national d'art moderne Collection, Centre
    Pompidou, Paris, France
AM 1986 - 27

THE PROPELLER GROUP
Uh…, 2007
Video projection
Edition 2/7 + 2 a.p.
1 video projector, 2 loudspeakers, 1 digital file, PAL,
    colour, stereo sound, 7′
Singapore Art Museum collection

Araya RASDJARMREARNSOOK
Two Planets, 2008
Video projection
Edition 1/5
2 video projectors, 2 loudspeakers, 4 digital files, PAL,
    colour, stereo sound (Thai with English subtitles), 15′,
    18′, 10′, 16′
Singapore Art Museum collection

Martial RAYSSE
Identité, maintenant vous êtes un Martial Raysse
    (Identity, Now You Are a Martial Raysse), 1967
Closed-circuit video installation
Limited edition 1/1
1 black-and-white camera
1 black-and-white monitor on a wood and metal
    support, Plexiglass
Musée national d'art moderne Collection, Centre
    Pompidou, Paris, France
AM 1991 - 83

Rachel REUPKE
Infrastructure, 2002
Video projection
1 video projector, 2 loudspeakers
1 videotape, PAL, black and white, sound, 14′
Musée national d'art moderne Collection, Centre
    Pompidou, Paris, France
AM 2005 - 161
Now Wait For Last Year, 2007
1 videotape, PAL, colour, sound, 9′20″
Musée national d'art moderne Collection, Centre
    Pompidou, Paris, France
AM 2008 - 104

Pipilotti RIST
A la belle étoile (Under the Sky), 2007
Audiovisual installation
Edition 1/3 + 1 a.p.
1 video projector, 1 amplifier, loudspeakers

1 videotape, HDCAM, PAL, colour, stereo sound, 10'26"
Commissioned by New Media department, Musée
national d'art moderne Collection, Centre Pompidou,
Paris, France
AM 2007 - 169

Sima SALEHI RAHNI
Circle, 2009
Audiovisual installation
Edition 1/1
3 video projectors, 3 loudspeakers, 1 synchroniser, 3
digital files, PAL, colour, stereo sound, 8'57"
Singapore Art Museum collection

SREY Bandol
See **Keith DEVERELL**

Richard STREITMATTER-TRAN
Missed Connections, 2004
Video projection
Edition 1/5
1 video projector, 2 loudspeakers, 1 digital file, PAL,
colour, sound, 8'
Singapore Art Museum collection

Shuntaro TANIKAWA and Shuji TERAYAMA
Video Letters, 1982–1983
1 videotape, NTSC, colour, sound, 75'
Musée national d'art moderne Collection, Centre
Pompidou, Paris, France
AM 1988 - 577

Shuji TERAYAMA
See **Shuntaro TANIKAWA**

THAN Sok
Negligence Leads to Loss; Attention Preserves, 2009
Video installation
Edition 1/3
1 video projector, 1 concrete spirit house, 1 digital file,
PAL, colour, sound, 9'42"
Singapore Art Museum collection

TRINH T. Minh-ha
The Fourth Dimension, 2001
1 videotape, PAL, colour, sound, 87'
Musée national d'art moderne Collection, Centre
Pompidou, Paris, France
AM 2005 - 229

Tun Win Aung and Wah Nu
Kekeke! Kebalaba!, 2009
Audiovisual installation
Edition 1/3
1 video projector, 1 monitor, 2 loudspeakers, 1set of
headphones, 1 pedestal, 2 digital files, NTSC, black
and white, colour, sound, 3'
Singapore Art Museum collection

Bill VIOLA
Hatsu Yume (First Dream), 1981
1 videotape, NTSC, colour, sound, 56'
Musée national d'art moderne Collection, Centre
Pompidou, Paris, France
AM 1985 - 447
Reverse Television/Portraits of Viewers, 1983–1984
1 videotape, NTSC, colour, mute, 44 sequences of 30"
Musée national d'art moderne Collection, Centre
Pompidou, Paris, France
AM 1988 - 543

Wah Nu
See **Tun Win Aung**

Apichatpong WEERASETHAKUL
Nokia Short, 2003
1 videotape, PAL, colour, sound, 2'17"
Musée national d'art moderne Collection, Centre
Pompidou, Paris, France
AM 2006 - 780

Apichatpong WEERASETHAKUL and Christelle
LHEUREUX
Ghost of Asia, 2005
Video installation
Edition 1/3 + 2 a.p.
2 video projectors, 1 synchroniser
2 videotapes, PAL, colour, sound (Thai with English
subtitles), 9'
Musée national d'art moderne Collection, Centre
Pompidou, Paris, France
AM 2007 - 154

YANG Fudong
Backyard - Hey! Sun is Rising, 2001
Video projection
1 video projector, 2 loudspeakers
1 videotape, PAL, black-and-white, sound, 13'
Gift of the Société des Amis du MNAM, Centre
Pompidou, PAC, 2003
Musée national d'art moderne Collection, Centre
Pompidou, Paris, France
AM 2004 - 448

Artist Biographies

Vito ACCONCI
Born in 1940 in New York, USA
Lives and works in New York, USA

Selected Exhibitions
Vito Acconci: Film-Landscape, Video Close Up, Castello di Rivoli, Museo d'arte contemporanea, Rivoli, 2010.
Temps de Vídeo: 1965–2005, Fundació La Caixa, Barcelona, 2005–06.
Vito Hannibal Acconci Studio – Word / Action / Architecture, Stedelijk Museum, Amsterdam, 2005.
Vito Hannibal Acconci Studio, Musée des beaux-arts, Nantes, 2004.
Vito Acconci: Panorámica, Museo Tamayo arte contemporáneo, Mexico City, 2004.
Rooms with a View: Environments for Video, Guggenheim Museum, New York, 1997.
3e Biennale de Lyon: Interactivité…, Lyon, 1995.
Acconci Studio, Centro Galego de arte contemporánea, Santiago de Compostela, 1996.
Vito Acconci: House of Streets, Parks and Plazas, Le Consortium, Centre d'art contemporain, Dijon, 1994.

Selected Bibliography
ACCONCI Vito, SCHACHTER Kenny, PFAFF Lilian, BECHTLER Cristina, *Art Becomes Architecture Becomes Art: A Conversation Betweeen Vito Acconci and Kenny Schachter*. Vienna; New York: Springer, 2006.
KARDON Janet, *Time*. Philadelphia: Philadelphia College of Art, 1977.
KIRSHNER Judith R., *Vito Acconci: A Retrospective, 1969 to 1980*. Chicago: Museum of Contemporary Art, 1980.
LINKER Kate, *Vito Acconci*. New York: Rizzoli, 1994.
MOORE Gloria, ACCONCI Vito, *Vito Acconci: Writings, Works, Projects*. Barcelona: Polígrafa, 2001 (20_21 Collection).
VAN ASSCHE Christine [ed.], *Temps de vídeo: 1965–2005*. Barcelona: Fundació La Caixa, 2006; *New Media Collection: 1965–2005, Centre Pompidou*. Taipei: Taipei Fine Arts Museum, 2006; *New Media Collection/Installations: 1965–2005*. Paris: Editions du Centre Pompidou, 2006.
WARD Frazer, TAYLOR C. Mark, BLOOMER Jennifer, *Vito Acconci*. London: Phaidon, 2002 (Contemporary artists).

Sonia ANDRADE
Born in 1935 in Rio de Janeiro, Brazil
Lives and works in Rio de Janeiro, Brazil

Selected Solo Exhibitions
Museu de arte moderna, Rio de Janeiro: *Conjunto de cinco vídeo-intalações*, 1999 | *Situações Negativas*, 1984 | *A Caça*, 1978 | *Instalação*, 1976.
Museu de arte contemporânea da Universidade de São Paulo, Sao Paulo: *Hydragrammas*, 1994 | *8 Vídeos de Sonia Andrade*, 1977.

Selected Bibliography
FIGUEIREDO Luciano, *Sonia Andrade: Videos 2005–1974*. Rio de Janeiro: Centro Cultural Banco do Brazil, 2005.

HAUSER Andreas, *8 videos de Sonia Andrade*. Sao Paulo: Museu de arte contemporanea, 1977.

ARAHMAIANI
Born in 1961 in Bandung, Indonesia
Lives and works in Jakarta and Yogyakarta, Indonesia

Selected Exhibitions
Contemporareity: Contemporary Art of Indonesia, MOCA Shanghai, Shanghai, 2010.
Global Feminisms, Brooklyn Museum of Art, New York, 2007.
50th Biennale di Venezia: Delays and Revolutions, Venice, 2003.
4th Gwangju Biennale: PAUSE, Gwangju, 2002.
5e Biennale de Lyon: Partage d'exotismes, Lyon, 2000.
2nd Asia Pacific Triennial of Contemporary Art, Brisbane, 1996.

Selected Bibliography
LUCIE-SMITH Edward, *Art Tomorrow*. Paris: Editions Pierre Terrail, 2002.
SUPANGKAT Jim, "Contemporary Art in Indonesia: Development beyond the 1970s". In *Art in Southeast Asia, 1997: Glimpses into the Future* edited by Kumagi Isao. Tokyo: Museum of Contemporary Art, 1997.
POSHYANANDA Apinan, "Roaring Tigers, Desperate Dragons in Transition" In *Contemporary Art in Asia: Traditions/Tensions*. New York: Asia Society, 1996.

Samuel BECKETT
Born in 1906 in Dublin, Ireland
Died in 1989 in Paris, France

Selected Exhibitions
Sounds, Kunst-Neue Musik, Neue Berliner Kunstverein, Berlin, 2010.
Samuel Beckett, Musée national d'art moderne-Centre de création industrielle, Centre Pompidou, Paris, 2007.
A Theater without Theater, Museu d'art contemporani, Barcelona, 2007.
Lights, Cameras, Action: Artists' Films for the Cinema, Whitney Museum of American Art, New York, 2007.
Corps étrangers, Musée du Louvre, Paris, 2006–07.
Temps de vídeo: 1965–2005, Fundació La Caixa, Barcelona, 2005–06.
Samuel Beckett, Bruce Nauman, Kunsthalle, Vienna, 2000.
Voilà, Le monde dans la tête, Musée d'art moderne de la Ville de Paris, Paris, 2000.

Selected Bibliography
DOUGLAS Stan [ed.], *Samuel Beckett, Teleplays*. Vancouver: Vancouver Art Gallery, 1988.
VAN ASSCHE Christine [ed.], *Temps de vídeo: 1965–2005*. Barcelona: Fundació La Caixa, 2006; *New Media Collection: 1965–2005, Centre Pompidou*. Taipei: Taipei Fine Arts Museum, 2006.

Louidgi BELTRAME
Born in 1971 in Marseilles, France
Lives and works in Paris, France

Selected Exhibitions
Louidgi Beltrame: Energodar, Fondation d'entreprise Ricard, Paris, 2010.
Project Room, Musée d'art moderne et contemporain, Strasbourg, 2008.
The City as a Script, Pinchuk Art Center, Kiev, 2007.
'Ondas Tropicais', Les Nuits Tropicales, Palais de Tokyo, Paris, 2006.

Selected Bibliography
BEAUSSE Pascal, STEELE Lisa, BELTRAME Louidgi, *Louidgi Beltrame, 2000–2005, 53 Stills, 3 Drawings, 72 Pages*. Toronto: Vtapes; Paris: AFAA, 2005.
JAVAULT Patrick, "Coïncidence des plans". In *Louidgi Beltrame*. Strasbourg: Musée d'art moderne et contemporain, 2008.

Peter CAMPUS
Born in 1937 in New York, USA
Lives and works in New York, USA,

Selected Exhibitions
Peter Campus: Optiks, BFI Southbank Gallery, London, 2009–10.
Edge of the Ocean: Video Work by Peter Campus, 1970–2008, Parrish Art Museum, New York, 2007–08.
Balance and Power: Performance and Surveillance in Video Art, Rose Art Museum, Brandeis University, Waltham, Massachusetts, 2006.
Temps de vídeo: 1965–2005, Fundació La Caixa, Barcelona, 2005–06.
Peter Campus, Bohen Foundation, New York, 1996.
Projects: Peter Campus, Museum of Modern Art, New York, 1976.

Selected Bibliography
CAMPUS Peter, HERZOGENRATH Wulf, SMITH Roberta, *Peter Campus, Video-Installationen, Foto-Installationen, Fotos, Videobänder*. Cologne: Kölnischer Kunstverein, 1979.
Peter Campus: Analog + Digital Video + Foto 1970–2003. Bremen, Kunsthalle 2003.
RUSH Michael, "Peter Campus at Leslie Tonkonow", *Art in America*. May 2006, 168.
VAN ASSCHE Christine [ed.], *Temps de vídeo: 1965–2005*. Barcelona: Fundació La Caixa, 2006; *New Media Collection: 1965–2005, Centre Pompidou*. Taipei: Taipei Fine Arts Museum, 2006; *New Media Collection/Installations: 1965–2005*. Paris: Editions du Centre Pompidou, 2006.

Keith DEVERELL
Born in 1976 in Saint Helier, Jersey
Lives and works in Melbourne, Australia

Selected Exhibitions
SONE Residency and Performance, The Bundanon Trust Artist in Residence Program, Bundanon, 2010.
Rear Window, Melbourne Laneways Commission, Melbourne, 2009.

Selected Bibliography
WILSON Catherine, "The Haunting Cry of the Street Hawker", *The Jakarta Post*. Indonesia: January 2010. Accessed 23 January 2010. http://www.thejakartapost.com/news/2010/11/01/the-haunting-cry-street-hawker.html.
TOFTS Darren, *Capturing the Art of Living*. Melbourne: Melbourne Laneways Commission, 2009.

Valie EXPORT
Born in 1940 in Linz, Austria
Lives and works in Vienna, Austria and Cologne, Germany

Selected Exhibitions
Fresh Hell: Carte Blanche à Adam McEwen, Palais de Tokyo, Paris, 2010–11.
Donna: Feminist Avant-Garde of the 1970s, Galleria nazionale d'arte moderna, Rome, 2010.
Waiting for Video: Works from the 1960s to Today, National Museum of Modern Art, Tokyo, 2009.
Held Together with Water, Istanbul Museum of Modern Art, Istanbul, 2008–09.
Feedback: The Video Data Bank, Video Art and Artist Interview, Museum of Modern Art, New York, 2007.
Temps de vídeo: 1965–2005, Fundació La Caixa, Barcelona, 2005–06.
Valie Export: Eine Werkschau, Kunst der Gegenwart, Sammlung Essl, Vienna, 2005.
Split: Reality, Museum moderner Kunst, Vienna, 1997.

Selected Bibliography
Auf den Lieb geschrieben, Vienna, Kunsthalle, 1995.
VAN ASSCHE Christine [ed.], *Temps de vídeo: 1965–2005*. Barcelona: Fundació La Caixa, 2006; *New Media Collection: 1965–2005, Centre Pompidou*. Taipei: Taipei Fine Arts Museum, 2006.

Jean-Luc GODARD
Born in 1930 in Paris, France
Lives and works in Rolle, Switzerland and Paris, France

Selected Retrospective Projections & Exhibitions
Paradise Now! Essential French Avant-garde Cinema, 1890–2008, Tate Modern, London, 2008.
Forever Godard, Centre Georges Pompidou, Paris, 2006.
Temps de vídeo: 1965–2005, Fundació La Caixa, Barcelona, 2005–06.
Godard: A Portrait of the Artist at 70, Museum of Modern Art, New York, 2004.
Jean-Luc Godard, les essais, Galerie nationale du Jeu de Paume, Paris, 1997.
Jean-Luc Godard, une rétrospective des films et vidéos de Godard depuis 1974, Museum of Modern Art, New York, 1992.

Selected Bibliography
BERGALA Alain [ed.], *Jean-Luc Godard par Jean-Luc Godard*. Paris: Cahiers du cinéma, 1998.
GODARD Jean-Luc, *Introduction à une véritable histoire du cinéma; Volume 1*. Paris : Albatros, 1986 (ça cinéma; 22).
KAGANSKI Serge, LALANNE Jean-Marc, GODARD Jean-Luc, "Le droit d'auteur ? Un auteur n'a que des devoirs". *Les Inrockuptibles*, May 2010, xvii–xxii.
MacCABE Colin, *Godard, Images, Sounds, Politics*. Bloomington: Indiana University Press, 1980.

MUSSMAN Toby [ed.], *Jean-Luc Godard, A Critical Anthology*. New York: E.P. Dutton, 1986.
TOWNSEND Chris, "Jean-Luc Godard, Centre Pompidou, Paris May 11 to August 14", *Art Monthly*, September 2006, 45.
VAN ASSCHE Christine [ed.], *Temps de vídeo: 1965–2005*. Barcelona: Fundació La Caixa, 2006; *New Media Collection: 1965–2005, Centre Pompidou*. Taipei: Taipei Fine Arts Museum, 2006.

Dan GRAHAM
Born in 1942 in Urbana, USA
Lives and works in New York, USA

Selected Exhibitions
Dan Graham: Beyond, Museum of Contemporary Art, Los Angeles, 2009.
Waiting for Video, Works from the 1960s to Today, National Museum of Modern Art, Tokyo, 2009.
The Art of Participation, 1950 to Now, San Francisco Museum of Modern Art, San Francisco, 2009.
Mapping the City, Stedelijk Museum, Amsterdam, 2007.
Temps de vídeo: 1965–2005, Fundació La Caixa, Barcelona, 2005–06.
Dan Graham: Oeuvres 1965–2000, Museu de arte contemporanea de Serralves, Porto, 2001.
Dan Graham: Architecture, Camden Arts Centre, London, 1997.
Dan Graham, Centro Galego de arte contemporánea, Santiago de Compostela, 1997.

Selected Bibliography
BUCHLOH B.H.D., *Video-Architecture-Television*. Halifax: Press of the Nova Scotia College of Art & Design; New York: New York University Press, 1979.
GRAHAM Dan, BRUYN Eric de, BUCHLOH B.H.D., DE DUVE Thierry, *Dan Graham, catalogue raisonné Works 1965–2000*. Dusseldorf: Richter, 2001.
GRAHAM Dan, *Rock My Religion*. Villeurbanne: Le Nouveau Musée; Dijon: Les Presses du Réel, 1993 (Ecrits d'artistes).
GRAHAM Dan, *Ma position, écrits sur mes œuvres*. Villeurbanne: Le Nouveau Musée; Dijon: Les Presses du Réel, 1992 (Ecrits d'artistes).
GRAHAM Dan, FUCHS R.H., BUCHLOH B.H.D., HERBERT A., *Dan Graham, Articles*. Eindhoven: Stedelijk Van Abbemuseum, 1978.
MOURE Gloria, VAN ASSCHE Christine, *Dan Graham*. Santiago de Compostela: Centro Galego de arte contemporánea, 1997.
VAN ASSCHE Christine [ed.], *Temps de vídeo: 1965–2005*. Barcelona: Fundació La Caixa, 2006; *New Media Collection: 1965–2005, Centre Pompidou*. Taipei: Taipei Fine Arts Museum, 2006; *New Media Collection/Installations: 1965–2005*. Paris: Editions du Centre Pompidou, 2006.

Johan GRIMONPREZ
Born in 1962 in Roeselare, Belgium
Lives and works in New York, USA and Ghent, Belgium

Selected Exhibitions
Dial H-I-S-T-O-R-Y, Hammer Museum, Los Angeles, 2008.
Looking for Alfred, Retrospektive 1992–2007, Pinakothek der Moderne, Sammlung moderne Kunst, Munich, 2007.
Temps de vídeo: 1965–2005, Fundació La Caixa, Barcelona, 2005–06.

Inflight! Stedelijk Museum voor Actuele Kunst, Ghent, 2000.
Prends garde ! A jouer au fantôme on le devient, Musée national d'art moderne, Centre Georges Pompidou, Paris, 1997.

Selected Bibliography
BODE Steven [ed.], *Johan Grimonprez, Looking for Alfred*. London: Film and Video Umbrella; Ostfildern: Hatje Cantz, 2007.
BONAMI Francesco, OBRIST Hans-Ulrich, GRIMONPREZ Johan, *Sogni=Dreams, 48th Biennale d'arte di Venezia*. Fondazione Sandretto Rebaudengo per l'arte Rome: Castelvecchi Arte, 1999.
GRIMONPREZ Johan [ed.], *Inflight*. Ostfildern-Ruit: Hatje Cantz, 2000.
GRIMONPREZ Johan, TAYLOR Simon, *Johan Grimonprez*. Brussels: Société des expositions du Palais des beaux-arts, 1994.
VAN ASSCHE Christine [ed.], *Temps de vídeo: 1965–2005*. Barcelona: Fundació La Caixa, 2006; *New Media Collection: 1965–2005, Centre Pompidou*. Taipei: Taipei Fine Arts Museum, 2006; *New Media Collection/Installations: 1965–2005*. Paris: Editions du Centre Pompidou, 2006.

Pierre HUYGHE
Born in 1962 in Antony, France
Lives and works in New York, USA and Paris, France

Selected Exhibitions
Pierre Huyghe: La estación de las fiestas = La saison des fêtes, Museo nacional Centro de arte Reina Sofía, Madrid, 2010.
Pierre Huyghe: Live Show as Exhibition, Reykjavik Art Museum, Reykjavik, 2007.
Pierre Huyghe: Je donne une règle du jeu, Musée d'art moderne de la Ville de Paris, Paris, 2006.
Pierre Huyghe: Celebration Park, Tate Modern, London, 2006.
Temps de vídeo: 1965–2005, Fundació La Caixa, Barcelona, 2005–06.
Pierre Huyghe: Streamside Day, Irish Museum of Modern Art, Dublin, 2005.
Pierre Huyghe: Float, Castello di Rivoli, Museo d'arte contemporanea, Rivoli, 2004.
Pierre Huyghe: Streamside Day Follies, Dia Art Foundation, Chelsea, 2003.
Pierre Huyghe: Les Grandes Ensembles, Modern Art Museum of Fort Worth, Fort Worth, 2003.
Pierre Huyghe: The Third Memory, Musée national d'art moderne, Paris, 2000.

Selected Bibliography
CHRISTOV-BAKARGIEV Carolyn, *Pierre Huyghe*. Castello di Rivoli: Museo d'arte contemporanea; Rivoli: Skira, 2004.
DEITCH Jeffrey [ed.], *Form Follows Fiction*. Rivoli: Museo d'arte contemporanea; Milan: Charta, 2001.
HUYGHE Pierre, PARRENO Philippe [ed.], *No Ghost Just a Shell*. Eindhoven: Van Abbemuseum, 2003.
VAN ASSCHE Christine, MASSÉRA, Jean-Charles, *Pierre Huyghe, The Third Memory*. Paris: Musée national d'art moderne; Editions du Centre Pompidou; Chicago: Renaissance Society at the University of Chicago, 2000.
VAN ASSCHE Christine [ed.], *Temps de vídeo: 1965–2005*. Barcelona: Fundació La Caixa, 2006; *New Media Collection:*

1965–2005, Centre Pompidou. Taipei: Taipei Fine Arts Museum, 2006; *New Media Collection/Installations: 1965–2005*. Paris: Editions du Centre Pompidou, 2006.

Mako IDEMITSU

Born in 1940 in Tokyo, Japan
Lives and works in Tokyo, Japan

Selected Exhibitions

elles@centrepompidou, Musée national d'art moderne-Centre de création industrielle, Centre Pompidou, Paris, 2009.
Modern Means, Mori Art Museum, Tokyo, 2004.
Image & Gender: The World of Mako Idemitsu, Waseda University, Tokyo, 2002.
Video Viewpoints, Museum of Modern Art, New York, 1986.

Selected Bibliography

BUTLER Cornelia, MARK Lisa Gabrielle, *WACK! Art and the Feminist Revolution*. Los Angeles: Museum of Contemporary Art; Cambridge: MIT Press, 2007.

Isaac JULIEN

Born in 1960 in Bow, UK
Lives and works in London, UK

Selected Exhibitions

Afro Modern, Tate Liverpool, Liverpool, 2010.
Lights, Cameras, Action: Artists' Films for the Cinema, Whitney Museum of American Art, New York, 2007.
Currents 99: Isaac Julien, Saint Louis Art Museum, Saint Louis, 2006–07.
The Secret Public: The Last Days of the British Underground 1978–1988, Kunstverein, Munich, 2006.
Temps de vídeo: 1965–2005, Fundació La Caixa, Barcelona, 2005–06.
Isaac Julien, Musée national d'art moderne-Centre de création industrielle, Centre Pompidou, Paris, 2005.
Isaac Julien: Paradise Omeros, Three and Frantz Fanon, Museum Boijmans Van Beuningen, Rotterdam, 2004.
Isaac Julien: Baltimore and Paradise Omeros, Artpace San Antonio, San Antonio, 2003.

Selected Bibliography

Isaac Julien. Montreal: Musée d'art contemporain, 2004.
Turner Prize, London, Tate Gallery, 2001.
ENWEZOR Okwui, BASUALDO Carlos [ed.], texts by FLORES Juan, HALL Stuart, JULIEN Isaac, et al., *Creolite and Creolization*, Documenta 11_Platform 3. Kassel: Documenta, 2002.
JULIEN Isaac, NASH M., VERGÈS F., *Frantz Fanon, peau noire, masque blanc*. Paris: K Films Edition, 1998.
VAN ASSCHE Christine, ZABUNYAN Elvan, VERGÈS Françoise, *Isaac Julien*. Paris: Musée national d'art moderne; Editions du Centre Pompidou, 2005.
VAN ASSCHE Christine [ed.], *Temps de vídeo: 1965–2005*. Barcelona: Fundació La Caixa, 2006; *New Media Collection: 1965–2005, Centre Pompidou*. Taipei: Taipei Fine Arts Museum, 2006; *New Media Collection/Installations: 1965–2005*. Paris : Editions du Centre Pompidou, 2006.

Sonia KHURANA

Born in 1968 in Saharanpur, India
Lives and works in New Delhi, India

Selected Exhibitions

Aichi Triennale 2010, Nagoya, 2010.
elles@centrepompidou, Musée national d'art moderne-Centre de création industrielle, Centre Pompidou, Paris, 2009.
7th Gwangju Biennale: Annual Report: A Year in Exhibitions, Gwangju, 2008.
Horn Please, Narratives in Contemporary Indian Art, Kunstmuseum, Bern, 2007.
Global Feminisms, Brooklyn Museum of Art, New York, 2007.

Selected Bibliography

MATT Gerald, FITZ Angelika, WÖRGÖTTER Michael, *Kapital & Karma, aktuelle Positionen indischer Kunst = Kapital & Karma, Recent Positions in Indian Art*. Vienna: Kunsthalle; Ostfildern-Ruit: Hatje Cantz, 2002.

Thierry KUNTZEL

Born in 1948 in Bergerac, France
Died in 2007 in Paris, France

Selected Exhibitions

L'opera video di Thierry Kuntzel, proiezioni e installazione, Académie de France à Rome, Villa Medicis, Rome, 2008.
In Memoriam: Thierry Kuntzel (1948–2007), Museum of Modern Art, New York, 2007.
Thierry Kuntzel: Lumières du temps, Musée des beaux-arts, Nantes, 2006.
Temps de vídeo: 1965–2005, Fundació La Caixa, Barcelona, 2005–06.
Thierry Kuntzel: Rétrospective, Galerie nationale du Jeu de Paume, Paris, 1993.
Projects 29: Thierry Kuntzel, Museum of Modern Art, New York, 1991.

Selected Bibliography

DUGUET Anne-Marie, *Thierry Kuntzel*. Paris: Galerie nationale du Jeu de Paume, 1993.
GUIBERT Hervé, *Thierry Kuntzel*. Dunkerque: Ecole régionale des beaux-arts Georges Pompidou, 1991.
KUNTZEL Thierry, *Title TK* [+ DVD] / edited by Anne-Marie DUGUET, texts by Raymond BELLOUR, Anne-Marie DUGUET, Jean-Paul FARGIER, et al., Paris: Les Presses du réel; Nantes: Musée des beaux-arts, 2006 (Anarchive).
KUNTZEL Thierry, DUGUET Anne-Marie, *Title TK: notes 1974–1992*. Paris: Anarchive; Nantes: Musée des beaux-arts, 2006.
VAN ASSCHE Christine, DUGUET Anne-Marie, KUNTZEL Thierry, *Nostos II de Thierry Kuntzel*. Paris: Musée national d'art moderne, Centre Georges Pompidou, 1984.
VAN ASSCHE Christine [ed.], *Temps de vídeo: 1965–2005*. Barcelona: Fundació La Caixa, 2006; *New Media Collection: 1965–2005, Centre Pompidou*. Taipei: Taipei Fine Arts Museum, 2006; *New Media Collection/ Installations: 1965–2005*. Paris: Editions du Centre Pompidou, 2006.

Dinh Q. LÊ

Born in 1968 in Ha Tien, Vietnam
Lives and works in Ho Chi Minh City, Vietnam

Selected Exhibitions

Project 93: Dinh Q. Lê, Museum of Modern Art, New York, 2010.

7th Busan Biennale: Living in Evolution, Busan, 2010.
4th Fukuoka Asian Art Triennale: Live and Let Live: Creators of Tomorrow, Fukuoka, 2009.
5th Asia Pacific Triennial, Brisbane, 2006.
50th Biennale di Venezia: Delays and Revolutions, Venice, 2003.

Selected Bibliography

CATALANI Stefano, MONROE Michael, NGUYEN Viet Thanh ROTH Moira, *A Tapestry of Memories: The Art of Dinh Q. Lê.* Bellevue: Bellevue Arts Museum, 2007.
CHIU Melissa, *Vietnam: Destination for the New Millenium; The Art of Dinh Q. Lê.* New York: Asia Society Museum, 2005.
MILES Chris, LÊ Dinh Q., ROTH Mara, *Dinh Q. Lê: From Vietnam to Hollywood*, Seattle: Marquand Books, 2003.

LEE Wen

Born in 1957 in Singapore, Singapore
Lives and works in Singapore, Singapore and Tokyo, Japan

Selected Exhibitions

The Artists Village: 20 Years On, Singapore Art Museum, Singapore, 2008.
Inward Gazes: Documentaries of Performance Art in China & Asia, Macao Museum of Art, Macao, 2008.
Made In China, Louisiana Museum of Modern Art, Humlebæk, 2007.
Situations, Museum of Contemporary Art, Sydney, 2005.
Rencontre international d'art performance et multimédia, Quebec, 1996.
5th Fukui International Video Biennale, Fukui, 1993.

Selected Bibliography

LEE Wen, *A Waking Dream: Drawings and Poetry.* Singapore: Select Books, 1981.
LEE Weng Choy, "Artist Essay on Lee Wen". In *3rd Asia Pacific Triennal of Contemporary Art*. Brisbane: Queensland Art Gallery, 1999.
NADARAJAN Gunalan, STORER Russell, TAN Eugene, *Contemporary Art in Singapore*. Singapore: Institute of Contemporary Arts; Singapore: LASALLE, 2007.
WOON Tien Wei, "Between Journeys: an Interview with Lee Wen". *Performance Research: A Journal of the Performing Arts*, 6 (I), 2001: 3–7.

Christelle LHEUREUX

Born in 1972 in Bolbec, France
Lives and works in Paris, France and Geneva, Switzerland

Selected Exhibitions

Pourquoi attendre ? Fonds André Iten, Centre d'Art Contemporain, Geneva, 2009.
7th Gwangju Biennale: Annual Report: A Year in Exhibitions, Gwangju, 2008.
International Triennale of Contemporary Art: *Re-reading the future*, Prague, 2008.
Playback, Musée d'art moderne de la Ville de Paris, Paris, 2007–08.
Biennale de Lyon, Lyon, 2007.

Selected Bibliography

International Incheon Women Artists' Biennale. Incheon: Unchein Metropolitan City, 2007.

LHEUREUX Christelle with WEERASETHAKUL Apichatpong, *La force de l'art, Je ne crois pas aux fantômes*. Paris: Galeries nationales du Grand Palais, 2006.

LIU Wei

Born in 1965 in Beijing, China
Lives and works in Beijing, China

Selected Exhibions

Rotating Views #1, Astrup Fearnley Collection, Astrup Fearnley Museum of Modern Art, Oslo, 2009.
China Now, Cobra Museum voor Moderne Kunst, Amstelveen, 2007–08.
Over One Billion Served: Conceptual Photography from the People's Republic of China, Asian Civilisations Museum, Singapore, 2005.
Between Past and Future, New Photography and Video from China, International Center of Photography, New York, 2004.
New Urbanism – Contemporary Art Project, Guangdong Museum of Art, Guangzhou, 2002.

Selected Bibliography

Thermocline of Art: New Asian Waves. Karlsruhe: ZKM, Zentrum für Kunst und Medientechnologie, 2007.
Kasseler Video-und DokumentarFilmFestival. Kassel: Kasseler Video-und DokumentarFilmFestival, 2005.

Joan LOGUE

Born in 1942 in McKeesport, USA
Lives and works in New York, USA

Selected Solo Exhibitions

Documenta 8, Documenta, Kassel, 1987.
Video Portrait Gallery, Centre Pompidou, Paris, 1981.
John Cage: Video Portrait, Walker Art Institute, Minneapolis; Anthology Film Archives, New York, 1980.
Video Portraits from California, Museum of Modern Art, New York, 1978.

Selected Bibliography

Documenta 8. Kassel: Documenta 8, 1987.
Southland Video Anthology 1976–1977. Long Beach: Long Beach Museum of Art, 1977.

Documentary Film

Monory, Editions du Centre Pompidou, Paris, 1983.

Sue McCAULEY

Born in 1955 in Sydney, Australia
Lives and works in Melbourne, Australia

Selected Exhibitions

re_VISION (with Olaf Meyer), Australian Centre for the Moving Image, Melbourne, 2003.
Antarctica: Secrets of the Frozen World, Museum of Victoria, Melbourne; Tasmania Museum and Art Gallery, Hobart, 1992.

Selected Bibliography

TOFTS Darren, *Capturing the Art of Living*. Melbourne: Melbourne Laneways Commission, 2009.

Chris MARKER

Born in 1921 in Neuilly-sur-Seine, France
Lives and works in Paris, France

Selected Exhibitions
Chris Marker: Abschied vom Kino, Museum für Gestaltung, Zurich, 2008.
Paradise Now! Essential French Avant-garde Cinema, 1890–2008, Tate Modern, London, 2008.
Temps de vídeo: 1965–2005, Fundació La Caixa, Barcelona, 2005–06.
Chris Marker: Chats perchés, Centre Pompidou, Paris, 2005.
Chris Marker: Owls at Noon Prelude: The Hollow Men, Museum of Modern Art, New York, 2005.
Chris Marker, Fundació Antoni Tàpies, Barcelona, 1999.
Chris Marker: Silent Movie 1994–1995, Museum of Modern Art, New York, 1995.

Selected Bibliography
ALTER Nora, *Chris Marker*. Urbana; Chicago: University of Illinois Press, 2006.
BAMCHADE Pourvali, *Chris Marker*. Paris: SCEREN-CNDP; Cahiers du cinéma, 2003 (Collection pédagigique, Les petits cahiers).
BAZIN André, BELLOUR Raymond, BLÜMINGER Christa, et al., *Chris Marker, retorno a la inmemoria del cineasta*. Valencia: Ediciones de la Mirada, 2000.
EXPÓSITO Marcello, *Chris Marker, José Val del Omar*. Séville: Centro andaluz de arte contemporáneo, 1999.
KÄMPER Birgit, TODE Thomas, *Chris Marker, Filmessayist*. Munich: CICIM, 1997.
HARBORD, Janet, *Chris Marker: La Jetée*. London: Afterall Publishing, 2009.
LAMBERT Arnaud, *Also Known as Chris Marker*. Laon: Editions Le Point du jour, 2008 (Le champ photographique).
LUPTON Catherine, *Chris Marker, Memories of the Future*. London: Reaktion Books, 2005.
VAN ASSCHE Christine [ed.], *Temps de vídeo: 1965–2005*. Barcelona: Fundació La Caixa, 2006; *New Media Collection: 1965–2005. Centre Pompidou*, Taipei: Taipei Fine Arts Museum, 2006; *New Media Collection/Installations: 1965–2005*. Paris: Editions du Centre Pompidou, 2006.

CD-ROM
MARKER Chris, *Immemory* / Pref. Christine VAN ASSCHE, Paris, Centre Pompidou, 1998.

Toshio MATSUMOTO

Born in 1932 in Nagoya, Japan
Lives and works in Tokyo, Japan

Selected Filmography
Dogura Magura, 1988; *War at the Age of Sixteen*, 1973; *Demons*, 1971; *Funeral Parade of Roses*, 1969.

Selected Experimental & Documentary Short Films
Disguise, 1992; *Sign*, 1990; *Trauma*, 1989; *Engram*, 1987; *EE Control, Vibration, Sway*, 1985; *Wawe, Delay Exposure*, 1984; *Formation*, 1983; *Votive Picture, Relation, Shift*, 1982; *Connection*, 1981; *Ki-Breathing*, 1980; *White Hole*, 1979; *Enigma*, 1978; *Black Hole*, 1977; *Kite*, 1976; *Everything Visible Is Empty, Young Girl, Phantom, Atman*, 1975.

Selected Bibliography
GEROW Aaron, "Matsumoto Toshio", *Documentarists of Japan, n. 9, Matsumoto Toshio*. Accessed 22 November 2010. http://www.yidff.jp/docbox/9/box9-2-e.html.

Ko NAKAJIMA

Born in 1941 in Tokyo, Japan
Lives and works in Tokyo, Japan

Selected Exhibitions
Video Art 1966–1996: Il Tempo, la Luce, la Materia, Museo Cantonale d'arte, Lugano, 1996.
The Arts for Television, Contemporary Arts Museum, Houston, 1989.
Western Front Video, Musée d´art contemporain, Montreal, 1984.

Selected Bibliography
FARGIER Jean-Paul, GATTINONI Christian, et al., *Esprits de sel, patrimoine photographique, photographies de François Sagnes, travaux vidéo de Ko Nakajima*. Montpellier: Frac Languedoc-Roussillon, 1992.

Bruce NAUMAN

Born in 1941 in Fort Wayne, USA
Lives and works in Galisteo, USA

Selected Exhibitions
A Rose Has No Teeth: Bruce Nauman in the 60s, University of California, Berkeley Art Museum, Berkeley, 2007.
Bruce Nauman: Make Me Think Me, Tate Liverpool, Liverpool, 2006.
Temps de vídeo: 1965–2005, Fundació La Caixa, Barcelona, 2005–06.
Bruce Nauman: Raw Materials, Tate Modern, London, 2005.
Bruce Nauman: Mapping the Studio I (Fat Chance John Cage), DIA Center for the Arts, New York, 2002.
Bruce Nauman: Image-Texte, 1966–1996, Musée national d'art moderne, Centre Georges Pompidou, Paris, 1997.
Bruce Nauman: Work from 1965 to 1986, Los Angeles County Museum of Art, Los Angeles, 1986.
Bruce Nauman: Neons, Baltimore Museum of Art, Baltimore, 1982–83.

Selected Bibliography
CROSS Susan, *Bruce Nauman, Theaters of Experience*. Berlin: Deutsche Guggenheim; New York: Guggenheim Museum Publ., 2003.
GLASMEIER Michael, HOFFMANN Christine, FOLIR Sabine, HARTEL Gaby, MATT Gerald, *Samuel Beckett, Bruce Nauman*. Vienna: Kunsthalle, 2000.
VAN ASSCHE Christine, *Bruce Nauman : Image-Texte, 1966–1996*. Paris: Musée national d'art moderne; Editions du Centre Pompidou, 1997–98.
VAN ASSCHE Christine [ed.], *Temps de vídeo: 1965–2005*. Barcelona: Fundació La Caixa, 2006; *New Media Collection: 1965–2005, Centre Pompidou*. Taipei: Taipei Fine Arts Museum, 2006; *New Media Collection/Installations: 1965–2005*. Paris: Editions du Centre Pompidou, 2006.

Jun NGUYEN-HATSUSHIBA

Born in 1968 in Tokyo, Japan
Lives and works in Ho Chi Minh City, Vietnam

Selected Exhibitions

Jun Nguyen-Hatsushiba, Kunstmuseum, Lucerne, 2007.
MAM Project 002, Mori Art Museum, Tokyo, 2004.
Jun Nguyen-Hatsushiba, Museo d'arte contemporanea Roma, Rome, 2003–04.
Matrix Program 2003, UC Berkley Art Museum, Berkeley, 2003.
Jun Nguyen-Hatsushiba, New Museum of Contemporary Art, New York, 2003.
Biennale de Lyon, Lyon, *Moscow Biennale of Contemporary Art*, Moscow, *51st Biennale di Venezia: The Experience of Art*, Venice, 2005.
Busan Biennale, Busan, *Tel Aviv Biennale*, *Bienal de São Paulo*, Sao Paulo, 2002.

Selected Bibliography

CAMERON Dan, GRAMBYE Lars, LIEW Fredrik, *Jun Nguyen-Hatsushiba*. Malmo: Malmo Konsthall, 2005.
CHRISTOV-BAKARGIEV Carolyn, HUBERMAN Anthony, GIANELLI Ida, *I Moderni = the Moderns*. Rivoli: Castello di Rivoli, Museo d'arte contemporanea, 2003.
HASEGAWA Yuko [ed.], *Jun Nguyen-Hatsushiba*, MACRO. Rome: Museo d'arte contemporanea, 2003.
KATAOKA Mami, VILIANI Andrea, TOMISAWA Haruko, *Jun Nguyen-Hatsushiba, MAM project 002*. Tokyo: Mori Art Museum, 2004.
VAN ASSCHE Christine [ed.], *New Media Collection/Installations: 1965–2005*. Paris: Editions du Centre Pompidou, 2006.

MEAS Sokhorn

Born in 1977 in Kandal, Cambodia
Lives and works in Phnom Penh, Cambodia

Selected Exhibitions

Meas Sokhorn: Trash-Fix, Centre Culturel Français Cambodge, Phnom Penh, 2010.
Global Hybrid II, Hancock University, Los Angeles, 2010.
Signature Art Prize, Singapore Art Museum, Singapore, 2008.
Surfacing, Sala Artspace, Phnom Penh, 2007.

Selected Bibiliography

VACHON Michelle, *Shaping the Arts*. Phnom Penh: Southeast Asia Globe, 2010.
MELLEN Greg, *Show Features Cambodian Artists*. Long Beach: Long Beach Press Telegram, 2010.

Tony OURSLER

Born in 1957 in New York, USA
Lives and works in New York, USA

Selected Exhibitions

Tony Oursler: LOCK 2,4,6, KUB, Kunsthaus, Bregenz, 2009–10.
Temps de vídeo: 1965–2005, Fundació La Caixa, Barcelona, 2005–06.
Tony Oursler at Art Museum Tennis Palace, Helsinki City Art Museum, Helsinki, 2005–06.
Tony Oursler: Dispositifs, Galerie nationale du Jeu de Paume, Paris, 2005.
Tony Oursler: Unk, Kunsthaus, Aahrus, 2004.
Tony Oursler: Station, Magasin 3: Stockholm Konstall, Stockholm, 2002.
Tony Oursler: the Influence Machine, Madison Square Park, New York; Soho Square, London, 2000.
Sphères d'influences: Tony Oursler, Musée national d'art moderne, Paris, 1985–86.

Selected Bibliography

Tony Oursler, capc. Bordeaux: Musée d'art contemporain, 1997.
JANUS Elizabeth [ed.], BELLOUR Raymond, CONRAD Tony, DEJONG Constance, *Tony Oursler*. Barcelona: Polígrafa; Valencia: IVAM, Instituto valenciano de arte moderno, 2001.
VAN ASSCHE Christine [ed.], Paul ARDENNE, Raymond BELLOUR, Tony OURSLER, *Tony Oursler*. Paris: Galerie nationale du Jeu de Paume; Flammarion, 2005.
VAN ASSCHE Christine [ed.], *Temps de vídeo: 1965–2005*. Barcelona: Fundació La Caixa, 2006; *New Media Collection: 1965–2005, Centre Pompidou*. Taipei: Taipei Fine Arts Museum, 2006; *New Media Collection/Installations: 1965–2005*. Paris: Editions du Centre Pompidou, 2006.

Nam June PAIK

Born in 1932 in Seoul, South Korea
Died in 2006 in Miami, USA

Selected Exhibitions

Nam June Paik: Video Artist, Performance Artist, Composer & Visionary, Tate Liverpool, Liverpool, 2010–11.
Paik 'n' Paik, Stiftung Museum Kunst Palast, Dusseldorf, 2010.
Bye Bye, Nam June Paik, Watarium Museum of Contemporary Art, Tokyo, 2006.
In memoriam, Museum of Modern Art, New York, 2006.
Temps de vídeo: 1965–2005, Fundació La Caixa, Barcelona, 2005–06.
Sons et lumières: une histoire de son dans l'art du 20ème siècle, Musée national d'art moderne, Centre Georges Pompidou, Paris, 2004.
Nam June Paik: Fluxus und Video Skulptur, Wilhelm-Lehmbruck-Museum, Duisburg, 2002.
The World of Nam June Paik, Guggenheim Museum, New York, 2000.
Nam June Paik, Fluxus-Video, Kunsthalle, Bremen, 1999–2000.

Selected Bibliography

BROCKHAUS Christoph, *Nam June Paik, Fluxus und Video Skulptur*. Duisburg: Stiftung Wilhelm Lehmbruck Museum, 2002.
DECKER-PHILLIPS Edith, *Paik Video*. New York: E. Decker-Phillips, 1997.
MÜLLER Christian [ed.], *Nam June Paik, Zeichnungen*. Basel: Museum für Gegenwartskunst, 2000.
FARGIER Jean-Paul, "Nam June Paik, le grand simulateur", *Cahiers du cinéma*, March 2006, 68–71.
The World of Nam June Paik. New York: Solomon R. Guggenheim Museum, 2000.
VAN ASSCHE Christine [ed.], *Temps de vídeo: 1965–2005*. Barcelona: Fundació La Caixa, 2006; *New Media Collection: 1965–2005. Centre Pompidou*, Taipei: Taipei Fine Arts Museum, 2006; *New Media Collection/Installations: 1965–2005*. Paris: Editions du Centre Pompidou, 2006.

CD-ROM
Nam June Paik and Charlotte Moorman, Munich, Systhema, 1998.

THE PROPELLER GROUP
Formed in 2006 in Ho Chi Minh City, Vietnam

Phunam born in 1974 in Saigon, Vietnam
Matt LUCERO born in 1976 in Upland, USA
Tuan Andrew NGUYEN born in 1976 in Saigon, Vietnam
Live and work in Ho Chi Minh City, Vietnam and Los Angeles, USA

Selected Exhibitions
3rd Singapore Biennale: Open House, Singapore, 2011.
Against Easy Listening, 1A Space, Hong Kong, 2010.
8th Shanghai Biennale: Rehearsal [with Superflex], Shanghai, 2010.

Selected Bibliography
ArtAsiaPacific Almanac 2008. New York: ArtAsiaPacific Publishing LLC, 2007.
BUTT Zoe [interview], "The Pilgrimage of Inspiration – Artists as Engineers in Vietnam: The Propeller Group interview with Tuan Andrew Nguyen, Phu Nam Thuc Ha, and Matt Lucero", *Independent Curators International, Dispatch*, 13 May 2010. Accessed 30 November 2010. http://www.ici-exhibitions.org/images/uploads/propeller.pdf.
VU Thi Quynh Giao [interview], "Vietnam the World Tour: The Propeller Group", *diacritics: Diasporic Vietnamese Artists Network*, October 9, 2010. Acessed 30 November 2010. http://diacritics.org/2010/10/09/vietnam-the-world-tour-the-propellor-group/.

Araya RASDJARMREARNSOOK
Born in 1957 in Trad, Thailand
Lives and works in Chiang Mai, Thailand

Selected Exhibitions
17th Biennale of Sydney: The Beauty of Distance, Sydney, 2010.
Six Feet Under: An Autopsy of Our Relation to the Dead, Kunstmuseum, Bern, 2006.
6th Gwangju Biennale: Trace Root: Unfolding Asian Stories, Gwangju, 2006.
T1 Turin Triennal: The Pantagruel Syndrome, Rivoli, 2005–06.
8th International Istanbul Biennial: Poetic Justice, Istanbul, 2003.
Araya Rasdjarmrearnsook: At Nightfall Candles are Lighted, Contemporary Art Museum, Chiang Mai; Chulalongkorn University Art Gallery, Bangkok, 2000.

Selected Bibliography
CAMERON Dan, *Taipei Biennale: Dirty Yoga*. Taipei: Taipei Fine Arts Museum, 2006.
COOKE Lynne, *10th Biennale of Sydney: Jurassic Technologies Revenant*. Sydney: Biennale of Sydney, 1996.
HOPTMAN Laura, *54th Carnegie International*. Pittsburgh: Carnegie Museum of Art, 2004.
RASDJARMREARNSOOK Araya, *In This Circumstance, the Sole Object of Attention should be the Treachery of the Moon*. Bangkok: Ardel Gallery of Modern Art, 2009.

Martial RAYSSE
Born in 1936 in Golfe-Juan, France
Lives and works in Issigeac, France

Selected Exhibitions
Daimler Art Collection, MUMOK, Museum Moderner Kunst Stiftung Ludwig, Vienna, 2010.
Temps de vídeo: 1965–2005, Fundació La Caixa, Barcelona, 2005–06.
Retrospective Martial Raysse, Galerie nationale du Jeu de Paume, Paris, 1992.
Martial Raysse 1970–1980, Musée national d'art moderne, Centre Georges Pompidou, Paris, 1981.
Martial Raysse: obrazy a objekty, Národní Galerie, Prague, 1969.

Selected Bibliography
HAAS Patrick de, *Martial Raysse 1970–1980*. Paris: Musée national d'art moderne; Editions du Centre Pompidou, 1981.
SEMIN Didier [ed.], *Martial Raysse*. Paris: Editions du Jeu de Paume, 2002.
VAN ASSCHE Christine [ed.], *Temps de vídeo: 1965–2005*. Barcelona: Fundació La Caixa, 2006; *New Media Collection: 1965–2005, Centre Pompidou*. Taipei: Taipei Fine Arts Museum, 2006; *New Media Collection/Installations: 1965–2005*. Paris: Editions du Centre Pompidou, 2006.

Rachel REUPKE
Born in 1971 in Henley-on-Thames, UK
Lives and works in London, UK

Selected Exhibitions
10 Seconds or Greater, Picture This, Bristol, 2010.
Biennale of Contemporary Art, Prague, 2005.

Selected Bibliography
STIWER Pierre, DI FELICE Paul [ed.], *Le bâti, le vivant*. Luxembourg: Café-crème, 2002.

Pipilotti RIST
Born in 1962 in Grabs, Switzerland
Lives and works in Zurich, Switzerland and Los Angeles, USA

Selected Exhibitions
Elixir: the Video Organism of Pipilotti Rist, Museum Boijmans Van Beuningen, Rotterdam, 2009.
elles@centrepompidou, Musée national d'art moderne-Centre de création industrielle, Centre Pompidou, Paris, 2009.
Yuyu, Marugame Genichiro-Inokuma Museum of Contemporary Art, Marugame, 2008. *I Want to See How You See*, Sprengel Museum, Hanover, 2006.
Stir Heart, Rinse Heart, San Francisco Museum of Modern Art, San Francisco, 2004.

Selected Bibliography
JULIN Richard [interview], RIST Pipilotti, NEUMAN David, *Congratulations*. Stockholm: Konsthall; Baden: L. Müller Publ., 2007.
PHELAN Peggy, OBRIST Hans Ulrich, BRONFEN Elisabeth, et al., *Pipilotti Rist*. London: Phaidon, 2001.
Pipilotti Rist. Tokyo: Hara Museum of Contemporary Art; Karakaracan, 2007.

RIST Pipilotti, *Himalaya, Pipilotti Rist 50 kg*. Paris: Paris-Musées; Cologne: Oktagon, 1999.
RIST Pipilotti, *Pipilotti Rist, Apricots Along the Streets*. Zurich; Berlin; New York: Scalo, 2001.

Sima SALEHI RAHNI
Born in 1967 in Tehran, Iran
Lives and works in Singapore, Singapore

Selected Exhibitions
Seven-Day Weekend / Le week-end de sept jours, Ecole nationale supérieure des beaux-arts, Paris, 2010.
Singapore Art Exhibition: ART BUFFET SINGAPORE!, Singapore Art Museum, Singapore, 2009.

SREY Bandol
Born in 1973 in Battambang, Cambodia
Lives and works in Battambang, Cambodia

Selected Exhibitions
IMPACT: An Art Exhibit About Landmines in Cambodia, Cartagena Summit for a Mine-Free World, New York, 2010.
Chambuk, French Cultural Centre, Phnom Penh, 2005.

Richard STREITMATTER-TRAN
Born in 1972 in Bien Hoa, Vietnam
Lives and works in Ho Chi Minh City, Vietnam

Selected Exhibitions
Singapore Biennale 2008: Wonder, Singapore, 2008.
Post-Doi Moi. Singapore Art Museum, 2008.
52nd Biennale di Venezia: Think with the Sense – Feel with Mind: Art in the Present Tense, Venice, 2007.
Thermocline of Art, New Asian Waves, ZKM, Zentrum für Kunst und Medientechnologie, Karlsruhe, 2007.
5th Gwangju Biennale: A Grain of Dust A Drop of Water, Gwangju, 2004.

Selected Bibilography
CHIU Melissa, GENOCCHIO Benjamin, *Asian Art Now*. New York: Monacelli Press, 2010.
STREITMATTER-TRAN Rich, "Mapping the Mekong". In *6th Asia Pacific Triennial of Contemporary Art*. Brisbane: Queensland Art Gallery, 2009.

Shuntaro TANIKAWA
Born in 1931 in Tokyo, Japan
Lives and works in Tokyo, Japan

Filmography
Video Letters, 1982–83.

Selected Bibliography
LONDON Barbara, "Video Letter by Shuntaro Tanikawa and Shuji Terayama: An Introduction", *Camera Obscura*, 1990, 8 (3, 24), 195–203.

Shuji TERAYAMA
Born in 1935 in Aomori, Japan
Died in 1983 in Tokyo, Japan

Selected Filmography
Farewell to the Arch, 1984; *Video Letters*, 1982–83; *The Fruits of Passion*, 1981; *Grass Labyrinth*, 1979; *Marudororu no uta | Shadow Film: A Woman with Two Heads*, 1977.

Selected Bibliography
LONDON Barbara, "Video Letter by Shuntaro Tanikawa and Shuji Terayama: An Introduction", *Camera Obscura*, 1990, 8 (3, 24), 195–203.

THAN Sok
Born in 1984 in Takeo, Cambodia
Lives and works in Phnom Penh, Cambodia

Selected Exhibitions
Tragedy, Bophana Audiovisual Resource Centre, Phnom Penh, 2010.
Accumulations, French Cultural Centre, Phnom Penh, 2009.
< In Transition >, Reyum Institue of Arts & Culture, Phnom Penh, 2007.
On Site Lab Series-1 + hand, Tokyo Wonder Site Aoyama, Tokyo, 2006.

Selected Bibliography
JANES Dianne, "Home of spirit and memory", *The Phnom Penh Post*, 18 January 2010. Accessed 24 November 2010. http://khmernz.blogspot.com/2010/01/home-of-spirit-and-memory.html.
CATCHING Rebecca, "Earth, Water, and Fire", *ArtSlant*, 18 November 2009. Accessed 24 November 2010. http://www.artslant.com/ew/articles/show/11594.

TRINH T. Minh-ha
Born in 1952 in Hanoi, Vietnam
Lives and works in Berkeley, USA

Selected Exhibitions
GAGARIN the Artists in their Own Words: the First Decade, SMAK, Ghent, 2009–10.
Le rêve de l'artiste et du spectateur, second volet, Trinh T. Minh-ha et Teresa Hak Kyung Cha, Galerie nationale du Jeu de Paume, Paris, 2008.
Power, Casino, Luxembourg, 2002.

Selected Filmography
Night Passage, 2004; *The Fourth Dimension*, 2001; *A Tale of Love*, 1995; *Shoot for the Contents*, 1991; *Surname Viet Given Name Nam*, 1989; *Naked Spaces, Living is Round*, 1985; *Reassemblage*, 1982.

Selected Bibliography
TRINH T. Minh-ha, *Cinema Interval*. New York: Routledge, 1999.
TRINH T. Minh-ha, BOURDIER Jean-Paul, *Drawn from African Dwellings*. Bloomington: Indiana University Press, 1996.
TRINH T. Minh-ha, *Framer Framed*. New York: Routledge, 1992.
TRINH T. Minh-ha, *The Digital Film Event*. New York: Routledge, 2005.
Trinh T. Minh-ha. Munich: Kunstverein, 1995.

Tun Win Aung and Wah Nu

Tun Win Aung
Born in 1975 in Yalutt, Myanmar
Lives and works in Yangon, Myanmar

Wah Nu
Born in 1977 in Yangon, Myanmar
Lives and works in Yangon, Myanmar

Selected Exhibitions
Videozone V: 5th International Video Art Biennial in Israel, Tel Aviv, 2010.
6th Asia Pacific Triennial of Contemporary Art, Brisbane, 2009.
11th Asian Art Biennale Bangladesh, Dhaka, 2004.

Selected Bibliography
Po Po, "Even S/superman Can Be Able to Come Back in Punk Style", *The 3rd Fukuoka Asian Art Triennale 2005 – Parallel Realities: Asian Art Now*. Fukuoka: Fukuoka Asian Art Museum, 2005.
Po Po, "*Mask Dance*", Yangon, *Rati Magazine*, 3 (9), 2003, 66–71.
STREITMATTER-TRAN Rich, "Tun Win Aung and Wah Nu: Between the Two", In *6th Asia Pacific Triennial of Contemporary Art*. Brisbane: Queensland Art Gallery, 2009.

Bill VIOLA

Born in 1951 in Flushing, USA
Lives and works in Long Beach, USA

Selected Exhibitions
Bill Viola: Obras figurativas, Museo Picasso, Málaga, 2010.
Bill Viola: Las Horas invisibles, Museo de bellas artes, Granada, 2007.
Bill Viola: NORD/LB's Kunstpreis 2005, Kunsthalle Bremen, Bremen, 2006.
Temps de vídeo: 1965–2005, Fundació La Caixa, Barcelona, 2005–06.
Bill Viola: Going Forth by Day, Deutsche Guggenheim, Berlin, 2002.
Bill Viola: The Twenty-Five-Year Survey, Whitney Museum of American Art, New York, 1998.
Bill Viola, ARC, Musée d'art moderne de la Ville de Paris, Paris, 1983–84.
Projects: Bill Viola, Museum of Modern Art, New York, 1979.

Selected Bibliography
DECKER Edith, HERZOGENRATH Wulf, MALSH Friedemann, *Video-Skulptur, Retrospektiv und Aktuel 1963–1989*. Cologne: DuMont, 1989.
LONDON Barbara [ed.], *Bill Viola: Installations and Videotapes*. New York: Museum of Modern Art, 1987.
ROSS David, WALSH John, VIOLA Bill, *Bill Viola, las horas invisibles*. Grenada: Museo de bellas artes, 2007.
ROSS David, WALSH John, VIOLA Bill, ELLIOT David, OBIGANE Akio, *Bill Viola: Hatsu-Yume, First Dream*. Tokyo: Mori Art Museum, 2006.
VAN ASSCHE Christine [ed.], *Temps de vídeo: 1965–2005*. Barcelona: Fundació La Caixa, 2006; *New Media Collection: 1965–2005, Centre Pompidou*. Taipei: Taipei Fine Arts Museum, 2006; *New Media Collection/Installations: 1965–2005*. Paris: Editions du Centre Pompidou, 2006.

Apichatpong WEERASETHAKUL

Born in 1970 in Bangkok, Thailand
Lives and works in Bangkok, Thailand

Selected Exhibitions
Primitive, Musée d'art moderne de la Ville de Paris, Paris, 2009–10.
Primitive, eine Filminstallation, Haus der Kunst, Munich, 2009.
Unknown Forces, Redcat, Los Angeles, 2007.
29th Bienal de São Paulo, Sao Paulo, 2010.

Selected Bibliography
KIM Young-Ha, TOUFIC Jalal, KIM Clara, SCHAFHAUSEN Nicolaus, SUMIMOTO Fumihiko. *Media City Seoul 2010-Trust*. Seoul: Seoul Museum of Art, 2010.
QUANDT James, *Apichatpong Weerasethakul*. Vienna: Filmmuseum, 2009 (Filmmuseum;12).
WEERASETHAKUL Apichatpong, SCHERF Angeline, *Primitive*. Paris: Musée d'art moderne de la Ville de Paris, 2009.

YANG Fudong

Born in 1971 in Beijing, China
Lives and works in Shanghai, China

Selected Solo Exhibitions
... in the bamboo forest ..., Kunsthaus Baselland, Muttenz, 2010.
The General's Smile, Hara Museum of Contemporary Art, Tokyo, 2009–10.
Dawn Mist Separation Faith, Zendai Museum of Modern Art, Shanghai, 2009.
Seven Intellectuals in a Bamboo Forest, Asia Society and Museum, New York, 2009.
Recent Films and Videos, Stedelijk Museum, Amsterdam, 2005–06.
New Generations, Castello di Rivoli, Museo d'arte contemporanea, Rivoli, 2005.
Don't Worry, It Will Be Better…, Kunstahalle, Vienna, 2005.

Selected Bibliography
BECCARIA Marcella, *Yang Fudong*, Rivoli, Castello di Rivoli; Milan: Skira, 2006.
FAN Di'an, KNAPSTEIN Gabriele, *Living in Time*. Berlin: Staatliche Museen zu Berlin-Preußischer Kulturbesitz, 2001.
WECK Ardalan Ziba de, OBRIST Hans Ulrich, *No Snow on the Bridge, Film and Video Installations by Yang Fudong*. London: Parasol Unit Foundation for Contemporary Art; Zurich: JRP-Ringier, 2006.

Essay Author Biographies

Toshiya Kuroiwa
Born in 1966, video and media artist Toshiya Kuroiwa has been Professor in Image Arts and Animation at the Department of Design, Kyushu Sangyo University since 1999. From 1992 to 1999, he was Assistant Professor at the Kyushu Institute of Design after graduating in audio and visual studies at the same institute. He is a member of the Japan Society of Image Arts and Sciences and the Japan Society for the Science of Design. He is also video designer and technical director for stage performances.

Patricia Levasseur de la Motte
Patricia Levasseur de la Motte earned an MA in Museology and an MRes in Art History (Asian Arts) from the Ecole du Louvre, Paris. She then worked as a Research Assistant at the National Museum of Asian Arts-Guimet, Paris. In her current role as Assistant Curator for Photography and New Media at the Singapore Art Museum (SAM), she co-curated several exhibitions including *TRANSPORTASIAN: Visions of Contemporary Photography from Southeast Asia*, SAM (2009); *Rainbow Asia*, Seoul Arts Center (2010); and *Video, an Art, a History 1965–2010: A Selection from the Centre Pompidou and Singapore Art Museum Collections*, SAM (2011).

Jacqueline Millner
Jacqueline Millner is one of Australia's major critical voices in art. She lectures in art history and theory at Sydney College of the Arts, University of Sydney. She has published widely on contemporary art for the last 15 years, with particular emphasis on installation and video art. Her recent book *Conceptual Beauty* (2010) is an anthology of her most significant writings on Australian contemporary artists. She is currently working on a book on street art under the auspices of a research grant from the Australia Council for the Arts.

Krisna Murti
Since 2003, Krisna Murti has been a guest lecturer in new media studies at the Post Graduate School of Indonesian Arts Institute, Yogyakarta. He initiated research and mapping of ASEAN New Media Art 2010 (COCI) and his publications include *Video Publik* (1999) and *Essays on Video Art and New Media: Indonesia and Beyond* (2009). He has participated in *Impakt*, Utrecht, the Netherlands (2000); Havana Biennale, Cuba (2000); Gwangju Biennale, Korea (2000); Venice Biennale, Italy (2005); and *transmediale*, Germany (2005).

Mark Nash
Mark Nash was a co-curator of *Documenta 11* (2002). He has also curated *Experiments With Truth*, Fabric Workshop and Museum, Philadelphia (2004–05); *Pere Portabella*, Museum of Modern Art, New York (2007); *Reimagining October* (with Isaac Julien), Calvert 22, London (2009); and *The View from Elsewhere* (with Kathryn Weir) Gallery of Modern Art, Brisbane (2009). He has curated the film elements of international exhibitions including *The Short Century* (2001); the Berlin Biennale (2004); and the Sharjah Biennial (2007). He is Professor and Head of Department, Curating Contemporary Art at the Royal College of Art, London.

Nguyen Nhu Huy
Nguyen Nhu Huy is a video artist, independent curator, translator and art writer based in Ho Chi Minh City, Vietnam. He has widely published on contemporary Vietnamese art in Vietnam and acted as official speaker at several international art conferences. Having curated exhibitions in Vietnam, South Korea and USA, Nguyen is also the co-founder and artistic director of ZeroStation (www.zerostation.vn), an alternative space devoted to the development of the contemporary art community in Ho Chi Minh City.

Adeline Ooi
Adeline Ooi is a curator and arts writer from Malaysia. She has written essays, reviews and criticism for private publications and international exhibition catalogues. Publications she has recently contributed to include *Agus Suwage: Still Crazy After All These Years* and *Mella Jaarsma: Fitting Room*. She was the recipient of The Nippon Foundation's Asian Public Intellectual (Junior) Fellowships Grant 2002/3. She is a director, and co-founder of RogueArt.

Steven Pettifor
Writer, curator and artist Steven Pettifor is an authority on contemporary Thai and Asian art. From the United Kingdom, Pettifor studied art at Wimbledon School of Art and then John Moores University in Liverpool, where he graduated with a BFA in 1990. He migrated to Asia in 1992, and now lives in Bangkok. He has contributed to several international newspapers and journals, and is presently the Thailand editor for *Asian Art News*. In 2004 he published the book *Flavours – Thai Contemporary Art*.

David Teh
David Teh works in the Department of English Language and Literature, National University of Singapore, researching contemporary art and visual culture in Southeast Asia. He received his PhD in critical theory from the University of Sydney (2005), before working as an independent critic and curator in Bangkok (until 2009). His curatorial projects included *Platform* (2006); *The More Things Change…* The 5th Bangkok Experimental Film Festival (2008); and *Unreal Asia*, a programme for the 55th International Short Film Festival, Oberhausen, Germany (2009).

Christine Van Assche
Christine Van Assche is Chief Curator of Centre Georges Pompidou's New Media Department. She founded its collection of 120 audiovisual installations by artists like Nam June Paik, Dan Graham, Bill Viola, Mona Hatoum and Jun Nguyen-Hatsushiba. The collection also includes 1,600 videotapes, CD-ROMs, CDs and websites representative of the diverse contemporary trends. She is author of numerous *catalogues raisonnés* and monographs on Stan Douglas, Pierre Huyghe, Isaac Julien, Chris Marker, Bruce Nauman, Tony Oursler, Zineb Sedira, David Claerbout, etc. She has curated many international travelling and solo exhibitions.

Beverly Yong
Beverly Yong has written extensively on Malaysian art over the past 10 years, and has edited a number of publications on local and regional art, including recently, *Between Generations: 50 Years Across Modern Art in Malaysia* (with Hasnul J. Saidon, University of Malaya, Universiti Sains Malaysia, and Valentine Willie Fine Art, Kuala Lumpur, 2008). She wrote a regular art column for the *Business Times*, and the *New Sunday Times* from 2000 to 2003. She is a director and co-founder of RogueArt, an art consultancy based in Kuala Lumpur.

Further Readings

GENERAL READING

COMER Stuart, *Film and Video Art*. London: Tate Publishing, 2009.

CONOMOS John, *Mutant Media: Essays on Cinema, Video Art and New Media*. Sydney: Artspace and Power Publications, 2007.

CUBITT Sean, *Videography: Video Media as Art and Culture*. New York: St. Martin's Press, 1993.

DE MÈREDIEU Florence, ELLIOTT Richard [trans.], *Video and Media Art*. Edinburgh: Chambers, 2005.

GRAU Olivier [ed.], *MediaArtHistories*. Cambridge; London: MIT Press, 2007.

HALL Doug [ed.], *Illuminating Video: An Essential Guide to Video Art*. New York: Aperture in association with Bay Area Video Coalition, 1990.

MARTIN Sylvia, *Video Art*. Cologne: Taschen, 2006.

PAUL Christiane, *New Media in the White Cube and Beyond: Curatorial Models for Digital Art*. Berkeley: University of California Press, 2008.

REINKE Steve, TUCKER Tom [eds.], *LUX: A Decade of Artists' Film and Video*. Toronto: YYZ Books, 2000.

RUSH Michael, *New Media in Art*. London: Thames & Hudson, 2005.

—, *Video Art*. London: Thames & Hudson, 2003.

VAN ASSCHE Christine [ed.], *New Media Collection/ Installations: 1965–2005*. Paris: Centre Pompidou, 2006.

WALKER John A., *Art in the Age of Mass Media*. London: Pluto Press, 1990.

EXHIBITION AND FESTIVAL CATALOGUES

4th Fukuoka Asian Art Triennale: Live and Let Live: Creators of Tomorrow. Fukuoka: Fukuoka Asian Art Museum, 2009.

Between Past and Future: New Photography and Video from China. New York: International Center of Photography, 2004.

Crosscurrents: New Media Art from Beijing, Hong Kong and Singapore. Singapore: Osage Singapore, 2008.

Digital Paradise. Daejeon: Daejeon Museum of Art, 2005.

Fast Forward: New Chinese Video Art. Macau: Contemporary Art Center, 1999.

Feedback: The Video Data Bank: Video Art and Artist Interview. New York: Museum of Modern Art, 2007.

FRIELING Rudolf, HERZOGENRATH Wulf, *40 Years Videoart. de: Digital Heritage: Video Art in Germany from 1963 to the Present*. Ostfildern: Hatje Cantz, 2006.

From Message to Media. Bangkok: Bangkok University Art Gallery, 2007.

HANHARDT John G., et al., *Moving Pictures: Contemporary Photography and Video from the Guggenheim Collection*. New York: Harry N. Abrams, 2004.

KOOP Stuart, DELANY Max, *Screen Life: Videos from Australia*. Madrid: Reina Sofia Museum, 2002.

LONDON Barbara, DELANY Samuel, *Video Spaces: Eight Installations*. New York: Museum of Modern Art, 1995.

LOSCHMANN Jorg, *Identities versus Globalisation?* Bangkok: Thailand National Gallery, 2004.

Move on Asia 2007: _single channel video art festival. Seoul: Gallery Loop, 2007.

OK. Video: Jakarta Video Art Festival. Jakarta: National Gallery of Indonesia, 2003.

Performance Art and Video Installation. London: Tate Gallery, 1985.

Pioneers of Brazilian Video Art 1973–1983. Los Angeles: Getty Center, 2004.

SAIDON Hasnul J., RAJAH Niranjan [eds.], *Pameran Seni Elektronik Pertama (The First Electronic Exhibition)*. Kuala Lumpur: National Art Gallery Malaysia, 1997.

STORER Russell [ed.], *Video Logic*. Sydney: Museum of Contemporary Art, 2008.

Thermocline of Art: New Asian Waves. Karlsruhe: Center for Art and Media, 2007.

Videoprogramme: Single Screen Video Art from Asia. Singapore: Institute of Contemporary Arts Singapore, 2003.

Waiting for Video: Works from the 1960s to Today. Tokyo: National Museum of Modern Art, 2009.

REGIONAL SURVEYS

MURTI Krisna, *Essays on Video Art and New Media: Indonesia and Beyond*. Yogyakarta: IVAA, 2009.

STREITMATTER-TRAN Richard, "Making the Mekong". In *6th Asia Pacific Triennal of Contemporary Art*. Brisbane: Queensland Art Gallery, 2009.

Index

About the Centre Pompidou

The Centre national d'art et de culture Georges Pompidou was the brainchild of President Georges Pompidou who wanted to create an original cultural institution in the heart of Paris completely focused on modern and contemporary creation, where the visual arts would rub shoulders with theatre, music, cinema, literature and the spoken word. Housed in the centre of Paris in a building designed by Renzo Piano and Richard Rogers, whose architecture symbolises the spirit of the 20th century, the Centre Pompidou first opened its doors to the public in 1977. After renovation work from 1997 to December 1999, it opened to the public again on 1 January 2000, with expanded museum space and enhanced reception areas. Since then it has once again become one of the most visited attractions in France. Some 6 million people pass through the Centre Pompidou's doors each year, a total of over 190 million visitors in its 30 years of existence.

In a unique location under one roof, the Centre Pompidou houses one of the most important museums in the world, featuring the leading collection of modern and contemporary art in Europe, a vast public reference library with facilities for over 2,000 readers, general documentation on 20th-century art, a cinema and performance halls, a music research institute, educational activity areas, bookshops, a restaurant and a café. Unswerving in its interdisciplinary vocation and its core mission - to spread knowledge about all creative works from the 20th century and those heralding the new millennium - each year the Centre Pompidou holds 30 or so public exhibitions plus international events - cinema and documentary screenings, conferences and symposiums, concerts, dance and educational activities - many of which go on to other venues in both France and abroad.

The Centre Pompidou has been an innovator in the field of new media (video, sound and multimedia installations). Its commitment to this discipline is demonstrated by the creation of the New Media Collection which is housed in the Musée national d'art moderne and comprises over 120 international multimedia installations and 1,600 videotapes, soundtracks, CD-ROMs and websites. New Media Encyclopedia: www.newmedia-art.org.

About the Singapore Art Museum

The mission of the Singapore Art Museum (SAM) is to preserve and promote the art histories and contemporary art practices of Singapore and the Southeast Asian region. Opened in January 1996 as a museum under the National Heritage Board of Singapore, SAM has amassed one of the world's largest public collections of modern and contemporary Southeast Asian artwork. Since 2009, SAM has focused its programming and collections development initiatives around contemporary Southeast Asian art and art practices. Through strategic alliances with arts and cultural institutions and community organisations. SAM facilitates visual arts education, exchange, and research and development within the region and internationally. SAM is also the organiser of the Singapore Biennale 2011.

Photo Credits

Credit Suisse: Innovation In Art Series

The Credit Suisse: Innovation In Art Series began in 2007 as a long-term partnership between the Singapore Art Museum (SAM) and Credit Suisse AG. The Series enables SAM to showcase important Asian contemporary art practices, ground-breaking artists, as well as significant exhibitions from around the world. Exhibitions presented under the Series include *Seeing. Feeling. Being: Alberto Giacometti*, *Accelerate: Chinese Contemporary Art*, *FX Harsono: Testimonies* and the prestigious *President's Young Talents*. In 2009, as part of Credit Suisse AG's commitment to promoting emerging artistic talent, the Bank also sponsored the inaugural *President's Young Talents Credit Suisse Artist Residency Award* which confers a cash award and sponsored artist residency to the winning President's Young Talent.

With the visual arts as a key focus, Credit Suisse AG builds lasting relationships with important museums and other institutions around the world. The Bank's support has given SAM the creative freedom and resources to plan ahead, while supporting the Museum's efforts to offer unique, varied experiences to its visitors and create a stimulating environment through contemporary art. For its contributions to SAM, Credit Suisse AG has been conferred the National Heritage Board's *Partner of Heritage* award.